SPANISH–
LIVE IT AND LEARN IT!

"I recommend this book to anyone interested in studying Spanish in Mexico. It's the most comprehensive guide I've seen on the topic — an incredibly helpful resource."

— *Steven D. Larson, High School Guidance Counselor*

"*Spanish – Live It and Learn It!* made me want to go back to Mexico immediately and attend a language school there. Martha Racine Taylor gives us so much to choose from and makes the possibilities exciting and accessible; the book provides everything necessary to choose a school; it's an invaluable resource, whether you're a beginning Spanish speaker or looking to sharpen your existing language skills."

— *Carla Jupiter, Chairperson, Book Selection Committee,*
Mendocino Community Library

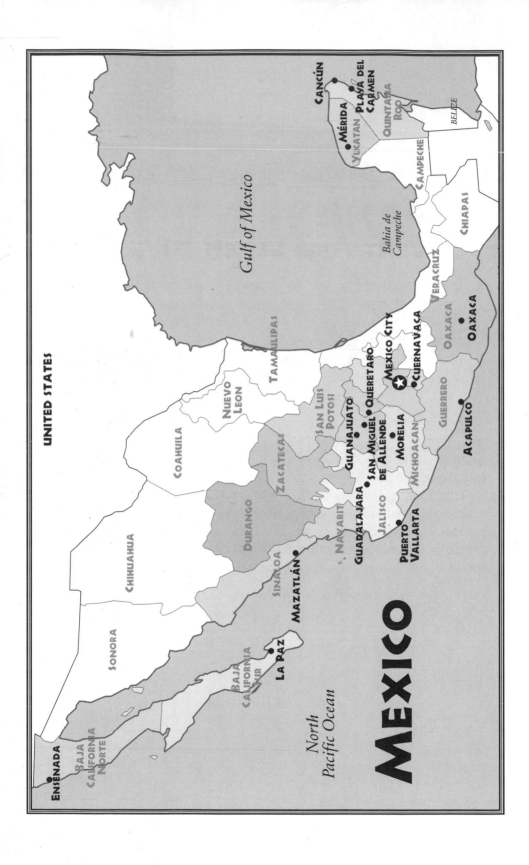

SPANISH–
LIVE IT AND LEARN IT!

The Complete Guide to
Language Immersion Schools in Mexico

MARTHA RACINE TAYLOR

Cypress House

Spanish – Live It and Learn It!
The Complete Guide to Language Immersion Schools in Mexico

Cypress House
155 Cypress Street
Fort Bragg, California 95437
800-773-7782
Fax: 707-964-7531
http:\\www.cypresshouse.com

Book production by Cypress House

Publisher's Cataloging-in-Publication Data

Taylor, Martha Racine.
 Spanish--live it and learn it! : the complete guide to language immersion schools in Mexico./
Martha Racine Taylor. -- 1st ed. -- Fort Bragg,
CA : Cypress House, 2005.
 p. ; cm.
 ISBN: 1-879384-64-7
 ISBN-13: 978-1-879384-64-4
 1. Language schools--Mexico--Directories. 2. Education, Bilingual. 3. Immersion method (Language teaching) 4. Spanish
language--Study and teaching--Immersion method. I. Title.
 P57.M6 T39 2005
 370.117/5/0972--dc22 0510   2005931156

Manufactured in the USA

9 8 7 6 5 4 3 2 1

First edition

To my husband, Thomas A. Taylor,
without whose encouragement, patience, and devotion
I would not have been able to complete this project.

CONTENTS

CONTENTS

SPANISH—
LIVE IT AND LEARN IT!

INTRODUCTION

Have you ever taken a foreign-language class? As a result, do you feel comfortable speaking that language? How many times have you heard someone say, "I took three years of Spanish in college, but I can't speak it!"

When you take a Spanish class at your local college or university, you're back in the English-speaking world as soon as you leave the classroom. Your Spanish is usually put aside until the next class, with the exception of homework or listening to recordings in a language lab.

What if that language lab were all around you? What if you didn't emerge into an English-speaking world but were plunged into an environment where the only way you could order a sandwich or find out how to get to the beach was to speak and understand Spanish? Studying Spanish in a Spanish-speaking country propels language learning beyond the classroom by placing you in a living language lab. Your fluency will improve from the very first day. If you've had some prior Spanish instruction, most of what you've already learned will come flooding back. After a few weeks staying with a Spanish-speaking family and taking care of your basic and not-so-basic needs in Spanish, you'll be speaking the language effortlessly. You may even be thinking in Spanish!

Real language learning takes place in the real world. Most students can absorb vocabulary and grammatical concepts and even enter into simple conversations in the classroom, but the true test of their language skills is their ability to communicate with native speakers in a country where the language is spoken. While leading study tours in Mexico, I have observed the seemingly miraculous progress many of my students made in their ability to communicate in Spanish after just a few days. Anyone who really wants to learn to speak a foreign language must reach beyond the classroom and "live" the language where it is spoken.

This book will help you choose the Spanish-language school that best suits your needs and interests. All the schools presented specialize in language-immersion programs designed to improve your fluency through a combination of classes and real-life practice with native speakers. A key component of an immersion program is staying with a Mexican family. This experience provides you with opportunities to speak Spanish outside the classroom. Your host family will contribute significantly to your language learning, but they'll teach you more than just the language. Interacting with your Mexican family will help you feel at ease in their country and appreciate their culture. Your relationship with them and the time you spend in Mexico will also give you a better understanding of the Mexican people you encounter back home.

WHY STUDY IN MEXICO?

There are twenty-two countries where Spanish is spoken, so why Mexico? The main reason is simple and compelling: according to the March 2002 Current Population Survey published by the U.S. Census Bureau, two-thirds of all Hispanics in the U.S. are of Mexican origin. In addition, Mexicans account for nearly 30 percent of all foreign-born residents of the U.S. Because many of these individuals are monolingual and others are barely able to communicate in English, there is a need for bilingual workers in many areas. Fluency in Spanish can greatly enhance employment prospects for job seekers in a variety of careers.

Mexicans immigrate to the U.S. to find better jobs and provide a better standard of living for their families. They are our customers, patients, employees, and students. They are often the family next door who shop at the same stores and attend the same church but are more fluent in Spanish than in English.

To communicate with Mexicans, you need to speak their dialect of Spanish, know their expressions and slang, and understand their culture. What better way to accomplish that than to study in Mexico? You'll interact with Mexicans on a daily basis and learn about their way of life, their culture, and their history. Your ability to speak Spanish as it is spoken in Mexico, and your understanding of the Mexicans themselves—what they believe and how they live—will be invaluable in your interactions with them in your hometown.

My relationship with Mexico and its people has been fascinating and fulfilling, sometimes even exciting and adventurous. I have visited almost every part of the country in the course of more than forty trips in thirty-five years, staying from a few days to more than six months. The immersion program I attended while earning my master's degree enhanced my fluency in Spanish and gave me an insider's view of Mexican culture. With every visit to Mexico, my fluency in Spanish improves, simply because I use it to communicate at all times without having to revert to English.

While researching this book I traveled throughout Mexico, visiting language schools, attending classes, talking with teachers and students, and staying with families. I made many friends, had wonderful experiences, and learned a great deal. I am more enthusiastic than ever about the benefits of studying Spanish in Mexico. I hope your experience will be just as rewarding and inspiring as mine. May you return home speaking Spanish, with a special place in your heart for Mexico and the warmth and generosity of its people.

CHOOSING YOUR SCHOOL

Where should you go to school? Your personal preferences will drive this decision. Do you love to explore old towns steeped in history? Does archaeology fascinate you? Are you into snorkeling or scuba diving? Is beach access important to your happiness? If you're unfamiliar with Mexico's geography and culture, read the introduction to each area discussed in this book. You'll also find a wealth of information in a good Mexico guidebook, such as the *Lonely Planet Guide to Mexico*.

Once you've decided where in Mexico you would like to study, look for a school with a well-established Spanish-language program that offers the courses you need and activities that suit your interests. Most schools include classes, tours, and events designed to acquaint foreign students with Mexican culture. In Oaxaca, for example, you can learn the ancient art of back-strap weaving from native weavers; in San Miguel de Allende you can combine Spanish instruction with art classes; and in Yucatán you can visit ancient Mayan ruins. Some schools in Quintana Roo (on the Mexican Caribbean) offer scuba certification. Many schools offer specialized language programs, such as medical or business Spanish, and certain schools offer children's programs.

When you contact a school directly, remember that the quality and speed of their response could be an indicator of the effectiveness of their programs. I suggest comparing two or three schools if possible, forwarding your questions to them by email. Choose a school that answers your questions completely and seems interested in having you as a student.

When investigating a school, it helps to have input from students who have actually studied there. Some schools post student comments on their websites. Of course, you may get a more balanced assessment directly from these students. Don't be afraid to ask the school for email addresses or other contact information for former students.

Some Spanish-language schools also teach English to Mexican students. This won't detract from your experience, but will enhance it by providing opportunities to practice your Spanish with native speakers. Many schools have informal language interchanges (*intercambios*) set up for English- and Spanish-speaking students to practice with one another. Participating in an *intercambio* is also a good way to meet the locals, to learn more about the area, and even to get involved in community activities.

You can also prepare yourself to teach English as a Second Language by getting the TEFL or TESL certification offered by some Spanish/English schools. The cost of earning one of these internationally recognized certifications in Mexico is a fraction of what it costs elsewhere.

The risk in signing up for Spanish courses at a school that mainly teaches English is that the Spanish program may be just an afterthought, and the quality of the instruction may not be up to standard. In this book, I've included some English schools that have strong Spanish programs. There are, however, some schools that would have you believe that they specialize in teaching Spanish to foreigners, when they exist almost exclusively to teach English. They seem to be trying to capitalize on the success of more established Spanish programs. I found several schools in this category while doing my research. Needless to say, they're not included in this book.

In summary, look for a school that you feel good about, in an area that intrigues you. Don't settle for just any school. By reading this book carefully, doing some Internet research, and communicating with schools by email or phone, you can find the school that's just right for you!

Below is a form to help you evaluate and compare schools. To use it effectively, make a photocopy for each school you're considering. Most of the information you need is in this book, but don't hesitate to contact the school by email to get answers to your questions.

SCHOOL EVALUATION FORM

School Name:

Location:

Positive and Negative Aspects of Location:

Cost per week/Hours of instruction per day:

Special Programs:

Cultural Activities:

Credit from: Cost of Credit:

Excursions: Cost:

Number of students per host family:

Extra services:

Comments:

FINANCING YOUR STUDY PROGRAM

If you're enthusiastic about studying Spanish in Mexico but are limited by your financial circumstances, there are some viable options for financing your study program.

FINANCIAL AID

The U.S. Department of Education permits colleges to release federal aid for payment toward a study-abroad program. To receive federal financial aid, you must attend the foreign school long enough to earn at least six semester units, which qualifies you as a half-time student. The study program must also be approved for credit by your home college or university. It should also be advancing you toward a degree, and not just providing an enrichment experience. If you can comply with these criteria, you may be able to receive Title IV funding, such as a Pell grant or Stafford student loan. The best way to accomplish this may be to go as a participant in a credit program sponsored by an American university. Check with the foreign-language or counseling department at your school. If your home institution doesn't have such a program, consider signing up for one at another college whose credits will transfer to your school. The transfer of financial aid is not automatic. Always check with your college's financial aid office to find out if you can use your loan or grant under those circumstances.

CAMPUS-BASED OR INSTITUTIONAL AID

"Institutional aid," loans, grants, and scholarships funded or administered by your home institution may in some cases be used to finance a study-abroad program. Scholarships come from a variety of sources, including alumni, campus clubs, faculty, and endowments. Some grant and loan funds may originate with the U.S. government but are administered by a college or university. This type of financial aid is usually based on need. If you feel that you qualify, inquire about local or state scholarships, a Perkins Loan, or a Federal Supplemental Educational Opportunity Grant (FSEOG) at the financial aid office in your college or university.

PRIVATE SCHOLARSHIPS

Private organizations, corporations, foundations, and civic groups provide scholarships. The Chrysler Corporation, the Coca-Cola Foundation, and the Gates Foundation, for example, have granted funds to students for study abroad. Rotary International has its own scholarship program that provides funds for study abroad. If you are Hispanic, you may find funding through the League of United Latin American Citizens.

Organizations that arrange study-abroad programs also offer scholarships for students. The American Institute for Foreign Studies (AIFS) offers scholarships for their semester or summer programs in Mexico. For information, call 800-727-2437 or go to the AIFS website: www.aifs.com. Cultural Experiences Abroad (CEA) offers scholarships for Spanish-language study at CEPE (*Centro de Estudios Para Extranjeros*) at the University of Guadalajara. A CEA scholarship provides $1,000 if you enroll for a semester, and $500 if you enroll for a summer session. For information, go to their website: www.gowithcea.com or call 800-266-4441. A similar opportunity is offered by the Council for International Exchange of Scholars (CIEE) for their summer program at the University of Guanajuato. To investigate the CIEE scholarship, go to www.ciee.org and click on *Scholarships.*

The Cemanáhuac Educational Community in Cuernavaca offers a scholarship in the amount of $860 for educators who enroll in their two-week summer program. For information and an application, visit Cemanáhuac's website: www.cemanahuac.com.

TIMELINE

Most scholarships require you to apply at least a year in advance. The lead times for student loans may be shorter, but considerable advance planning is necessary for applying for any type of financial aid.

SOURCES OF INFORMATION

The following are online and published sources of information on scholarships, loans and grants for students in study-abroad programs.

WEBSITES

AllScholars.com: www.allscholar.com

American Institute for Foreign Studies (AIFS): www.aifs.com

Alternative Student Loan: www.alternativestudentloan.com or 866-301-3637

Broke Scholar: www.brokescholar.com

Council for International Exchange of Scholars: www.ciee.org

Institute of International Education (IIE): www.iie.org or 800-4445-044

International Education Finance Corporation: www.finaid.com

International Student Loan Center (ISLC):
www.internationalstudentloan.com or 617-328-1565

BOOKS

Financial Resources for International Study: A Guide for U.S. Students and Professionals, Editors: Sara J. Steen and Marie O'Sullivan, published by Institute of International Education

Financial Aid for Study and Training Abroad by Gail A. Schlachter & R. David Weber, published by Reference Service Press.

WORKING IN MEXICO

Like other developing nations, Mexico has a high unemployment rate, which has resulted in strict regulations prohibiting foreigners from taking jobs that would otherwise go to Mexican citizens. You are not permitted to work in Mexico if you were admitted under a tourist or student visa, and getting a work permit is very difficult. Employees of international firms with Mexican subsidiaries can work in Mexico, provided they receive their salaries directly from the foreign company, and not from a Mexican firm. The Mexican government sometimes issues work permits to foreigners who have specific skills needed in Mexico, but these permits are given only to people sponsored by Mexican companies.

If you're staying in Mexico for a year or more, you may be able to support yourself by teaching English in a private school or language center. To teach in a Mexican school legally, you'll need a TEFL or TESL certificate and an FM3 visa. As mentioned in chapter One, there are some Spanish-language schools that offer the certifications you need to teach English at home or abroad. You can get your TEFL or TESL certificate at a fraction of what it would cost in the U.S. or Europe. Vancouver Language Centre, a Canadian school with a branch in Guadalajara, employs foreign nationals to teach English. For information on these jobs, visit their website: www.study-mexico.com.

IMPORTING GOODS FOR SALE

Some entrepreneurial students bring back traditional Mexican arts and crafts to sell. If you are not a licensed importer, you should be aware of your country's laws regarding how much you can bring back without paying duty. The U.S. allows its citizens to bring back up to $800 worth of goods from a foreign country. Anything over this value is subject to import duties. The $800 exemption applies to items in your possession when you return to the U.S., not items that you ship back. For more information on customs regulations and exemptions, see the "Know Before You Go" brochure on the U.S. Customs and Border Protection website: www.cbp.gov.

GETTING COLLEGE CREDIT

A re you working toward a college degree? If so, there are a variety of ways to earn college or university credit for the classes you take at private immersion schools in Mexico.

UNIVERSITY CREDIT

CREDIT FROM YOUR COLLEGE OR UNIVERSITY. Check with the foreign-language department at your college or university to determine whether they will grant credit for your independent studies in Mexico. Some U.S. institutions offer independent study credit to their students, but most do not. Two students I met in La Paz were receiving three units of credit for conversational Spanish from a California State University where they were full-time students.

If your college does not offer credit for independent study, they may have a scheduled language study program in Mexico. These programs begin and end on specific dates and are accompanied by faculty from the sponsoring institution. Although they're often reserved for full-time students, others can sometimes join these groups, especially those offered by a community college or a university extension program.

UNIVERSITY OF SOUTHERN MISSISSIPPI. You can attend one of the following Spanish-language schools and earn credits from the University of Southern Mississippi:

Baden-Powell Institute – Morelia

Cemanahuac Educational Community – Cuernavaca

Centro de Idiomas – Mazatlán

Instituto Allende – San Miguel de Allende

Instituto Cultural Oaxaca – Oaxaca

Centro De Idiomas Del Sureste (CIS) – Mérida

In addition to the tuition you pay to your Mexican school, you will pay tuition to U.S.M., which ranges from $495 for three quarter units, to $1195 for twelve quarter units. For information about college credit through the University of Southern Mississippi, contact:

> Susan Steen, Director, or Melissa Ravencraft, Coordinator
> Office of International Programs
> University of Southern Mississippi
> 118 College Drive #10047
> Hattiesburg, MS 39406-0001
> Tel: 601-266-4344 or 601-266-5009
> Fax: 601-266-5699
> Email: s.l.steen@usm.edu or melissa.ravencraft@usm.edu

UNIVERSITY OF LAVERNE. Four weeks of study at Cuauhnáhuac Spanish Language Institute in Cuernavaca may qualify you for six units if you register for credit through the University of LaVerne in Southern California. In addition to the tuition at Cuauhnáhuac, you pay $60/unit to University of LaVerne. For more information, contact.

> Dr. Andrea Labinger
> University of LaVerne
> 1950 3rd Street
> La Verne, CA 91750
> Tel: 909-593-3511
> Email: labinger@ulv.edu

AUSTIN PEAY UNIVERSITY. This Tennessee university offers credit for studies at two schools: Becari in Oaxaca and Encuentros in Cuernavaca. Students must register through the university's Mexico study program and pay $140/unit of credit. For more information, contact:

> Dr. Ramón Magrans
> Austin Peay State University
> PO Box 4487
> Clarkesville, TN 37044
> Tel: 931-221-7847 or 800-747-1894
> Email magransr@hotmail.com

NICHOLLS STATE UNIVERSITY. You can earn university credit through Nicholls State University in Louisiana for courses at Spanish Language Institute (SLI) in Cuernavaca. For more information, contact:

Cynthia Webb
Department of Study Abroad
PO Box 2080
Thiodaux, Louisiana 70310
Tel: 985-448-4440

ASHLAND UNIVERSITY. If you happen to be a teacher, you can earn one semester unit of graduate credit from Ashland University in Ohio for each week of study at Cuauhnáhuac Spanish Language Institute in Cuernavaca. For more information, contact:

Marcia Snell
519 Park Drive
Kenilworth, IL 60043
Tel: 877-745-3562

NATIONAL REGISTRATION CENTER FOR STUDIES ABROAD (NRCSA). NRCSA will work with a student's home university or any university that grants credit for the particular program the student is attending. The credit courses available depend upon the school. They range from elementary Spanish through graduate literature. In general, NRCSA charges double to triple the normal tuition of the schools they approve:

Cemanahuac - Cuernavaca

Universal - Cuernavaca

CEPE - Puerto Vallarta

OLE - Querétaro

Centro de Idiomas - Mazatlán

Centro de Idiomas del Sureste (CIS) – Mérida

Detailed information on NRCSA's services and fees is available on their website: www.nrcsa.com. You can also contact them by phone, fax, and Email:

NRCSA
PO Box 1393, Milwaukee, WI 53201
Tel: 414-278-0631 • Fax: 414-271-8884
Email: info@nrcsa.com or study@nrcsa.com

ACADEMIC ASSESSMENT ASSOCIATES INTERNATIONAL. Although some of the schools in this book may still list Academic Assessment Associates International (AAAI) as a credit-granting organization, AAAI has apparently discontinued its services and abandoned its website: www.aaaix.org.

MEXICAN UNIVERSITIES. Some Spanish-language schools are maintained by accredited Mexican universities authorized to grant their own credit by the *Secretaria de Educación Pública* (Secretary of Public Education). CEPE, with campuses in Guadalajara and Puerto Vallarta, offers credit through the University of Guadalajara. Instituto Allende in San Miguel de Allende is associated with the University of Guanajuato. Universidad Internacional in Cuernavaca is an accredited private university. A word of caution: do not assume that your college or university will accept credits earned from a Mexican university. Always check with the admissions and records department before registering for your Mexican study program.

COMMUNITY COLLEGE CREDIT

SEATTLE CENTRAL COMMUNITY COLLEGE (SCCC). This U.S. community college offers lower-division undergraduate credit for study at almost any Spanish-language school in Mexico. You sign up through their independent study program, choosing the course that best fits your language level and goals. Tuition is $300 for five quarter units. You can get more information on Professor Steve Tash's website: www.westudyabroad.com. You can contact Steve Tash directly by email, phone, or mail:

Professor Steve Tash c/o WeStudyAbroad.com
23786 Villena
Mission Viejo, CA 92692 USA
Tel: 949-916-1096
Fax: 949-916-1499
Email: travelstudy@yahoo.com

Karen Kato, at Seattle Central Community College, handles credits earned through We Study Abroad. She can be reached by phone: 206-587-5422 or by email: kakato@sccd.ctc.edu.

IMPORTANT NOTE: *All credit-granting institutions require that you sign up through them before leaving for Mexico.*

PREPARING FOR YOUR TRIP

W hat do you absolutely need to take? What can you live without? Make a list and check it more than twice! Some essentials will make life easier and more comfortable for you in Mexico. Some items may be problematic, but there are things you should not take under any circumstances: firearms, illegal drugs, or large quantities of any item for resale. For complete information on what is allowed and not allowed, see the U.S. State Department website: www.travel.state.gov. Click on *International Travel*, then *Regional Information*, and finally *Tips for Travel to Mexico*.

HEALTH-RELATED ITEMS

PRESCRIPTION DRUGS. Of course you should bring a supply of any prescription drugs you take on a regular basis. Always carry them in the original bottles with labels attached. If you take any controlled substances, such as anticonvulsants, sleep, or pain medications, ask your doctor for a letter explaining why you need them. If you can't get a letter from your doctor, take a copy of the prescription. Many prescription drugs are available over the counter in pharmacies in Mexico; however, if you need a controlled substance you must have a prescription from a Mexican doctor to get it. If you lose your medicine, a letter from your doctor or a copy of your original prescription may be necessary to replace it.

ANTIBIOTICS. It may be a good idea to take along a broad-spectrum antibiotic. Tell your doctor where you are going and ask if there is an appropriate medication you can take along in case you become ill.

PREVENTATIVES AND REMEDIES. In addition to cosmetics, toothpaste, and shampoo, here's a list of preventatives and over-the-counter medical supplies that I routinely take to Mexico:

- Sunscreen and lip balm
- Mosquito repellent
- Antiseptic or Antibiotic ointment
- Band-Aids and an elastic bandage
- Antibacterial hand wipes
- Water purification drops or portable water purifier
- Allergy medication or nasal spray

- Sore-throat lozenges and/or cough drops
- Tylenol, Excedrin, Ibuprofen, or Aleve (not readily available in Mexico)
- Vitamins
- Anti-diarrheal (Pepto-Bismol or Kaopectate, for example)
- Moleskin or corn pads

This is a very basic list; add to it according to your personal needs and preferences.

EYEGLASSES. If you wear glasses, take two pairs and at least one pair of good polarized sunglasses. It's also a good idea to take your eyeglass prescription in case you should need to replace them. Opticians are very common in Mexican cities and towns. With your prescription, you can easily get a new pair of glasses.

CLOTHING AND JEWELRY

Although the ads in travel magazines may show Mexico as a tropical paradise with weather to match, that description applies mainly to the coastal resort areas. If you're planning to study in Mazatlán, Puerto Vallarta, Cancún, or Playa del Carmen, your wardrobe should include shorts and beachwear. If, however, your school is located in one of the mountain cities such as Guadalajara, Guanajuato, or Oaxaca, you will encounter cooler weather and possibly even rain, so pack accordingly. (See "Climate" in the description of the city where your school is located.)

Wherever you go to school, take at least one set of "good" clothes: a dress or skirt outfit for women; long pants and a conservative shirt for men. You will most likely be invited out to dinner or to a party, whether through school or with your host family. On special occasions, Mexicans tend to dress more formally than Americans and Canadians do.

Avoid taking too much clothing or clothing that requires special care such as dry cleaning. Leave expensive jewelry at home. In fact, there's no need to take much jewelry, since attractive handmade necklaces, earrings, and bracelets are available at very low prices and make great souvenirs.

TOURIST CARDS AND VISAS

A student from the U.S. or Canada enrolled in a study program of six months or less may enter Mexico with a tourist card, also called an FMT. These are distributed on the plane before landing in Mexico, and are available at border stations if you're entering the country by car or bus.

You will be required to present the proper identification at the immigration counter in the airport. You'll also be asked how long you plan to stay. The maximum stay on a tourist card is 180 days (six months). Although your tourist card might not look like much, it's a very important document, as it is your legal permission to be in the country. Safeguard your tourist card during your stay, and remember that you'll be asked to surrender it upon leaving Mexico. For more information on Mexican tourist cards, including a picture of one, go to www.mexperience.com, and click on Planning a Trip to Mexico and Entry Requirements.

If you intend to study for more than six months at a Mexican college or university, you must apply for a student visa or FM3 at a Mexican consulate before leaving the U.S. or Canada. You'll be required to provide an acceptance letter from the Mexican school you plan to attend, proof of financial resources, several passport photos, and a certificate of good health. You'll also pay a small consular fee. More information on student visas and a list of Mexican consulates in the U.S. and Canada can be found on the Mexonline website: www.mexonline.com. If visa and consulate information is not listed in the links on the left side of the page, use the search feature to find *Visas* or *Consulates*. Visa and travel information for Canadian citizens is available in English on the Mexican Embassy's Canadian website: www.embamexcan.com.

IDENTIFICATION

U.S. and Canadian citizens can enter Mexico and get a tourist card with only a certified copy of their birth certificate; however, I recommend traveling with a passport, because it provides a much better means of identification. To apply for a passport, get an application from your local travel agency or post office at least six weeks before your departure date. You will then need to have passport photos taken, which can be done by a photography studio, a travel agency, or even some post offices. You'll also need a certified copy of your birth certificate to send with the passport application. (Order an extra copy to include in your emergency envelope as described in the next paragraph.) More information on applying for a U.S. passport is available on the U.S. State Department's website: www.travel.state.gov.

Before you leave home, prepare an emergency envelope with copies of your passport and airline ticket in case you lose the originals. It's a good idea to include a certified copy of your birth certificate as well. If you lose your passport, the birth certificate should allow you to leave the country or get the passport replaced at an American consulate or embassy. Just in case, you should have the address and phone number of the American consulate nearest your school in Mexico. American consulates are listed on the Internet at www.mexonline.com/consulate.htm.

IMMUNIZATIONS

No immunizations are required for travel to Mexico, unless you are coming from a country where there is an outbreak of cholera or some other dread disease. You may want to consider getting some shots before leaving, though. Hepatitis is more common in Mexico than in other parts of North America, and it is recommended that you get inoculated against hepatitis A and B. Also, make sure your tetanus shots are up to date. For possible outbreaks of other diseases, such as malaria, refer to the Centers for Disease Control website: www.cdc.gov. Look for *Travelers' Health*, click on *Destinations*, and *Central America* and *Mexico.* Anti-malaria medications such as chloroquine are available from your local health department, but are only recommended if you plan to spend time in the jungle areas of Yucatán, Chiapas, or Tabasco.

INSURANCE

HEALTH INSURANCE. If you have health coverage, check with your insurance carrier to find out if you're covered should you become ill or get hurt in Mexico. Some insurance companies will reimburse you for any covered medical expenses you incur; however, you may need to pay the doctor or hospital at the time you are treated. When you return home, you can then submit a claim to your insurance company. If you don't have health insurance or your plan doesn't cover you abroad, there are short-term health insurance plans you can purchase. At least two companies offer medical coverage for U.S. citizens traveling abroad: International Medical Group (IMG) 877-328-1565 or www.internationalstudentinsurance.com, and Cultural Insurance Services International 800-303-8120 www.culturalinsurance.com. Rates vary, depending on your age, the amount of coverage you need, and the deductible. Check out these or any other Internet-based insurance company thoroughly before applying and paying your premium. Make sure they are licensed in the U.S. or your country of residence. Make sure you'll be covered in Mexico, and find out how they pay claims — directly to the doctor or hospital or to you as a reimbursement.

TRAVEL INSURANCE. Trip-cancellation insurance covers nonrefundable travel costs should illness or accident force you to return home sooner than you had planned. Like travel health insurance, trip-cancellation policies are in effect only for the duration of your trip. This type of insurance is available at travel agencies and on the Internet. There are a variety of companies to choose from, including Travel Insured International, Travelex, CSA Travel Protection, Travel Guard, and HTH Protection. You can get comparison quotes tailored to your trip on two websites: www.quotetravelinsurance.com and www.totaltravelinsurance.com. Your airfare and other travel-related expenses will automatically be covered. Before purchasing a policy, find out whether it will cover your prepaid school expenses, such as tuition and room and board.

COMMUNICATIONS

The Mexican mail system is notoriously slow. Mexicans will tell you stories about how long it took a letter to get to its destination. If you need to communicate with the folks back home, your best options are email and telephone.

Email access is relatively easy in Mexico due to the large number of Internet cafés where you can check your email and surf the web at very low rates ($1 to $3/hour). The school you attend may also offer you free Internet access. In rare cases, students are able to use their host family's Internet connection; however, most Mexicans do not have home Internet service. If you don't know how to access your email from a remote computer, make sure to contact your provider and find out how to do so before you leave for Mexico.

The least expensive way to make local and long-distance calls in Mexico is to use a prepaid phone card. Public phones are plentiful throughout the country, and almost all of them are card phones. Mexican phone cards are available in denominations from 35 to 100 pesos (about $3.50–$10). You can buy them at many locations, from tiny shops to large supermarkets, newsstands, and pharmacies. TelMex phone cards can now be purchased online before you leave home. To buy one, or for more information on TelMex, visit the TelMex U.S.A website: www.telmexusa.com.

Several different phone cards are available, but TelMex and Ladatel cards seem to work in more phones than the others. To use a phone card, just insert it into the phone and dial a number within Mexico or in almost any country in the world. A digital display will let you know how much money is left on your card. The cost in U.S. currency ranges from 25 cents/minute for calls within Mexico, to 50 cents/minute for calls to the U.S. and Canada. Calls to other parts of the world cost $1–$2/minute. You should find these rates a considerable saving over using an MCI or AT&T credit card or your cell phone.

Though common in Mexico, public telephones are not always available when you need one. If you prefer the convenience of your cell phone, ask your wireless provider if it will work in Mexico. Some do and some don't, depending on the agreements that wireless providers maintain with their Mexican counterparts. Also inquire about the roaming charges, which can be substantial, and whether you'll need to sign up for an additional service. For example, Cingular's regular service works only near the U.S. border, but their international service works all over Mexico.

When calling from the U.S. to Mexico, you must always dial the international access code (011) before the country code (52). If you leave Mexican phone numbers with family and friends in the U.S., be sure to let them know that 011 must precede the Mexican phone number.

To call from Mexico to the U.S. or Canada, you must first dial 001, followed by the U.S. or Canadian area code and phone number.

MONEY MATTERS

First, determine how much money you'll need. Since your tuition, housing costs, and most of your meals will most likely be included in your study program, you won't need to take a large amount of money. $10–$15/day should be enough to cover your incidental expenses such as bus fare, snacks, and entry fees to museums and ruins. To make sure you have enough money while in Mexico, I suggest that you have at least four sources of funds:

- Money in your checking account, which you can withdraw at any ATM;

- A major credit card (MasterCard or VISA is best);

- U.S. dollars in small denominations for tips and bargaining power when shopping;

- Traveler's checks in case your ATM card or credit card are lost or stolen.*

---

* Although traveler's checks are good to have in reserve, they're no longer the best way to carry money while traveling in Mexico. Some Mexican banks don't cash them, and those that do offer a much less favorable exchange rate for traveler's checks than for ATM and credit card transactions. An ATM card is the best way to get money quickly while avoiding the long lines at many banks.

Exchange Rate. The exchange rate has averaged ten Mexican pesos per U.S. dollar for the past few years. The rate is not fixed, however; it varies slightly from day to day and can range from 9.5 to 11 pesos per dollar over a period of a few months.

The following form contains line items for the significant expenses you'll incur while studying in Mexico. Using the form, you should be able to estimate the total cost of your study program and create your own budget based on your spending habits. It's best to overestimate rather than run short of money while in Mexico. You may want to include a sum (at least $100) for unexpected (emergency) expenses, although your ATM card or credit card can serve this purpose.

BUDGET

Expenses	Totals
Round-trip airfare	
Airport Hotel	
Transportation to/from home airport	
Transportation to/from Mexican airport to host family	
Tuition per week times number of weeks	
Home stay or lodging per week	
Bus fare to/from school (allow $1 per day)	
Extra meals	
Entertainment	
Excursions	
Shopping	
Emergency Funds	
Grand Total:	

Transportation

Getting to Mexico. Many international airlines fly to Mexico, but sometimes it's difficult to find flights to out-of-the-way places. If you wish to fly directly to the city where your school is located, contact ABS Travel, an agency in Miami. This agency's website, www.abstravel.com, shows all airlines serving cities and towns in Mexico. Another very helpful web-site belongs to Exito Travel: www.exitotravel.com. They offer inexpensive airfares to Mexico and other parts of Latin America.

PUBLIC TRANSPORTATION

The public transportation system in Mexico is much more extensive and less expensive than in the U.S. or Canada. Buses go everywhere, from the largest cities to the smallest towns high in the mountains. Taxis are readily available, and fares are very reasonable. Walking is safe in most cities, but always ask your host family before setting out on your own. Getting to school on foot affords you the opportunity to get to know your neighborhood and feel more connected to the local culture.

BUSES. The rickety, overloaded Mexican bus negotiating a mountain road is a thing of the past. Although there are still a few older buses that go to small towns and rural areas, even second-class bus service has improved. When Mexico's bus lines upgraded, they relegated the former first-class buses to second-class service. The new first-class buses are reminiscent of small airliners. The seats recline into mini beds, and American movies with subtitles are shown on longer routes. There are restrooms, and a refreshment area offers coffee and cold drinks. Some bus lines even provide a box lunch for passengers. All first-class buses are air conditioned, but they can be overly cold, especially at night, so bring a jacket or sweater.

Most Mexicans travel between cities by bus, principally because of the high domestic airfares. For example, a round-trip flight from Mazatlán to León/Bajío airport near Guanajuato costs nearly $700, even though the length of the trip is about 500 miles, roughly equal to the distance between San Francisco and Los Angeles. The trip on a first-class bus takes about twelve hours each way and costs less than $100.

TAXIS. Except in large cities like New York or Toronto, taxis are not a common method of transportation in the U.S. and Canada. In Mexico taxis are almost always available, even in small towns and rural areas. Most taxis are safe and their drivers congenial; there have, however, been incidents of kidnapping and robbery linked to taxis in Mexico City, Guadalajara, and Cuernavaca. It's best to avoid hailing a taxi on the street in those cities. Ask your school or family to call a taxi for you if at all possible. Also, find out how to distinguish legitimate taxis from possible *pirata* (pirate) taxis in case you must flag one down.

STAYING HEALTHY

Mexico is an old and proud nation. It's also a developing nation. In the many years I have been traveling to Mexico, I have seen great improvements in transportation, technology, and communications. However, Mexico's water and sewer systems are often antiquated and inadequate. Poor sanitation can result in illnesses caused by water- and food-borne bacteria.

PREVENTING ILLNESS

The main health complaint of visitors to Mexico is the gastrointestinal distress and diarrhea better known as turista or "Moctezuma's Revenge." You can avoid this malady by taking a few precautions and watching what you eat, especially when dining out. Avoid lettuce, strawberries, and any unpeeled fruit. Forego ice in your drink. Have a beer instead of a margarita. And don't forget the lactobacillus acidophilus! I recently spent six months in Mexico with nary a stomach cramp, but I took acidophilus regularly. This ingredient in yogurt is available in capsules in most health-food stores in the U.S. It's a little harder to find in Mexico, so take a supply with you. Some visitors to Mexico claim that taking chewable Pepto Bismol tablets regularly also helps avoid diarrhea.

WATER. That timeworn advice to world travelers, *Don't drink the water*, is still valid in Mexico. Tap water in many places in Mexico can make you sick. Stick to bottled water, even to brush your teeth, and you'll avoid most water-borne bacteria. Remember that tap water is often used to make ice, so drink cold beverages without ice while in Mexico. Bottled soft drinks and beer are not likely to be contaminated, but wipe the top of the container clean before drinking from it. If you're using a glass, make sure it's dry and has not just been rinsed in tap water.

Street vendors often sell *aguas,* which are iced juice drinks made with water and served from large glass jars. They look wonderful, especially on a hot day, but for the sake of your stomach, get a safe bottled drink instead. In tropical areas, there's a fresh fruit beverage you can safely enjoy: coconut milk is refreshing and pure. You drink it directly from the coconut with a straw. The vendor should open the coconut in your presence and hand it to you shell and all. Avoid coconut milk in plastic bags, as it could be diluted with tap water.

STREET FOOD. It's best to avoid eating from the inviting food stands you'll see on the streets in most Mexican towns and cities. I sometimes make an exception for baked goods, like bread, pastries, or amaranth cakes. Do not eat chicken, fish, or meat dishes on the street, unless they're hot off the grill. Even then, you're taking a risk, because the meat may have been unrefrigerated for some time before being cooked. It's also best to avoid raw, cut up fruit and vegetables at food stands or in marketplaces. If you want to eat a piece of fruit, remember that it's safest if you can peel it yourself. Get an orange or a banana, peel it, and eat it. Lime juice is also reputed to be a disinfectant of sorts, so I use it liberally whenever I'm served a fruit plate in a restaurant.

FRUITS, VEGETABLES, AND SEAFOOD. There are two reasons why raw fruits and vegetables can cause illness. First, they usually come directly to the store from local farms, are usually unwashed, and may be contaminated by fertilizer or manure. Your host family will most likely purify raw fruit and vegetables by soaking them in a solution of iodine and water, but you can't be sure that restaurants and street vendors have done this. Secondly, when you eat out, someone must cut up and prepare your salad or fruit plate. In restaurants, produce is often washed in tap water, introducing water-borne contaminants. If you're unsure whether they have been decontaminated, avoid salads and all uncooked fruits and vegetables.

One culprit for illness can be fresh salsa. In some restaurants it sits out all day and the same salsa is used for multiple customers. Even if the salsa is changed with every patron, remember that it's usually made from raw vegetables.

Seafood can make you very sick if it is spoiled or mishandled. Cooked seafood is safest, but don't eat it if it looks or smells bad. A typical dish in the coastal areas of Mexico is *ceviche*, which is made from raw fish or shellfish marinated in lime juice. Eat *ceviche* and other raw seafood at your own risk, as it may contain microorganisms that can cause illness.

If you're wondering what you *can* eat safely in Mexico, the answer to that question is just about anything, as long as it's prepared properly. Don't be afraid to eat whatever your host family serves. Aware that visitors to Mexico are susceptible to gastrointestinal ailments, they will be careful to prepare foods you can eat safely. Also, most families routinely use an iodine or chlorine solution to decontaminate fruits and vegetables for their own consumption.

PERSONAL HYGIENE. Contaminated water and raw or improperly prepared foods are not the only source of harmful bacteria. You can unwittingly ingest bacteria from things you have touched: toilet flush handles, doorknobs, items in the market, and park benches, etc. At home these bacteria may cause you no problem because your body is accustomed to them, but in Mexico you'll encounter different strains of bacteria. Make a habit of washing your hands frequently, and always use soap, not just water. Carry antibacterial hand wipes with you to use when there's no way to wash your hands before eating. If neither soap and water nor hand wipes are available, rub your hands with lime juice, which is said to have antiseptic properties.

ALCOHOLIC BEVERAGES. Young Americans often overindulge in alcohol while in Mexico because the drinking age there is eighteen instead of twenty-one as in the U.S. As has been publicized by the wild scenes of college students on spring break in Cancún, things can get out of hand quickly. This is partly due to the effects of tequila, rum, beer, and sometimes a mixture of all three. Don't underestimate the strength of tequila and its homemade cousin, mezcal; both are distilled from cactus plants and both are hard liquors. A common way to drink tequila is as a "popper," alternating shots of tequila with lime and salt. Since the tequila is full strength, it doesn't take long for the drinker to become intoxicated. Drinking too much tequila, mezcal, or even beer will impair your judgment, and this could put you in danger. Drink moderately while in Mexico, and drink only in safe places with a group of friends.

SUNBURN AND HEAT EXHAUSTION. Most of Mexico is south of the Tropic of Cancer and is therefore officially tropical. The angle of the sun in the tropics makes it much stronger than in the northern temperate zones. It's easier to get sunburned, even when it's not especially hot. To avoid sunburn, always use sunscreen on your face and any other exposed areas of your body. Don't stay out in the sun for long periods of time, especially during the midday hours. Too much sun and heat may also cause you to become dehydrated, which can eventually result in a condition called heat exhaustion or even life-threatening heat stroke. Be sure to drink plenty of fluids. Carry a small bottle of water with you as you go about your daily activities. If you do get overheated, go into an air-conditioned café, sit down, and have a cool drink. Symptoms of dehydration include thirst, headache, and weakness. If you become dehydrated, replace your fluids, rest, and try to stay cool. (See "What to do in Case of Illness".)

Mexico's coastal and lowland areas are hot and humid. If you're not used to this type of climate, you may feel overheated and listless for the first few days. Try not to overexert yourself, stay as cool as possible, and keep hydrated. Restrict strenuous activities to the morning and evening hours when it's cooler. Try taking a *siesta* (nap) during the hottest part of the afternoon. There's a reason for this Latin American custom! If you take it easy for the first few days, you should be able to resume your normal activities without adverse consequences.

ALTITUDE. Many of the cities featured in this book are at altitudes over 5,000 feet. Guanajuato and San Miguel de Allende are over 6,000 feet. If you have a medical condition that may worsen at altitude, consider studying in one of the coastal cities or in Merida, Yucatán, which is close to sea level. If you do experience symptoms of altitude sickness, such as headache, dizziness, or shortness of breath, slow down and rest frequently. The symptoms should disappear as soon as your body gets accustomed to the thinner air.

MOSQUITOES. Mosquitoes are a problem in the low-lying coastal areas of Mexico, where you should always take precautions not to get bitten. Wear mosquito repellent, long pants, and a long-sleeved shirt when going into rural areas or jungles where there are likely to be mosquitoes. Always carry mosquito repellent with you. There are two common mosquito-borne diseases in Mexico: malaria and dengue fever. Malaria is more serious, but dengue is very debilitating and painful. The best preventative for both is to avoid being bitten by mosquitoes. For information on where in Mexico there is a risk of malaria or dengue fever, check the Travelers Health section of the Centers for Disease Control website: www.cdc.gov. For a list of immunizations recommended for Mexico, see chapter 5, "Preparing for Your Trip."

Assuming you're in good health when you leave home, you can stay healthy by following some simple guidelines while in Mexico. Your overall experience will be much more enjoyable if it's not marred by illness.

GUIDELINES FOR AVOIDING ILLNESS

- Drink bottled water, not tap water.
- Avoid drinks made with ice.
- Always wash your hands before eating.
- Carry antibacterial hand wipes.
- Avoid eating from open-air food stands on the street.
- Drink plenty of non-alcoholic fluids and do not become dehydrated.
- Take lactobacillus acidophilus tablets throughout your stay.
- Take it easy the first few days. Take a *siesta* (nap) each afternoon.
- Use sunscreen, and avoid spending too much time in the sun and getting overheated.

- Wear mosquito repellent in coastal and lowland areas.
- Respect the strength of tequila, mezcal, and other alcoholic beverages.

WHAT TO DO IN CASE OF ILLNESS

REHYDRATE. Diarrhea, vomiting, and overexertion in the heat can cause dehydration. The Centers for Disease Control (www.cvc.gov) recommends the World Health Organization oral rehydration salts, sold as CeraLyte in many parts of the world. In the U.S. you can purchase CeraLyte from the travel supply company Magellan's: www.magellans.com. It costs about $10 for four foil packets. CeraLyte is easy to pack but must be mixed with purified water. If you don't have CeraLyte, the CDC suggests a homemade oral rehydration solution that also relieves diarrhea. To make it, you'll need two glasses. Mix eight ounces of fruit juice with half a teaspoon of honey and a pinch of salt in one glass. In the other, mix a quarter teaspoon of baking soda with eight ounces of water. Slowly sip from one glass, then from the other. In an hour or two, you should feel better.

TAKE MEDICATION. Among the "absorbents" that the World Health Organization recommends for diarrhea are activated charcoal, bismuth subsalicylate (Pepto-Bismol), and kaolin and pectin (Kaopectate). They also suggest taking prescription antimotility agents such as Lomotil or natural opiates like codeine. These should be used with caution. Before you leave, consult your doctor to decide what to take with you in case you get a gastrointestinal illness.

SEE A DOCTOR. In rare cases, the symptoms of *turista* will persist for more than just a few days and be accompanied by weakness, fever, nausea, vomiting, abdominal cramps, or bloody stools. If this happens to you, ask to see a doctor. You may have something more serious, such as amebic dysentery, and you may need antibiotics or antimicrobial medication.

SAFETY CONCERNS

Like all countries, Mexico has its dangers. If you're aware of what can go wrong, you can avoid being the victim of a crime or getting hurt in an accident. The following are some safety concerns that are of particular importance for visitors to Mexico.

CRIME

There have been many recent news reports about crime in Mexico, but most of the violent crimes and kidnappings occur in the Mexico City area. With the exception of the capital, most Mexican cities are probably safer than their counterparts in the U.S. There are, however, neighborhoods to avoid, especially at night. Your host family may warn you away from these areas. If you're uncertain about the safety of a neighborhood, ask someone you trust before going there. Also, try to restrict your night-time activities to group outings. Don't go out alone after dark, and take the same precautions you would in a strange city at home.

THEFT. Much of the crime in Mexico is petty theft, principally by pick-pockets. How can you protect yourself? Thieves are looking for easy targets, so with a little common sense you can avoid a problem. In a crowded market or on the street, keep your money in a money belt or fanny pack placed on the front of your body where it's inaccessible to pickpockets. Don't carry it in your backpack or purse, and especially not in a wallet in your back pocket.

Beachgoers who leave their valuables on the beach and go swimming are often the victims of thieves. To avoid losing your money at the beach, take only what you might need, and keep it in an inside pocket in your swimsuit or in a waterproof "swim wallet" that you wear around your neck. Leave your watch and jewelry in your room. If you go to the beach with a group of friends, you can take turns watching each other's things.

WATER SAFETY

Even though the water is warmer in Mexico than in other parts of North America, the ocean is still dangerous, particularly along the Pacific coast, where large, powerful waves are common. Watch the waves for a while before you decide to go in swimming or body surfing. Use the buddy system. There are seldom lifeguards on even the most frequented Mexican beaches, so you are responsible for your own safety in the water.

VEHICLE SAFETY

BUSES. Mexican first-class buses are usually newer than those in the U.S., and many have safety features like anti-lock brakes and traction control. Most inter-city buses also have speed controls that keep the driver from exceeding 60 mph. It's safer to always take first-class buses. An older, run-down, second-class bus is more likely to have an accident. It's also best to take buses in the daytime hours. There have been incidents of highway robbery (asaltos) involving buses traveling lonely stretches of road at night.

TAXIS. Mexico City has had a recent increase in the number of *pirata* (pirate) taxis, unlicensed taxis that look exactly like all the others to the untrained eye. These *pirata* taxis also exist in Cuernavaca and Guadalajara. To avoid being picked up by one, inquire at your school or ask your host family how to identify an authorized taxi (*un taxi autorizado*). They may call one for you or suggest that you hail one from a particular company. Taxis are a common and relatively safe means of transport in most Mexican cities; however, as in the U.S., some taxi drivers tend to speed and take chances.

CROSSING THE STREET. Be alert when crossing the street in Mexico. In most areas of the country, pedestrians do not have the right of way, and drivers may be less pedestrian-friendly than you are used to at home. Never assume that a car, bus, or taxi is going to stop or even slow down to allow you to cross the street.

DRIVING. If you drive in Mexico, avoid driving at night. There are at least three reasons for this precaution. 1) It's difficult to see road hazards, such as potholes or *topes* (speed bumps) at night. 2) Many areas of Baja California and the Sonora desert are open range. It's difficult to see a cow or burro in the road in time to stop, even in the daytime. 3) Bandits ply some lonely stretches of road at night. They use four-wheel-drive trucks with extremely bright lights to blind drivers and run them off the road. During the day, these hazards disappear or are greatly diminished. On the positive side, there is a network of green trucks called the Green Angels that patrol highways looking for tourists having car problems. They carry gasoline, batteries, an air compressor for pumping up tires, and other useful tools and equipment.

  The rules of the road are different in Mexico than in the U.S. and Canada. Mexicans do drive fast, but they are defensive drivers as well. If you see a car coming toward you head-on, get out of the way, don't insist on staying in your lane. Drivers often flash their headlights to indicate that they are taking the right of way. For example, if two cars come to a one-lane section of the highway, the first car to flash its headlights has the right of way. Mexican truck drivers use their left blinker light to signal to other drivers that it's all right to pass. Sometimes this is confusing; the truck could just be turning left! Expect the unexpected. If you decide to pass a slow car or truck, always look in your rearview mirror first to see if anyone is passing you. If you're in an accident where the police are involved, do not admit to anything on the scene. The general rule in Mexico is to take everyone to the police station and sort it all out there. Call your Mexican insurance company as soon as possible so that they can represent you with the police and the other party involved in the accident.

When parking your car, always lock it and take your valuables with you. Make sure that anything you must leave in the car (backpacks, jackets, books, etc.) is in the trunk or otherwise out of sight and not a temptation to thieves.

Unexpected Hazards

Mexico doesn't have as many laws relating to personal safety as the U.S. and Canada. People are expected to watch out for themselves. For example, if there's a construction project on the street, there may not be barriers to keep pedestrians from falling into an excavation. Sometimes bricks or lumber can fall down onto the street from a building project. Sidewalks are often in disrepair, and you must watch out for "Gringo traps," drop-offs and holes in the concrete that could cause injury. There are usually no railings to prevent tourists from falling off the ancient buildings in Pre-Columbian archeological sites. Climbing one of the pyramids is often a harrowing experience involving narrow, steep steps; and coming down is always more difficult than going up. Sometimes there's a chain or rope to hold on to, but usually you're on your own. The reason for this lack of concern for public safety is mainly due to the fact that Mexican law does not allow personal-injury lawsuits. Be observant and know your own capabilities. Above all, remember that staying safe in Mexico is your responsibility.

Living with a Mexican Family

The most rewarding experience of your Spanish-language immersion program may be living with a Mexican family, which is referred to by most schools as a "home stay." A home stay extends language learning to the world outside the classroom and immerses you in Mexican culture, but it can provide even more benefits. Many students make lasting friendships that result in an ongoing interchange of correspondence. Others return to the same family year after year as their studies continue. Still others invite their Mexican host family to visit them in the U.S.

or Canada, and the families get to know each other. This type of interchange has helped many Americans and Canadians to understand the Mexican immigrant families living in their own communities, resulting in a small but significant step toward global understanding.

WHAT TO EXPECT

ARRANGING A HOME STAY. The school you plan to attend will usually arrange a home stay for you. Your only responsibility in most cases will be to fill out a placement questionnaire with your personal information, including your age, gender, smoking preferences, and special dietary considerations. The school will match you with a host family and should email you their name, address, and contact information. If you do not receive information about your host family within a reasonable time, contact the school. Never leave home without contact information in Mexico. Carry with you a card showing the name, address, and telephone number of both your host family and the school. Before leaving, make sure family members at home have your address and phone number in Mexico, contact information for your school, and the details of your flights and bus connections.

GETTING TO YOUR HOME IN MEXICO. Ask your school how to get from the airport or bus station to your host family's home. Sometimes your family will pick you up and drive you home. In other cases, the school may offer you transportation. Usually there is a charge for this service, and the cost can be substantial if your destination is far from the nearest airport. For example, to transport a student from the Mexico City airport to Cuernavaca, most schools charge $80 one-way. A little-known alternative is the frequent bus service that will take you from the domestic terminal in the Mexico City airport to Cuernavaca for about $10. It will cost an additional $3–$5 for a taxi from the bus station to your host family's home, but you'll save about $65.

Information about specific transportation options is shown in the "Getting There" section for each city. Details on each school's transportation service, including cost, can be found in the "Extras" section of the school's description. Most schools also show transportation options on their websites. If you're uncertain about the best way to get there, try emailing the school with your questions. Most schools have someone on staff whose job it is to answer email inquiries in English.

ARRIVAL. Upon arrival, your host family will greet you and introduce you to any other students who are staying with them. They'll take you to your room, make sure you're comfortable and can find the bathroom, and show you where to find extra blankets or how to turn on the fan or air conditioner. As soon as possible, verify the address and especially the telephone number you received from the school. If you haven't already done so, write your host family's name, address, and phone number on a card or a piece of paper and keep it in your wallet. The heading should read: "My host family in (name of city). This serves two purposes: if you're injured, emergency workers can check your wallet for identification to determine whom to call; and if you need to call your family or give the address to a taxi driver, you'll always have it with you.

THE HOME. Most schools provide their students with accommodations in middle-class homes, but middle-class Mexican homes are not always built to the same standards as middle-class American homes. The exterior of most houses is rather plain, but the interior is usually nicely decorated and has most of the conveniences you would expect in the U.S. Many homes feature an interior patio that serves as a second living room with tropical plants and garden furniture. Typically, your room will contain a twin or double bed, a night table and lamp, a desk or table, a dresser, and a closet, but it may seem rather plain. There may not be a television or even a radio in your room, but the warmth of your host family should more than make up for the simplicity of the accommodations. In rare cases, you may be placed with a wealthy family in a mansion with a swimming pool. Some schools in Cuernavaca will make sure you get luxurious accommodations if you choose their deluxe home-stay plan.

THE BEST SITUATION. If you really want the home stay to add to your language learning, ask to be the only student assigned to a particular family. Although it might be fun to live with a number of other students, you'd probably spend more time speaking English with your roommates than speaking Spanish with your host family. Once I was placed in a home that functioned like a boarding house. There were eight students staying there, and the language of choice at meals was English, even though the hostess did not speak a word of it! Although the host family was friendly and helpful, they also ran two small businesses, so they had little time to spend with the students. This situation did not promote language learning, and it might have been avoided had I let the school know I wanted to be the only student assigned to the home.

MEALS. You may find the meal schedule and diet in Mexico very different from what you expect. Some Mexican food is hot and spicy, but most dishes are not laced with chile, and hot sauces are usually served on the side to add if you wish. If you're accustomed to restaurant Mexican food in the U.S., "real" Mexican food may surprise you. Chances are you'll sel-dom eat tacos or burritos. A meal might consist of something as familiar as roast chicken, rice, and vegetables. On the other hand, your family may be eager for you to try a delicious regional specialty or some of the fruits and vegetables not commonly available in the U.S. Mexicans eat lots of fruit and vegetables but are principally carnivores. If you're a vegetari-an, be sure to mention that in the dietary section of the school question-naire. The school will make an effort to place you with a family sensitive to your dietary preferences. If you prefer mild food, or dislike or are aller-gic to certain foods, let your family know. Special health foods and sup-plements are difficult to find in Mexico, and you should bring a supply if they're an important part of your diet.

BREAKFAST (EL DESAYUNO): Usually served between 7 and 8 a.m., break-fast is often a casual meal. You can expect to have coffee, cold cereal or oatmeal, eggs with ham or sausage (*chorizo*) or pancakes, fresh fruit, and juice. Mexican specialties like quesadillas, chilaquiles, and tamales are sometimes served for breakfast. A special treat is the fresh-squeezed orange juice that Mexicans prefer to the frozen concentrated type most Americans drink.

LUNCH (EL ALMUERZO OR LA COMIDA): Served between 2 and 4 p.m., this is traditionally the big meal of the day, and your family will expect you to be home for it. This meal is more like dinner in the U.S., consisting of a variety of foods served in several courses. The main course is usu-ally chicken, pork, or beef, sometimes served Mexican style with *mole* (a rich, spicy sauce) or *pibil* (slow roasted). On Sunday, extended family and friends are often invited to share this meal. Your hostess may go to a great deal of extra effort to prepare the afternoon meal for you. Be sure to let her know *early* if you must miss it, and avoid spoiling your appe-tite with snacks or "street food."

SUPPER (LA CENA): Served between 8 and 10 p.m., this is a light meal often consisting of fruit, soup, a sandwich, quesadillas, tacos, tostadas, or some-times leftovers from the midday meal.

SNACKS AND FAST FOOD. Healthy snacks (and some not so healthy) abound in Mexico. You should have no trouble finding yogurt, granola bars, nuts, hot dogs, hamburgers, French fries, and several types of chips. Many familiar brands have migrated across the border: Frito-Lay, Yoplait, Kel-logg's, Nabisco, Nestlé, and Quaker, to mention just a few. Most U.S. soft-drink brands are available in Mexico, and for those who crave fast food, McDonald's and Burger King are common in larger towns and cities.

KFC, Pizza Hut, and Domino's Pizza have also established a presence in Mexico. If you prefer more traditional Mexican snacks, the old standby, the taco stand, is always an option. These little snack bars can be found almost everywhere, cooking tacos on a charcoal or gas stove and sending out delicious aromas. Ask your family or someone at the school to recommend one. They can point you in the direction of a taco stand where the food is tasty and safe. See chapter 6 – "Staying Healthy."

KITCHEN PRIVILEGES. Your hostess may appreciate your help, but don't assume that you can use the kitchen whenever you wish. In most families, the meals are prepared and served by the mother or a hired cook. If you would like to prepare some of your own food, ask first—and be sure to clean up afterward.

HOUSEHOLD HELP. Whether it is a cleaning woman who comes in a few times a week, or a cadre of live-in servants, normally someone other than family members will be cleaning your room. Although household help are usually quite trustworthy, as a precaution you should not leave valuables lying around. Some families will assign you a locked closet or other secure area for your valuables. In other situations, you may need to be creative. Hide your passport and extra money in odd places, such as in a sock in a locked suitcase. Never leave large amounts of cash or valuable jewelry in your room. Always carry a photocopy of your passport and your original Mexican tourist card with you, but leave your original passport at your Mexican home. The chances of losing your important papers in the street are much greater than the chances that they'll be stolen from your room.

LAUNDRY. Your hostess is not your mom, so don't expect her, or even the household help, to do your laundry. Most host families will explain their laundry policy in the beginning, but if you're unsure, ask before using the washing machine and especially the dryer. In areas where there's plenty of sunshine, most people hang their clothes outside rather than use the dryer. Some families will do your laundry for a minimal extra charge; others prefer that you take your dirty clothes to a commercial laundry or Laundromat. Many families wash their clothes by hand in a special concrete basin and washboard combination. If you do your own laundry by hand, ask where to hang it. Don't assume you can just hang your underwear in the bathroom. Get specific instructions on laundry to avoid any unpleasant or embarrassing situations.

ELECTRICITY. Electricity in Mexico is 110 volt, 60 cycle AC, the same as in the U.S., but the power isn't always reliable. Outages and power surges occur more frequently in Mexico than in the U.S. If you'll be using a lap-top or other electronic equipment, make sure to bring a surge protector. Mexicans also seem to be more concerned with saving electricity than most Americans. They avoid using the washer and dryer and turn out the lights whenever they leave a room. Your family will appreciate it if you observe and adopt their thrifty habits.

HEAT. It gets cold in the winter in mountain cities such as Guanajuato and San Miguel de Allende, and most Mexican houses lack central heat-ing or even portable room heaters. Check the altitude of the city you'll be visiting. If it's above 5,000 feet and you plan to be there in December, January, or February, bring some warm sleeping garments. In hot areas such as the Caribbean coast or Yucatán, it seldom gets cold, and you can expect to find a fan or air conditioner in your room. To get a glimpse of temperatures and weather conditions in the Mexican town or city where you'll be staying, find it on www.yahooweather.com a few days before you leave. The site shows current weather for cities and towns all over Mexico and will also give you a long-range forecast.

SMOKING. Smoking is more prevalent in Mexico than in the U.S., and mem-bers of your host family may be smokers. If you are a non-smoker, you may be able to request a smoke-free home on your school's registration questionnaire. If you smoke, avoid smoking in your room or even in the house unless you have specific permission from your host family.

WHAT THE FAMILY WILL EXPECT

Your host family will expect you to speak Spanish at all times. Even if they speak English, the school may prohibit them from speaking English with you except in certain crucial situations where understanding is im-portant to your health or well-being.

They will expect you to be on time for meals or to let them know if you won't be there. If you miss a meal without notice, it may be considered an insult and damage your relationship with your host family.

They will expect you to keep your room neat and clean. Hang up your clothes, and keep underwear and small items in drawers or your suitcase. Put laundry all together in a bag or in a receptacle they provide. If you keep snacks, water, or soft drinks in your room, store them in a box or a drawer. Do not leave open packages of food lying around.

They will expect you to avoid wasting valuable resources such as elec-tricity and water. Even though you feel like a member of the family, nev-er forget that you are a paying guest. To make sure your stay is profitable for your family, turn off lights and air conditioning when leaving a room, take short showers, and wash your clothes only with permission and only when necessary.

They will expect you to pay your room and board on time and in cash, unless it is paid to the school. Inquire at the outset whether they'd like you to pay each week or at the beginning or end of your stay. Do not assume that they will accept traveler's checks in payment. Most families prefer to be paid in cash. Home-stay prices are usually quoted in U.S. dollars, but in most cases you can also pay in Mexican pesos. If you pay in pesos, make sure that your host or hostess agrees to the exchange rate and total.

The best families will expect you to participate in family activities, and they'll often arrange to attend cultural events, visit places of interest, or meet with friends for your benefit. You should graciously accept their invitations, go with a positive attitude, and thank them for including you.

A Few Simple Rules

Some schools will give you a list of rules for your home stay, and some families also provide written rules. There are, however, some common-sense rules that may not be spelled out.

1. Do not use illegal drugs or alcohol in the home. As a general rule, you should avoid using, or associating with others who use illegal drugs. Drug abuse is a very serious crime everywhere in Mexico, and foreigners have gone to prison for years just for smoking marijuana.

2. Always let the family know where you are going, with whom, and when you will return. Mexican hospitality requires that they protect their guests. Your family will feel responsible for you as long as you are staying in their home, and this applies whether you are sixteen or sixty. It's all right to go out with friends or even take off on your own for a weekend, as long as you let your family know when you'll be back and stick to that time.

3. Get permission from your family before inviting friends to your home, especially into your room. Most families will welcome your friends, but they appreciate being asked first. If you have a friend coming over for a meal, offer to help with the preparations and be sure that you introduce him or her to everyone in the family.

4. Avoid making a lot of noise. If you're accustomed to listening to loud music and bring along a portable stereo, don't for-

get the headphones. Loud music emanating from your room will not be appreciated. Ordinarily, there is only one television set in the home. You may watch TV with family members from time to time, but don't expect to watch all your favorite programs on a regular basis.

Mexicans are some of the friendliest and most gracious people in the world. Chances are you will be accepted as "one of the family" very quickly. As a rule, your family will be helpful when you attempt to speak Spanish, tolerant of your habits, and understanding of your problems. You can show your gratitude for their hospitality by being a considerate guest.

FITTING IN: HOW TO AVOID BEING AN UGLY AMERICAN

When their bestseller *The Ugly American* was published in 1958, Eugene Burdick and William Lederer coined a term that stands for American arrogance and lack of understanding of foreign cultures. Although the book was written about Americans in Southeast Asia, over the years "ugly Americans" have appeared almost everywhere, including Mexico.

To avoid being thought of as an "ugly American," you must make an effort to appreciate the values that Mexicans hold dear. You will not be able to change Mexico or reform its people. Try to embrace rather than reject their customs, even though they may not fit your lifestyle or worldview. Remember that you are an ambassador for your country and that all Americans may be judged by your behavior. You can fit in by showing appreciation, respect, and understanding of the Mexican people and their culture.

WHEN IN MEXICO, DO AS THE MEXICANS DO!

Some things are done differently in Mexico. For example, it's acceptable to get someone's attention with a loud "PSSSST!" Drivers use the horn often and do not brake or swerve for animals or even for pedestrians. Vendors in marketplaces and on the street set a high initial price for their wares because they expect you to bargain. Taxis are often not metered, and fares must be negotiated beforehand. Safety and sanitation laws are either nonexistent or very lenient. Beggars are tolerated, especially around churches.

Try to accept these differences and not be overtly critical of them. After all, you are in Mexico to learn the language and absorb the culture.

Mexico even *looks* different from the U.S. Streets and sidewalks aren't always paved, and vacant lots are sometimes filled with trash. Construction often remains unfinished for tax reasons, and some buildings are substandard and even unsafe. Despite all this, you will also see delightful gardens, beautiful colonial buildings, ancient ruins, and even modern shopping centers. If you look for poverty and failure, you'll find them; if you learn to ignore the negative aspects and search out Mexico's beauty and culture, you'll find them, too.

MEXICAN TIME. One thing that can test your patience is the Mexican concept of time, which they call *"hora mexicana."* Mexican time can be very flexible, and there are different expectations under different circumstances. The times of social events are often the most indeterminate. For example, if you are invited to a party at 9 p.m., you probably shouldn't show up until 9:30 or even 10. If you arrive at 9, your hosts will most likely not be ready for you. You should, however, be on time for meals, classes, appointments, movies, and theater performances, which usually start promptly. Buses, trains, and airlines stick to a strict schedule as well. So how do you know whether to show up on time or be late? There's a double standard operating in some situations. If you've arranged to take a tour at 8 a.m., you should be prompt, but try not to get irritated if your guide doesn't get there until 9:15. Always expect that you might be kept waiting, and bring along a book or magazine to keep yourself occupied.

Another time-related problem for many visitors is the fact that traditional mealtimes in Mexico are much later than in the U.S. or Canada. This is especially true for lunch and supper. If you're used to eating lunch at noon and supper at 6 p.m., you'll need to adapt to a new schedule while in Mexico. Lunch is rarely served before 2 p.m., and supper could be as late as 9:30. To ward off the hunger pangs, try carefully timed snacking in the late morning and again at around 6 p.m., but avoid eating too much and spoiling the next meal with your family.

DRESSING APPROPRIATELY. Many Americans think of Mexico as a vacation spot requiring very little attention to dress. Although shorts and T-shirts may be standard issue for visitors to coastal resort towns such as Puerto Vallarta or Cabo San Lucas, they are not normally worn in inland cities like Guadalajara or Cuernavaca. Look around you and observe what people are wearing. As a rule, Mexicans dress more conservatively than Americans do, and sloppy or skimpy clothing will mark you as a tourist.

An exception to this rule may be the current trend toward tight jeans and low-necked, midriff-hugging tops on teenage girls all over Mexico. Teenagers aside, most adults pay careful attention to their dress, even to the point of wearing designer clothes. You don't need a Christian Dior wardrobe to fit in, however; if you're aware of a few simple rules, you'll be accepted in almost any situation.

1. Avoid wearing shorts or your bathing suit in the city. This type of dress (or undress) is acceptable on the beach or at a *balneario* (bathing resort or hot spring), but not downtown.

2. Don't wear jeans everywhere. Although jeans are becoming more popular, they aren't ubiquitous in Mexico, especially when eating out or attending a social function.

3. Elegance is the norm for most social occasions. If you're invited to a party or out to dinner, you should expect to dress up a bit. Women should wear a dress, a skirt, or a dressy pants outfit. Men should wear slacks and a neat shirt. Suits or sport coats and ties are not common except in very formal situations. A *guayabera*, which is an embroidered shirt, is often worn on special occasions in place of a sport coat and tie.

4. Dress up if you must have any contact with officialdom, such as the police or immigration authorities. Many officials will interpret overly casual or sloppy dress as a sign of disrespect.

My final advice is to observe what people of your age and social class are wearing in different situations; make your clothing choices accordingly and you'll always fit in.

INTERACTION BETWEEN THE SEXES

It is a common misconception among Mexican men that American, Canadian, and European women are flirty and promiscuous, and this transfers directly to men's attitudes and behavior toward foreign women. If you are female, you need to be prepared to interact differently with Mexican men than you would with their American or Canadian counterparts. Rule number one is to avoid direct eye contact at first and not to dazzle every man you meet in the street with your best smile and most inviting look. Mexican men will take you up on what they consider an invitation to sex. Approached properly, however, they will exude charm and chivalry, treating you very much like a lady. Be polite and friendly, but not flirty. Watch what you wear. Tight pants, short skirts, and décolletage will just reinforce the myth that *gringas* are fast and easy. Regardless of how you feel about gender equity, accept the reality that it has not yet caught on in Mexico.

Women should also be aware that they are not welcome in all bars in Mexico. Unlike American and Canadian cocktail lounges, some Mexican bars are exclusively for men. These places are usually called *cantinas*. Just walking into a *cantina* could identify you as a prostitute. In fact, women rarely enter a bar or nightclub alone in Mexico. Go and have fun, but go with a group or a male escort.

Men must also be cognizant of different expectations in their interactions with the opposite sex. You may be looking for friendship or a meaningful relationship with an attractive *mexicana,* but her family may be suspicious of you and your intentions to the point of hostility. Even if the family is not hostile, they may discourage your romantic interest in their daughter, especially if you are not Catholic. On the other hand, some families are eager to marry their daughters to a rich *gringo*. You may not consider yourself wealthy, but some Mexicans think that all *gringos* are rich. After all, why would they be studying or vacationing in Mexico instead of working eighteen hours a day to make ends meet as so many Mexicans do?

People say that Mexico is a land of paradoxes. This is borne out by the fact that, although it's not considered proper for a woman to look a strange man in the eye on the street, hugging and kissing perfect strangers of either sex is not only acceptable, it is expected in certain situations! Used as a greeting and a farewell, the *abrazo* or hug is accepted by Mexicans as "normal," but many Americans or Canadians might consider it too personal. Kissing on the cheek (often both cheeks) is also common. So how do you know when this behavior is acceptable? It's usually done among friends or relatives. Your Mexican family will treat you as a relative, so be prepared for their extended family and friends to hug you or kiss you on the cheek. Except among old friends, hugging and kissing is less common in business and academic settings. Your teacher will probably greet you with a handshake, and the attendant at the local Internet café may just nod and point out your computer.

MACHISMO

Most Mexican men and many women still believe in machismo, a doctrine of male superiority left over from the Middle Ages in Spain. The following are some of the unwritten rules of machismo:

- Men are superior to women in every way—intellectually, physically, and emotionally.

- Men must be respected simply because they are male.
- Men must never allow themselves to be shown up or humbled.
- Men must defend their superiority against challenges from other males.

Because of *machisimo*, men are treated with a certain deference in Mexico. This can work in your favor if you are male; however, if you are a woman who is an accomplished professional or a natural athlete and have a tendency to show off your abilities, suppress the urge to do so when interacting with a Mexican man. Men reign supreme, especially in sports and careers, and women are very seldom treated as "one of the guys." My advice: If you are female, don't try to impress everyone with your academic brilliance or athletic abilities. Chances are your intellect will shine through anyway, and you'll be accepted rather than resented as an outspoken *gringa*. Let your Mexican "brother" carry your backpack if he offers to, but don't let him know that you can run faster and hike farther than he can. Think of it as keeping peace in the family.

What does *machismo* mean for the male visitor to Mexico? Although you are accepted as "one of the guys," you may find Mexican men overly competitive, especially when it comes to charming the ladies and excelling in sports. Let them impress you with their prowess as Don Juans or their superior ability to play *fútbol*. It costs nothing and will win you friends.

If you consider *machismo* a sham, you're right. It is. More and more Mexican women are entering fields previously reserved for men, but they still behave in ways that uphold the old tradition of *machismo*. Whether women defer to men out of genuine respect or just because it's expected, no one really knows. However, as an outsider, and especially as a female outsider, you need to be aware of this aspect of Mexican culture and modify your behavior accordingly.

GUNS AND THE MILITARY PRESENCE

Throughout Latin America, armed guards and soldiers are routinely stationed at government offices, banks, post offices, telephone and telegraph offices, airports, and any place of strategic importance. These men are usually in uniform and armed with machine guns. Although they may seem intimidating, they are just doing their jobs. There is usually no reason for alarm, but you should always assume that the guns are loaded, and follow any instructions you may be given by police, guards, or soldiers.

POLITICS

Mexicans love to talk about politics. Mexico is a democracy, and its government structure was modeled on that of the U.S. The elected representatives (diputados and senadores) serve in the congress in Mexico City. Although they make the laws, once in power they have many opportunities to flaunt them and sometimes profit handsomely from their time in office. Most Mexicans will tell you how corrupt their government officials are and complain about their high taxes and low standard of living, but don't take this as a disavowal of their love of country—Mexicans are loyal to Mexico, whatever her failings.

Mexicans are very sensitive to the overshadowing presence of the U.S., which they perceive as their rich and powerful northerly neighbor. Many Mexicans still "remember" (from their history books) that the U.S. army invaded and attempted to take over Mexico City in 1847. All those monuments and streets you see dedicated to the *Niños Heroés* are commemorating the deaths at the hands of American troops of the teenage military cadets who defended the *Castillo de Chapultepec,* which was previously the seat of government. Mexicans also "remember" that the U.S. appropriated one-third of their territory, including all or part of Texas, New Mexico, Colorado, California, and Arizona in 1848. In the 1860s, forty years after Mexico had fought its bloody war with Spain and gained its independence, the country was invaded by France. The French were expelled after several years of strife. Mexicans celebrate a turning point in their struggle against the French occupation every year on May 5 (*Cinco de Mayo*). In the early 1900s, American industrialists established controlling interests in natural resources in many parts of Mexico. All of these experiences have made Mexicans very wary of foreign control.

The best way to familiarize yourself with Mexico's past, which is the basis for its modern political structure, is to read a history of Mexico. Before you go, also make a point of reading an English-language Mexican newspaper on the Internet to familiarize yourself with current events. Everyone in Mexico knows the name of the President of the United States. You should know the name of the current President of Mexico and have some basic knowledge of the country's history and future challenges.

RELIGION

Most outsiders don't realize how pervasive religion is throughout Mexico. Catholic Churches are everywhere and are usually the largest and most beautifully decorated buildings in any town or city. Shrines abound along highways, in parks, and on city streets. Religious symbols in the form of crucifixes and pictures of saints and the Virgin Mary are often prominently displayed in homes and vehicles as well. On his visits to Mexico, Pope John Paul II received unprecedented attention from the press and the populace. His popularity in Mexico rivaled that of a modern rock group. If you aren't Catholic, you won't be expected to attend mass every Sunday, but you must show respect for Catholicism, regardless of your own beliefs.

DON'T BE A COMPLAINER

There is no surer way to become an "ugly American" in the eyes of your hosts than by complaining about the way things are done in Mexico. If you are judgmental about behavior or picky about your food, leave your opinions at the border or keep them to yourself. Some things are just different in Mexico, and that's *why* it's Mexico. Complaining about things will not change the culture. If, however, you feel threatened or unsafe it's all right to let your host family or the director of your school know about it.

Mexicans are very proud of their nation. As a longtime visitor to Mexico, I assure you that the country has made tremendous progress in the past thirty years, but there's still room for improvement, particularly in utilities, sanitation, and construction. Instead of criticizing the lack of conveniences you may encounter in some parts of Mexico, comment on the positive aspects: the beauty of the countryside, the manicured parks, the beautiful churches and historic buildings, and the hospitality of the people.

As long as you don't insist on everything being done your way or let it be known that you consider everything in your country superior to everything in Mexico, you'll be treated as an honored guest. If you try to understand and adapt to cultural differences, approaching your study program and home stay with a positive attitude, you'll be accepted as a friend, a classmate, and a member of the family. When you return to your country, you will most likely consider the time you spent learning Spanish in Mexico to have been a life-changing experience.

MAKING THE MOST OF
YOUR TIME IN MEXICO

Your time in Mexico is precious, so make an effort to learn as much Spanish as you can. Take advantage of every opportunity to learn something new or have a unique cultural experience. The following are some activities that will help improve your Spanish:

- Converse with your host family whenever possible.
- Participate in activities such as picnics, parties, and card games.
- Attend *intercambios* (language interchanges) at your school.
- Make Mexican friends.
- Sign up for an *amigo* (buddy) program if your school offers it.
- Attend cultural workshops and tutoring sessions at your school.
- Don't miss fiestas or festivals!
- Go to concerts, plays, and Spanish-language movies.
- Play or observe such sports as soccer (*fútbol*) or basketball (*básquet-bol* or *baloncesto*).
- Go shopping in non-tourist areas.
- Read magazines, newspapers, or a short novel in Spanish.
- Watch television with your family.

Be curious and open to different experiences. Be aware that your host family may have a favorite *telenovela* (soap opera). Mexican soap operas are shown in the evening and a large percentage of the population watches them. They usually don't last longer than one year, and the last episode of a popular *telenovela* is an important event.

A REALITY WORD GAME. A friend of mine who has learned to converse in several languages, including Thai and Indonesian, uses this method: pick ten new words each day that relate to your activities. For example, if you're going to the market, choose food words you don't already know and verbs related to buying and selling. Make a point of using those ten words as many times as possible during the day. Before you know it, they'll have become part of your vocabulary.

SLANG OR STREET SPANISH. Mexican slang is abundant and colorful, but it can be a minefield for someone new to the language. Be wary of expressions you learn on the street, in bars, or even from some of your new Mexican friends. As in English, there are expletives in Spanish. There are also expressions too vulgar to use in polite company. To avoid insulting someone or embarrassing yourself, take a book on Mexican slang with you and refer to it each time you encounter a "cool" new saying; also, check new slang words and expressions with someone you trust, such as a member of your host family.

REVIEW YOUR SPANISH BEFORE LEAVING. Don't wait until you're in Mexico to review your Spanish. If possible, take a class before you go, or, if you have a Spanish book from a class you've taken, use it to go over what you learned and pick up some new words and phrases. Seek out some Spanish-language tapes or a CD to practice with. Former teachers and college libraries often have tapes or CDs you can borrow, or you can buy them in a bookstore or on the Internet. Finally, don't overlook Mexican friends or coworkers. Let them know you're going to Mexico and want to practice Spanish. Most will be delighted to help you out by conversing with you in their native language.

RECOMMENDED READING

BOOKS ON MEXICO

The following list contains some of the better books I have read about Mexican culture and history, and a few good travel guides. The list is alphabetized by title.

Bordering on Chaos, Mexico's Roller Coaster Journey Toward Prosperity, by Andrés Oppenheimer. Published in 1996, this book describes the economic and political struggles that took place in Mexico in the 1990s, including the assassination of a presidential candidate and the Zapatista rebellion in the southern state of Chiapas. It also reveals the disturbing details of political intrigue, murder, drug dealing, and other activities of Mexico's former ruling party, the PRI. Now that PRI is no longer in power, the situation has changed a bit, but some of the same activities are still going on in the background.

Distant Neighbors: A Portrait of the Mexicans, by Alan Riding. Published in 1989, *Distant Neighbors* is somewhat out of date, but it still provides a valuable overview of Mexican society and the Mexican personality within a historical context. It's also a good guide to understanding Mexico's long-standing love-hate relationship with the United States.

The Death of Artemio Cruz, by Carlos Fuentes. This classic novel of the Mexican Revolution during the early part of the 20th century provides insight into Mexico at the time of Pancho Villa.

Where the Air is Clear, by Carlos Fuentes. This novel, by the same celebrated Mexican author, deals with the same time period in Mexican history, the revolution of 1910.

History of the Conquest of New Spain, by Bernal Díaz del Castillo. If you want to know what really happened during the Spanish conquest of Mexico, read this eyewitness account by a soldier who was with Hernán Cortés at the time he arrived in Mexico. Originally published in the 16th century, this book reads like a novel but actually chronicles the overthrow of the Aztec empire and Spain's subsequent colonization of Mexico.

The Labyrinth of Solitude, by Octavio Paz. This classic work by Mexico's Nobel Prize-winning poet and essayist is an examination of the Mexican character that probes deeply into the soul of the people. It presents the Mexicans and their traditions and beliefs from the point of view of an insider who explains the stereotypes and myths surrounding his culture. A paperback edition of this book, combined with some of Octavio Paz's other essays on Mexico, was published by Grove Press in 1985.

The Maya, by Michael D. Coe. This classic description of the Mayan civilization of Yucatán, Chiapas, and Guatemala is particularly relevant if you plan to study in Mérida, Cancún, or Playa del Carmen.

Mexico from the Olmecs to the Aztecs, by Michael D. Coe and Rex Koontz. Written by two professors who are recognized experts on Pre-Columbian Mexico, this book traces the history of Mexico's ancient civilizations, from the mysterious Olmecs to the Mayas and the Aztecs.

The Mexican Nation, Historical Continuity and Modern Change, by Douglas Richmond. Used as a textbook in many Mexican history classes in the U.S., this very readable book tells how the concepts of regionalism, ethnicity, and religion have shaped the history of Mexico. It explains the multicultural dimension of the country and offers insight into some of the most important historical events in its history. If you want to know the stories behind *Cinco de Mayo* or the Mexican Revolution, read this book.

Sons of the Shaking Earth, by Eric Wolf. This wonderfully readable introduction to Mexican history was written in 1959, so it serves mainly as historical background for a country that has changed significantly since that time.

Time Among the Maya: Travels in Belize, Guatemala, and Mexico, by Ronald Wright. This book follows the author's travels throughout the Mayan region as he investigates the ancient Mayan culture, placing special emphasis on their concept of time.

Year of the Jaguar, by James Maw. The travel diary of a young man who goes in search of the father he has never met, this book contains excellent descriptions of travel in Mexico. The book covers many areas of Mexico, from the U.S. border to the state of Chiapas on the Guatemalan border.

Guidebooks

The Lonely Planet Guide to Mexico by John Nobel, Susan, Forsyth, Allison Wright, Andrew Dean Nystrom, Morgan Konn, and Ben Greensfelder, published by Lonely Planet. This is a good all-round guidebook that includes Mexican history, safety and health tips, sightseeing, hotels and restaurants, and a multitude of other information. More specialized Lonely Planet guidebooks cover specific regions of Mexico; some of these are *Lonely Planet Yucatan, Lonely Planet Baja California, and Lonely Planet: Mexico's Pacific Coast.*

Moon Handbooks. This small publisher provides several regional guides to Mexico, such as *Moon Handbooks Baja: Tijuana to Cabo San Lucas* and *Moon Handbooks Baja: La Paz to Cabo San Lucas,* both by Joe Cummings; and *Moon Handbooks: Puerto Vallarta Including 300 Miles of Coastal Coverage and Sidetrips to Guadalajara and Lake Chapala* by Bruce Whipperman.

The People's Guide to Mexico, by Carl Franz, Lorena Havens, and Steve Rogers. This is more of a survival guide than a sightseeing guide. It contains a wealth of practical and cultural information on Mexico, all presented in an interesting and humorous format and illustrated with line drawings. I highly recommend it to anyone who has never experienced traveling or living in Mexico.

The Rough Guide To Mexico by Peter Eltringham. This is a travel guide designed for budget travelers and those who want to visit places that are less touristy and off the beaten track. It contains useful practical information on everything from transportation to sightseeing as well as places to eat and hotel accommodations in each area.

FINANCIAL AID

Financial Resources for International Study: A Guide for U.S. Students and Professionals, Editors: Sara J. Steen and Marie O'Sullivan, published by Institute of International Education

Financial Aid for Study and Training Abroad by Gail A Schlachter & R. David Weber, published by Reference Service Press.

INTERNET RESOURCES

GENERAL INFORMATION ON MEXICO

www.mexperience.com: This excellent site contains a wealth of information about Mexico and is well worth a look. Here you can find a description and picture of a multitude of destinations within Mexico, including many smaller, less known cities, towns, archeological sites, and beach areas. There's also a great deal of practical information, such as guides to living and working in Mexico, and buying, leasing, or renting real estate. This site also offers comprehensive information on telephones and other methods of communication in Mexico, as well as tips on health and safety.

www.mexonline.com: Advertised as "The oldest & most trusted online guide to Mexico," MexOnline has information on everything from accommodations to the culture and history of Mexico. There are links to real estate, shopping, and businesses, as well as city guides and maps of some areas of Mexico.

www.math.ucr.edu/ftm/baja.html: Hosted by the Math Department at UC Riverside, this site has a wealth of information about Baja California. In addition to the usual info on transportation, accommodations, and dining, there is some hard-to-find information such as Baja highway conditions, information on tides for various places in Baja, and locations of ATMs in Baja.

MEXICO ENTRY AND EXIT REQUIREMENTS

www.travel.state.gov: This is the U.S. State Department's official website. It has information on traveling and studying abroad in almost any country in the world. Of particular use when traveling to Mexico is the section entitled "Tips for Travelers to Mexico." To find it, click on

International Travel and *Regional Information*, then scroll down and click on *Tips for Travelers to Mexico*. In this section, you'll find information on visas and passports.

www.mexonline.com/consulate.htm: This page in the Mexonline website shows the locations of Mexican consulates in the U.S.

TRANSPORTATION

www.bajaferries.com.mx: This company runs a ferry from La Paz to Topolobampo, near Los Mochis on the mainland Pacific coast of Baja California. Schedules, fares, and contact information are shown on this website.

www.simplonpc.co.uk/SEMATUR.html: This British site has information on SEMATUR ferries from La Paz to Mazatlán and Topolobampo as well as from Santa Rosalia to Guaymas. SEMATUR is the main ferry company serving the routes from Baja California to the Mexican mainland, but it doesn't have an official website.

www.bajatravel.com: Transportation information for Baja California is available by clicking on *Baja Travel Guidebook* or *Baja WWW Yellow Pages*.

www.abstravel.com: This travel agency, located in Miami, shows schedules and flights into even the smallest cities in Mexico. It also allows you to purchase tickets on smaller, local airlines that aren't listed with mainstream travel services like Expedia or Orbitz.

www.exitotravel.com: Exito Travel is a Latin American travel agency recommended by many Spanish-language schools. They advertise specifically to the student of Spanish and offer low fares, extended trips, and special rates for groups. If you call them, Exito can get you information on flights that don't appear on the normal booking engines.

IMMUNIZATIONS AND HEALTH CONCERNS

www.cdc.gov: The official website of the U.S. Centers for Disease Control allows you to find out about any diseases that may be threats in the area where you plan to study. To begin, click on *Travelers' Health* in the navigation bar on the right. By selecting *Mexico and Central America* from the long list of destinations, you can read about every disease ever known to occur in the region you'll be visiting. Don't let this scare you, but do check for outbreaks and read up on immunizations and other preventative measures.

INSURANCE

www.internationalstudentinsurance.com: This website offers short-term international health, medical, and travel insurance especially for students traveling abroad. Their policies cover medical fees, evacuation, trip interruption, and accidental death or dismemberment. Policies may be issued for trips varying in length from five days to two years.

www.culturalinsurance.com: Cultural Insurance Services International (CISI) specializes in travel and medical insurance coverage for students in study-abroad programs. This company's minimum coverage is one month; premiums are quoted on a monthly basis.

www.quotetravelinsurance.com: This travel-insurance site from Square-mouth.com compares rates and coverage from more than sixty different insurance plans. Check each plan carefully to determine exactly what is covered. If you're uncertain about what type of coverage to buy, scroll to the bottom of the home page to read descriptions of the major categories.

www.totaltravelinsurance.com: Total Travel Insurance provides information on dozens of insurance plans. To read descriptions of the different types of travel-insurance coverage, scroll down to FAQs and click on *What is Travel Insurance?* Carefully compare insurance-plan coverage and maximum payments before buying.

FINANCIAL AID

Finding loans, grants, and scholarships for study-abroad programs is difficult. Most programs require that applicants be currently enrolled in an approved U.S. or Canadian college or university. The following websites contain information on and links to various sources of funding for study-abroad programs.

www.allscholar.com: This site offers a free scholarship search; however, they share your personal information with colleges and universities and other organizations. If you use this service, be aware that you may receive information from colleges and universities and businesses offering products and services for students.

www.alternativestudentloan.com: If you're registering for credit through the University of Southern Mississippi or Seattle Central Community college, you may be able to use a private loan through Alternative Student Loan to finance your study-abroad costs. Applications are taken online or by telephone: 866-301-3637.

www.teri.org: The Education Resources Institute (TERI) is a nonprofit organization that offers education loans. A TERI-approved school is used as a benchmark by other loan agencies.

www.iefc.com: International Education Finance Corporation (IEFC) offers information and applications to the International Student Loan Program (ISLP), the Stafford Loan program, and the Plus Loan program. These programs provide opportunities for U.S. students who wish to study outside of the United States but will be receiving their degree from their U.S. schools.

www.finaid.org: To use the International Education Finance Corporation site, search for *study abroad*. This organization lists financial aid for currently enrolled college and university students.

www.brokescholar.com: Broke Scholar lists hundreds of thousands of scholarships including some for study abroad. You must register for the free search service and be currently enrolled as a student in a U.S. or Canadian college or university. Your personal information may be shared with other organizations.

Spanish-language Schools

E ach school description features an "At a Glance" box, which contains essential contact information, tuition costs, and maximum class size. A five-star rating system represents my evaluation of the school's facilities, location, and programs. This concise overview is followed by more detailed information, including tuition and home-stay costs shown in U.S. dollars, a list of classes and programs, teaching methods, textbooks, and extra services. A section entitled "What Distinguishes This School?" highlights the qualities that set each school apart from the others.

The schools are arranged into four geographic regions: Baja California, the Pacific Coast, Mountain Cities, Yucatan and the Caribbean Coast, and are further organized by the city in which they are located. My impressions introduce each city, followed by comments on its history and points of interest. A "Getting There" section contains detailed information on how to travel to each city, including both air and ground transportation.

Baja California

Ensenada

The Mexican port city of Ensenada is just eighty miles south of San Diego, but it's a world away culturally from the subdivisions and shopping centers of Southern California. Ensenada is a typical Mexican city in many ways. Except on the days when cruise ships dock in the harbor, you won't hear much English spoken, and life goes on as it does anywhere in Mexico. The city's Mediterranean climate and friendly atmosphere are inviting, as are its shops and sidewalk cafés. Ensenada has a large working harbor where you can feed the ever-present sea lions and watch fishermen come in with their catch of the day. You can also observe the comings and goings of large ships and private yachts. Ensenada is Mexico's second most popular port of call for major cruise lines and pleasure boats. Near the waterfront is the *Riviera del Pacifico,* once a huge gambling casino owned by boxing great Jack Dempsey. Today it houses the Ensenada Cultural Center, which hosts events such as concerts, exhibits, and theater performances throughout the year.

South of Ensenada there are many good beaches as well as *La Bufadora*, an amazing blowhole at the end of Punta Banda. Popular activities include surfing, sailing, and fishing. Just north of the city is the elegant Bajamar Golf Resort with its eighteen-hole course. Ensenada is close to the best wine-producing area in Mexico, *El Valle de Guadalupe,* which offers winery tours and tasting. It's also the starting point for off-road races such as the Baja 500 and the Baja 1000.

GETTING THERE

BY PLANE

The nearest major airports are Lindbergh Field in San Diego and Rodríguez International Airport in Tijuana. The airport in Ensenada is restricted to private planes, so you'll need to get there by road from San Diego or Tijuana.

BY CAR

Ensenada is about an hour's drive south of the Mexico-U.S. border at Tijuana. The highway is a scenic, well-maintained four-lane toll road. There are three toll stops en route, each with a cost to autos of about $2.50 (the charge fluctuates along with the value of the Mexican peso). If you plan to rent a car or drive your own vehicle, be sure to purchase Mexican insurance at the border, as U.S. auto insurance is not valid in Mexico. If you're renting, you'll also need written permission to take the rental car into Mexico.

As you cross the border from San Ysidro, California, into Tijuana, a light in front of you will show either green (*PASE*) (pass through) or red *(REVISION)* (search), which triggers a bell. This is a random process, but if the red light comes on, you will be directed into an inspection area, questioned, and possibly searched.

After crossing the border, continue through Tijuana following the signs for Rosarito-Ensenada Scenic Road. When you reach the on-ramp to the highway, it should be marked Rosarito-Ensenada Scenic Road and *Ensenada Cuota. Cuota* is the Spanish word for toll. *Ensenada Cuota* indicates the toll road that begins at Playas de Tijuana and ends at the village of San Miguel, just north of Ensenada.

BY BUS

Taking a bus is relatively simple and very inexpensive. The San Diego trolley and Greyhound bus both travel to Tijuana from San Diego several times a day. Autotransportes de Baja California ("ABC") runs hourly air-conditioned buses to Ensenada from Tijuana.

There are two methods of getting from San Diego to Ensenada by public transportation.

OPTION 1. This is the most convenient route to Ensenada, but is the slowest and most expensive. This option is recommended for students who have never been to Mexico, have a lot of luggage, or have little or no ability to speak Spanish.

1. Take a taxi from the San Diego Airport (Lindberg Field) to the Downtown San Diego Greyhound Station at 120 West Broadway in San Diego. Cost: about $7.

2. Purchase a one-way ticket to *Tijuana Central*, the main bus terminal in Tijuana. As you board, confirm with the Greyhound driver that the bus is going to *Tijuana Central*. Cost: about $12.

3. The bus will stop in San Ysidro, California, and you may be asked to get off to identify your luggage stowed underneath. After crossing the border, the bus will again stop for passengers to go through Mexican customs.

4. Depending on the traffic and the number of stops, you should arrive at *Terminal Tijuana Central* about forty minutes after leaving Mexican Customs.

5. At *Terminal Tijuana Central,* go to the ticket counter for ABC Bus Lines *(Autotransportes de Baja California)* and buy a one-way ticket to Ensenada. Cost: about $8.00. The bus will arrive at the main Ensenada bus terminal located at Avenida Riveroll and Calle 11 in about ninety minutes. From the terminal you can either walk or take a taxi to your school or host family's residence.

OPTION 2. Although this way of getting to Ensenada is quicker and less expensive, it's not recommended for everyone. If you haven't traveled internationally or experienced life in a developing country, crossing the border on foot may make you uncomfortable. On the other hand, if you're an experienced traveler, and especially if you can already speak some Spanish, this is the way to go.

1. Take a taxi or a city bus from the San Diego Airport (Lindberg Field) to the nearest San Diego trolley stop. The staff at the airport information desks can show you where to catch the trolley. You can also find trolley stops, fares, and timetables on www.sdcommute.com. Cost of taxi ride: about $7.

2. Purchase a trolley ticket to the border (San Ysidro). The trip to the border by trolley takes about an hour. Cost: $2.

3. At the trolley's last stop in San Ysidro, walk through the turnstiles at the border and over the pedestrian overpass directly into Mexico. Once across, you'll be immediately approached by taxi drivers and vendors trying to sell their wares. Walk past the taxi stands and turn right on the first main street that runs parallel to the border. Next to a pharmacy you'll see the small Plaza Viva bus terminal where buses leave for Ensenada about every forty minutes.

4. Purchase a one-way ticket to Ensenada on the ABC bus line. Cost: about $8.

5. You'll arrive at the main Ensenada bus terminal located at Avenida Riveroll and Calle 11 in about ninety minutes.

Baja California Language College

At a Glance

Location: ★★★★
Facilities: ★★★ ½
Programs: ★★★★
Overall Rating: ★★★★
Cost: $245/week (six hours/day)
Maximum number of students per class: five
Mailing Address:
  Rolle Enterprise International
  PO Box 7556
  San Diego, CA 92167
Street Address:
  Colegio de Idiomas de B.C., S.A. de C.V.
  Avenida Riveroll #1287, Zona Centro
  Ensenada, Baja California, México

Tel/Fax: 52 646-174-1741 • **U.S. Tel:** 877-444-2252 (toll-free)
or 619-758-9711 • **U.S. Fax:** 619-758-9742
Email: college@bajacal.com • **Website:** www.bajacal.com
President: Keith Rolle
Director: Yolanda Camacho Carballo

Baja California Language College occupies two shell-pink buildings on a street corner not far from downtown Ensenada and within two blocks of the ABC bus station. There are several classrooms on two levels, a terrace, and a balcony area where informal classes are sometimes held. The school also has a large kitchen where students gather for coffee, lunch, and snacks. The atmosphere is very friendly; students and teachers seem like one big happy family.

ACADEMIC BACKGROUND

President Keith Rolle holds bachelor's degrees in communication and political science from the University of Minnesota as well as a master's degree in international management from St. Thomas University. He minored in French and attended the Alliance Française in Paris. Yolanda Camacho has a BS in biology from the University of Torreón as well as a Spanish as a Foreign Language teaching certificate from the Universidad de Baja California. The principal teachers have bachelor's degrees in various disciplines. In addition, they all have Spanish as a Foreign Language teaching certificates.

CREDIT

Students can earn up to six units of community college credit through Arizona Western College of Yuma, Arizona (www.azwestern.edu). You must register for credit at AWC before attending Baja California Language College. For enrollment materials or more information, contact Ms. Linda Elliott-Nelson (email linda.elliott-nelson@azwestern.edu).

Community college credit may also be arranged through Seattle Central Community College. *See "Getting College Credit," page 8.*

COSTS

Nonrefundable deposit (applied to tuition): $40

SMALL GROUP IMMERSION PROGRAM

Weekly (six hours/day, thirty hours/week): $245/week
Weekend (Saturday & Sunday, twelve hours): $145
Hourly: $25/hour
Daily (six hours): $60/day

PRIVATE IMMERSION PROGRAM

Weekly (six hours / day, thirty hours / week): $495 / week

Summer Rate (June, July, and August): $529 / week

Weekend (Saturday and Sunday, twelve hours): $190

Hourly: $35 / hour

Daily (six hours): $95 / day

NOTE: *The summer rate (June, July, and August) is slightly higher.*

EXECUTIVE IMMERSION PROGRAM

Weekly (thirty-nine hours): $690 / week

Transcript or Certificate of Completion: $25

DISCOUNTS

Seniors (sixty-four years old and older): 10 percent discount

EXTENDED STUDY

Five weeks prepaid: 20 percent discount

Ten weeks prepaid: 25 percent discount

FAMILY RATE

(Three or more family members enrolled together):
15 percent discount

LODGING

HOME STAY

Private room: $27 / day

Shared room: $22 / day

OTHER OPTIONS

Oceanfront Condominium: $1490 / month

Hotels: $45 to $250 / night

RV Parks: Rates vary with the season

PROGRAMS AND SCHEDULES

Orientation is held at 2 p.m. every Sunday. Classes meet Monday through Friday from 8:30 a.m. until 2:30 p.m.

SMALL GROUP IMMERSION PROGRAM

There are nine levels of course work appropriate for beginning to advanced students. The emphasis in the small-group courses is development of verbal communication and listening skills. The first four hours of each day are dedicated to classes in grammar and verbal communication. Each afternoon there is a two-hour activity period, during which the students can participate in games, field trips, or other activities designed to apply what they have learned in the morning session.

Special topics classes may be arranged for any group, including teachers, health professionals, attorneys, police, and fire and rescue personnel.

PRIVATE IMMERSION PROGRAM

This very flexible program features one-on-one instruction covering the material best suited to the student's needs. You can decide how many hours a day you will study Spanish; classes can be scheduled any day of the week, and even on weekends.

EXECUTIVE IMMERSION PROGRAM

Executive classes meet six days per week, Monday through Saturday, six and a half hours per day. The school develops individualized curriculum for this program, incorporating the Spanish terminology appropriate to the type of business. Afternoon sessions include visits to local businesses to meet Spanish-speaking professionals in similar fields. Also included are a personal email account and fax and courier service, as well as health club, spa, and tennis club guest privileges.

METHODS

Baja California Language College provides a casual learning environment where both grammar and conversation are taught with an emphasis on communication. After completing a course, students evaluate their ability to communicate comfortably in Spanish, and may choose to remain at the same level until they have mastered the concepts.

TEXTBOOKS

This school uses no textbooks, but teachers use a variety of materials and handouts in the classroom.

EXTRAS

MEDICAL SERVICES. The Baja California Language College is very close to the Ensenada Red Cross hospital. Their emergency room is open twenty-four hours a day. They also have a doctor of internal medicine on call for their students should medical emergencies arise.

U.S. MAIL SERVICE. A free weekly courier service delivers mail to the U.S. post office in San Diego, thus avoiding the several-week delay of sending mail through the Mexican postal service.

EMAIL. Students can reserve ten minutes per day to use the school's email account free of charge. There is no general Internet access at the school, but Ensenada has numerous Internet Cafés, which are open to the public and charge about $1/hour.

EXCURSIONS. Each Thursday, in lieu of the afternoon activity, the school coordinates an off-campus excursion to a place of interest in Ensenada.

WHAT DISTINGUISHES THIS SCHOOL?

LOCATION. Ensenada is only about an hour and a half south of the border at San Diego. Students from California and neighboring states can drive to the school or take the trolley/bus connection from San Diego, thereby saving on airfare.

FULL-TIME INSTRUCTORS. Most instructors at Baja Language College work full time at the school, which is not always the case in other schools.

FAMILY ATMOSPHERE. The enthusiasm of the teachers and students is palpable. Everyone seems to be working toward a common goal.

THE CENTER OF LANGUAGES

AT A GLANCE

LOCATION: ★ ★ ★ ★ ½
FACILITIES: ★ ★ ★ ★
PROGRAMS: ★ ★ ★ ★ ½
OVERALL RATING: ★ ★ ★ ★ ½
COST: $270/week (six hours/day)
MAXIMUM NUMBER OF STUDENTS PER CLASS: six
MAILING ADDRESS:
   PO Box 130715 • Carlsbad, CA 92013

STREET ADDRESS:
   Calle Felipe Ángeles #15
   Colonia Empleados • Ensenada, Baja California, México

TEL: 52 646-178-7600 • **FAX:** 52 646-178-0304
U.S. TOLL-FREE: 800-834-2256 • **U.S. FAX:** 760-476-9730
EMAIL: thecenteroflanguages@sdccu.net
WEBSITES: www.spanishschoolbaja.com or www.mexonline.com/cllas.htm
PRESIDENT: Ernesto Ledezma
DIRECTOR: Guillermina Fuentes

Set in the foothills of Ensenada with views of the city and port from the outdoor patio where students often congregate, the Center of Languages is a tranquil place to study Spanish. The relatively new building was originally designed as a residence but has been converted nicely to a school. Because of its connections with UC San Diego, CSU Stanislaus, and Palomar Community College, this school is a good choice for California students who need to earn college credit for their studies.

ACADEMIC BACKGROUND

President Ernesto Ledezma has twenty-five years' experience teaching Spanish as a Second Language and holds a Spanish instructor certificate from the Universidad de Baja California. He also has a bachelor's degree in professional sport training. Guillermina Fuentes has fifteen years' experience teaching Spanish as a Second Language. She holds a BA in biology and an MA in Education. Most instructors have bachelor's degrees and all have been trained in teaching Spanish as a Second Language by the Center of Languages. Instructor Karla Solís Cárdenas holds a degree in communication. Irma Cruz Soto has a bachelor's degree in computer science, and Susana Meixueiro Pineda has a law degree.

CREDIT

Students may earn community college credit through Seattle Central Community College. *See "Getting College Credit," page 8.*

The following California institutions offer credit for study programs held on specific dates:

UNIVERSITY OF CALIFORNIA AT SAN DIEGO (UCSD). Students may earn one to three quarter units, depending on length of program, plus continuing education for nurses and CLAD credit for California teachers. For application forms and enrollment information, contact the university directly:

Address:

Travel Study Programs
UCSD Extension 0170-A
9500 Gilman Dr.
La Jolla, CA 92023-0170

Tel: 858-964-1050

Fax: 858-964-1099

Email: travelstudy@ucsd.edu

PALOMAR COMMUNITY COLLEGE. One to three semester units are available for group classes originating at Palomar College in San Marcos, California. Application and enrollment information may be obtained by contacting:

Palomar Community College

Department of Foreign Languages

1140 West Mission Rd.

San Marcos, CA 92069

Tel: 760-744-1150, ext. 234

COSTS

Nonrefundable deposit (applied to tuition): $100

TUITION

WEEKDAY PROGRAM (THIRTY HOURS / WEEK)

Off Season (September through May)			
One week	*Two weeks*	*Three weeks*	*Four weeks*
$270	$480	$630	$720
Summer (June through August)			
One week	*Two weeks*	*Three weeks*	*Four weeks*
$295	$530	$705	$840

WEEKEND COURSE

Saturday and Sunday (inquire for dates): $205

Materials fee: $35 (includes two books and handouts)

Discounts: Significant discounts are built into the fees for multiple weeks. Senior Citizens over age fifty-five can study for half price in September or November.

All previous students are eligible for a $100 discount.

LODGING

HOME STAY (INCLUDING THREE MEALS A DAY)

One to three weeks:

Private Room: $30/day

Shared Room: $25/day/person

Four or more weeks:

   Private Room: $22/day

   Shared Room: $19/day/person

OTHER OPTIONS

   Hotels: $50 and up/night

   RV Parks Rates vary with the season

PROGRAMS AND SCHEDULES

Weekday classes are held year round, Monday through Friday, 8 a.m. to 2 p.m. in summer and 9 a.m. to 3 p.m. in winter. Weekend classes are held on alternate weekends.

INTENSIVE SPANISH (TEN LEVELS OF INSTRUCTION)

These courses include three hours of Spanish grammar, two hours of Spanish conversation, and an additional hour's "mini-course" study of Mexican and Latin American history, literature, grammar, art, and music.

SPECIAL COURSES

CALIFORNIA TEACHERS – BILINGUAL EXAMINATION PREP COURSE

This is a preparatory course for teachers preparing for the CLAD bilingual examinations given by the state of California. The school will provide personal referrals of teachers who have passed their exams after attending this class.

SPANISH LANGUAGE TRAINING FOR HEALTH PROFESSIONALS AND CONTINUING EDUCATION CREDITS FOR NURSES

The Center of Languages is a recognized provider approved by the California Board of Registered Nursing (Provider No. CEP 10423 for thirty contact hours, Receipt No. 19200646, BRN). For information, contact the school and mention the Accredited Spanish Language Training Course for Health Professionals.

SPANISH LANGUAGE TRAINING FOR LAW ENFORCEMENT OFFICERS

This special training course focuses on the acquisition of language for emergency situations and working more effectively in Spanish-speaking areas.

METHODS

The Spanish dialect taught at the Center of Languages is that of the Latin American business professional. They use a combination of methods: the natural approach, the Total Physical Response method, and the silent way.

TEXTBOOKS

The school provides its students with texts and materials. In-house textbooks for each of the ten levels are currently being developed, and two have been published.

EXTRAS

FIELD TRIPS. Tours to local museums and sites of historical and cultural interest are included in the programs. The Center of Languages regularly takes students to the local historical museum, the Ensenada Cultural Center, the Museo de Ciencias, and an art gallery.

SOCIAL ACTIVITIES. Thursday evenings are devoted to social activities accompanied by at least one faculty member. Students pay their own way to dine out, got to the movies, bowl, or visit one of the city's discos for dancing.

EMAIL ACCESS. The school provides email access. For full Internet access, students must go to one of Ensenada's many Internet cafés.

WHAT DISTINGUISHES THIS SCHOOL?

DIRECT CONNECTIONS WITH CALIFORNIA COLLEGES. University of California San Diego, California State University Stanislaus, and Palomar Community College offer courses for credit at The Center of Languages.

CONTINUING EDUCATION COURSES. Special courses are available for continuing education credit for professional groups, including teachers and medical professionals.

ACADEMIC EXCELLENCE. The Center of Languages was rated the top school of its type in Mexico by Foreign Studies International Associates, a panel of U.S. Spanish teachers who evaluated Spanish-language schools in Mexico, Costa Rica, and other areas, including Spain.

LA PAZ

L a Paz, the city whose name means "the peace," is indeed peaceful.
Even though its population of nearly 200,000 qualifies it as a small
city, La Paz retains the atmosphere of a small town. Although it functions
as the gateway to the Sea of Cortez, the city is decidedly non-touristy,
especially when compared with its jet-set neighbor, Cabo San Lucas. As
the capital of Baja California Sur, the economic base of La Paz is not entirely dependent on tourism; there's a large middle-class working community in this small port city.

Founded in 1535 by Herman Cortés, La Paz was not colonized by the
Spanish until a mission was established there in 1720. Until the Trans-
peninsular Highway was completed in 1973, the settlement languished,
but then became the capital of the newly formed state of Baja California
Sur the next year. Today La Paz is a thriving regional center and conduit
for nearly all trade between Baja and the Mexican mainland, thanks to
the ferry links to Topolobampo and Mazatlán.

Surrounded by desert, the city is set amid laurel trees and coconut and
date palms. It is laid out in a classic grid pattern with streets radiating
from the lovely waterfront promenade, or *malecón*. A few blocks from
the bay is the main plaza, Plaza Constitución, with its pink quartz ga-
zebo, tiled walkways, and 19th-century church. Surrounding the plaza
are many different shops, including a large department store and a variety of restaurants. A modern shopping center has recently been built on
the outskirts of the city.

La Paz may be the eco-tourism capital of Mexico. It is the starting
point for natural history tours into the surrounding desert and cruises
to the islands of the Sea of Cortez. The region offers a complex variety
of wildlife, plant life, and geology. Whale watching, island camping and
trekking, scuba diving, sport fishing, sea kayaking, bird watching, sailing, and sunbathing are some of the recreational activities that abound
in and around La Paz.

GETTING THERE

BY PLANE

AeroMexico and AeroCalifornia fly directly from the U.S. into La Paz; however, the normal online reservation services (Travelocity, Orbitz, etc.) may not find AeroCalifornia flights or flights of most "local" airlines in Latin America. To access flight information for AeroCalifornia, go to www.abstravel.com, the website of ABS Travel, an agency in Miami. It shows all airlines serving Mexican cities and can be very helpful when you're trying to fly to out-of-the-way places.

FLYING TO LOS CABOS. If you're going to La Paz from the U.S. or Canada, compare the cost of flying to Los Cabos airport, near Cabo San Lucas, with flying directly to La Paz. Although reaching your final destination requires a bus ride, a ticket to Los Cabos may be less expensive because more airlines fly there than to La Paz. Alaska Airlines, American Airlines, Mexicana, AeroMexico, and America West all fly to Los Cabos from the West Coast of the U.S. Delta and Continental fly there from Atlanta and Houston respectively.

BY BUS

FROM LOS CABOS AIRPORT. If you fly into Los Cabos, you'll need to transfer from the airport to the bus station in San José del Cabo. Buses run between San José del Cabo and La Paz about every two hours during the day. The schedule changes frequently; but the last bus usually leaves around 7 p.m. It's best to allow at least two hours between your arrival at the airport and your departure by bus from San Jose del Cabo. This will give you time to go through customs and immigration and catch the shuttle into town. Make it clear to the person who sells you the shuttle ticket that you're going to the bus station (terminal de autobuses) in San José del Cabo, not Cabo San Lucas, which is much farther away. The shuttle bus should cost $15 or less. An alternative is to take a taxi into San Jose del Cabo. You'll get there much faster, but you can expect to pay $50 or more. All taxi fares are centrally controlled and collected in the airport, so there's no bargaining.

Once at the San José del Cabo bus station, you'll see a schedule on the wall behind the counter. After buying a ticket, you can then go to the little café in the bus station, get a cold drink or a snack, and relax until the bus shows up.

FROM TIJUANA. If you're up for a twenty-two-hour bus ride, you can get to La Paz fairly cheaply from Tijuana. The fare each way is about $80, and buses normally leave at noon and 6 p.m. Autotransportes de Baja California (ABC) runs buses from Tijuana to all points along the Trans-peninsular Highway. As fares and schedules change frequently, you'll need to contact the bus company for current information. They have a website, but it's frequently under construction: http://abc.com.mx. If you can't access their website, you can call ABC from the U.S. at 52 664-621-2424. Alternatively, you can try calling the Tijuana bus terminal: 52 664-626-7101.

To get to Tijuana, the best option is to take the Greyhound bus from the station at 120 West Broadway in San Diego. You can get schedule and fare information by calling 619-239-3266 or 800-231-2222 or at www.greyhound.com. The Greyhound bus will take you to Tijuana's Central Bus Terminal (*Central Camionera*) where you can catch the ABC bus to La Paz. The San Diego to Tijuana fare at press time was $5.

BY CAR

La Paz is about 950 miles from San Diego. Only one road travels the entire Baja California peninsula from north to south. It is aptly named the Trans-peninsular Highway or Highway 1 (Carretera 1). Its condition is generally very good, but there are occasional washouts in the winter. For road conditions, you can check the following website: http://math.ucr.edu/ftm/baja.html. This extremely useful site contains information on all aspects of driving in Baja California. It is maintained by Fred Metcalf with server space provided by the math department at UC Riverside. Another useful site is www.baja.com. Road information can be found in their message boards (click on "9 message boards" on the banner at the top of the page). Getting to La Paz by car can be a beautiful two-to-three-day drive along a scenic road with spectacular landscapes, or it can be a grueling trip fraught with delays and discomfort. Much depends on the road conditions and the weather, which can bring floods in winter or extreme heat during the summer months.

Don't forget to purchase Mexican insurance for your car at the border or online before leaving home. For more information on driving in Mexico, see "Driving," page 26.

Centro de Idiomas, Cultura y Comunicación (CICC)

At a Glance

Location: ✮✮✮
Facilities: ✮✮
Programs: ✮✮✮
Overall Rating: ✮✮✮
Cost: $220/week (twenty-two hours total)
$250/week (twenty-six hours total)
Maximum number of students per class: five
Street Address:
   Madero 2460 y Legaspi
   La Paz 23000
   Baja California Sur, México

Tel: 52 612-125-7554
Fax: 52 612-125-7388
Email: cicclapaz@yahoo.com
Website: www.cicclapaz.com

Centro de Idiomas, Cultura y Comunicación is a small school on a residential street within walking distance of downtown La Paz and the waterfront. Located in a converted home, the school has a friendly, home-like atmosphere. European as well as American students study here.

Academic Background

The director, Marc Nicolet, is a U.S. and Swiss citizen with a degree in Economics from University of Fribourg in Switzerland. He speaks French, English, and Spanish and teaches French at the University of Baja California. There are three principal teachers: Martha Nava Gomez has a degree in business administration and twenty-five years' experience teaching Spanish and English; Ana Belén Castro has a degree in linguistics and teaches both Spanish and English to beginners; Fernando Abad is experienced in teaching both English and Spanish, especially to teenagers.

Credit

Community college credit may be arranged through Seattle Central Community College. *See "Getting College Credit," page 8.*

Costs

Nonrefundable registration fee: $80

Intensive Group Spanish Classes (materials included)

Hrs/week:	22	26
One week:	$220	$250
Two weeks:	$420	$495
Three weeks:	$620	$730
Four weeks:	$810	$955
Extra week:	$180	$200

Individual Spanish Classes

Individual (one-on-one) classes are available for 50 percent more than group classes.

Discounts

Early-bird Deal (for registering four months in advance): 15 percent discount

Two students (registered on the same online form): 10 percent plus $80 discount

Spanish for Travelers (ten hours/week): $99/week

BUSINESS SPANISH AND MEDICAL SPANISH

(Six to ten hours/week only in addition to Intensive Spanish program.)
One week: $90–150
Two weeks: $165–270
Three weeks: $230–380
Four weeks: $290–480
Extra week: $55–95

GROUP RATES

(For classes of three to six students)
Three students: $7/hour/student
Four students: $6/hour/student
Five students: $4.80/hour/student
Six students: $4/hour/student

LODGING

HOME STAY (INCLUDING TWO MEALS)

Private Room $17/day,
paid directly to the family

PROGRAMS AND SCHEDULES

TWENTY-TWO-HOUR INTENSIVE SPANISH

Monday through Friday 8:30 a.m.–1 p.m.

TWENTY-SIX-HOUR INTENSIVE SPANISH

Monday through Friday 8:30 a.m.–1 p.m. and Sat. 9:30 a.m.–1 p.m.

SPANISH FOR TRAVELERS

Held two hours/day Monday through Friday, this program covers more than 600 useful Spanish words, common expressions, and idioms useful to tourists. Home-stay accommodations are not available with this program.

Medical Spanish

Designed for medical professionals, this course includes instruction in admissions, medical history, illnesses, body and organs, emergencies, surgery, and pregnancy. The situations covered depend on the students' specialty and level. Practice is available with the local Red Cross. Visits to a private clinic and to the local psychiatric hospital can also be arranged.

Business Spanish

For business people interested in trading with Latin America or Spain, this course includes language relating to correspondence, invoicing, choosing a market, distribution, advertising, investing, banking, insurance, and currencies.

Note: Medical and Business Spanish are offered six to ten hours / week in the afternoons, but only as a complement to Intensive Spanish.

Methods

CICC uses its own method, which is interactive, dynamic, and personalized. Recognizing that each student has different learning abilities, teachers may use different approaches with different students.

Textbooks

The school produces and uses its own textbooks. Instructors also use other material such as newspapers, magazines, various readings, videotapes, and songs.

Extras

Language lab. A forty-five-minute language lab is offered daily at no extra charge. In the lab, students work from tapes to increase vocabulary and improve pronunciation.

Cultural activities. Free weekly activities are scheduled, including cooking and dance.

Sports and tour information. The school posts information for students about sports and nature excursions offered by a local company that gives discounts for small groups.

Free airport / La Paz Bus terminal pickup. The school will pick you up at the La Paz airport or at the local bus terminal and drive you to your host family or hotel.

SPECIAL SCHEDULES. Special schedules are available for groups of three or more students who wish to study fewer days per week or at different times.

INTERNET ACCESS. Although CICC does not offer Internet access, there is an Internet café very close to the school that gives discounts for CICC students.

WHAT DISTINGUISHES THIS SCHOOL?

FLEXIBILITY. The school can adapt its teaching methods to a student's needs and abilities.

PERSONAL ATTENTION. CICC is small and specializes in personal attention to each student. The director holds a daily briefing with the teachers to review each student's progress.

HOMELIKE ATMOSPHERE. The school is located in a converted house in a middle-class neighborhood; the atmosphere is informal, and most students seem to feel at home here.

Se Habla La Paz

At a Glance

Location: ★★★★½
Facilities: ★★★★
Programs: ★★★★
Overall Rating: ★★★★
Cost: $220/week (four hours/day)
Maximum number of students per class: five

Street Address:
Francisco I. Madero #540
(between Republica & Guerrero)
La Paz 23000 BCS, México

Street Address:
Lázaro Cárdenas #3022 at Avenida Chapilita
Guadalajara, Jalisco, México

Tel/Fax: 52 612-122-7763
Website: www.sehablalapaz.com
Email: info@sehablalapaz.com
Director: Juli Goff
Director of Education: Antonio Reynoso

Se Habla La Paz occupies a large multistory house on a residential street two blocks from the waterfront. The classrooms are spacious, with lots of light, and decorated with Mexican art and handicrafts. The house has multiple balconies and terraces, some with views of the bay and the Sea of Cortez. There is a small pool for student use, as well as an in-house library. The recent addition of a branch campus in Guadalajara provides the opportunity for students to study in a large metropolitan area. *See Guadalajara.*

ACADEMIC BACKGROUND

Director Julie Goff has a degree in Physical Therapy from the University of Kansas. She has worked in hospitals and public schools and has fourteen years' experience in hospital administration. Director of Education Antonio Reynoso has a degree in teaching Spanish and English and is also qualified in detecting and treating learning problems in children. He is the author of Se Habla's general and medical teaching materials. Instructor Merit Bernice Rochin Iriarte has a degree in education. Esteban Ramírez Soriano has degrees in communication engineering and electronics. In addition to teaching Spanish, he oversees Se Habla's website.

CREDIT

Community college credit may be arranged through Seattle Central Community College. *See "Getting College Credit," page 8.*

Continuing education credit for healthcare professionals is available through the Arizona State Nurses Association. Contact Se Habla La Paz for more information on this program.

COSTS

General/Conversational Program (twenty hours/week), includes all materials.

Registration fee: $75

WEEKLY RATES

Group classes (twenty hours): $220
Private classes (ten hours): $220

HOURLY RATES

Private tutoring: $22/hour

Couples, per person: $16.50/hour

Group, per person: $11/hour

HEALTHCARE PROGRAM (40 HOURS / WEEK)

One week: $550

Four weeks: $2090

LODGING

HOME STAY (INCLUDING TWO MEALS A DAY)

Private room: $120/week

Home-stay fees are paid directly to the host family. Most families can accommodate couples or small families. Home-stay matching is done well in advance of arrival, and students are given prior information about their families.

PROGRAMS AND SCHEDULES

GENERAL CONVERSATIONAL PROGRAM

Conversational Spanish classes meet for twenty hours per week. Before starting classes, students take a placement exam to determine the level of their language proficiency. Individual language programs can be designed for specific interests and for any length of time needed to successfully accomplish a student's language goals.

HEALTHCARE PROGRAM

Students in the Healthcare Program attend Spanish-language classes for twenty hours weekly and spend up to twenty hours in clinical environments with their medical counterparts. This program is designed for the student to be present, observe, listen, converse, and relate to the professionals and their patients in local hospitals, private offices, clinics, and community-based outreach programs. Instruction can be tailored for a variety of healthcare workers: nurses, doctors, therapists, social workers, religious associates, psychologists, psychiatrists, administrators, and volunteers.

METHODS

Se Habla uses an individualized communicative approach. After each student's language level is assessed to determine their most appropriate level of instruction, individualized educational materials are compiled.

TEXTBOOKS

Since Se Habla compiles each student's materials separately, the materials used depend on the individuals' particular needs, their levels of proficiency, and their areas of interest. All educational materials are included in the tuition and produced at the school, but each student is expected to bring an adequate Spanish-English bilingual dictionary.

EXTRAS

AIRPORT PICKUP. Free pickup at the La Paz airport is included in the tuition.

FREE ACTIVITIES. The school organizes weekly cultural activities and fiestas, and screens Spanish-language films.

POOL. There is a pool available for students to use.

LIBRARY. The school has a small library of Spanish-language books that students can borrow.

FREE SNACKS. There is a snack break each day with coffee and other beverages and typical Mexican foods.

PAYPAL PAYMENTS. This school accepts payment through the online service PayPal. For more information on how to pay with this method, visit www.paypal.com.

WHAT DISTINGUISHES THIS SCHOOL?

HEALTHCARE PROGRAM. In addition to attending Spanish classes, healthcare professionals have the opportunity to observe and practice the language in a clinical setting for up to twenty additional hours weekly.

CUSTOMIZED PROGRAMS. Your individual language program can be matched to your specific interests and designed for any length of time you need to accomplish your language goals.

SPECIAL SPORTS PACKAGES. Se Habla La Paz can combine Spanish-language study with scuba diving, camping, kayaking, sailing, wind surfing, kite boarding, fishing, and surfing.

TWO LOCATIONS. By arranging a study program that includes both Se Habla schools, students have the opportunity to experience a small coastal city in Baja California (La Paz) as well as a very large metropolitan area (Guadalajara).

MAZATLÁN

Mazatlán means "land of the deer" in the ancient Nahuatl language. Although there are no longer any deer in this seaside resort city, it does retain some of its former charm. A city with a split personality, Mazatlán is both a booming tourist center and a sleepy old coastal town. Along the miles of beach north of the city, in the area called La Zona Dorada (The Golden Zone), there are numerous hotels, restaurants, nightclubs, and gift shops. In La Zona Dorada, beach activities such as swimming, sunbathing, water skiing, and parasailing predominate. In the downtown area near the old port, one can still walk through a traditional marketplace, visit the historic cathedral, or admire the old buildings. Life seems to go on there as it always has, despite the changes brought about by tourism. Mazatlán has many good seafood restaurants, and the nightlife is lively in the beach areas. There are several fine art galleries and handicraft markets in the downtown area. In February, during Carnaval (Mardi Gras), thousands of costumed celebrants throng the resort's streets and beaches.

Mazatlán's Carnaval is reputed to be the third largest in the world.

Mazatlán's population is nearly 600,000. With the largest port facility between Los Angeles and the Panama Canal, the city is home to Latin America's biggest fleet of commercial shrimp vessels (over 800 boats). Nearly 40,000 tons of shrimp are processed each year, making Mazatlán "The Shrimp Capital of the World." The large harbor near the city center also accommodates commercial vessels and cruise ships. Deep-sea fishing is very popular. Sport-fishing boats, motor yachts, and sailboats operate out of two new marinas north of the city.

GETTING THERE

BY PLANE

Alaska Airlines, America West, Mexicana, and AeroMexico fly to Mazatlán from San Francisco and Los Angeles. Round-trip airfares begin around $300. As this is a popular destination, there are sometimes charters and specials that lower the fares to $200.

BY BUS

It is possible to take a bus from the U.S./Mexico border to Mazatlán. Autobuses Crucero (www.autobusescrucero.com). offers transportation to Mexico from many western U.S. cities, including Tucson, Phoenix, Los Angeles, Stockton, Las Vegas, Santa Barbara, Fresno, Portland, and even Yakima, Washington. Cruccro buses are allied with Greyhound Mexico and usually leave from a Greyhound bus terminal. For more information, call Greyhound in the U.S. at 800-229-9424. An alternate bus line, TBC, leaves for Mazatlán from its own bus station at in Tucson. You can call TBC in Tucson at 520 903-2801 or in Phoenix at 602-258-2355 or 602-258-2445 for current schedules and fares.

BY CAR

After crossing the border in California or Arizona, you can drive to Mazatlán in two or three days. From California, take Mexico Highway 2 out of Mexicali to Highway 15, the main Pacific route in Mexico. From Arizona, take Highway 15 directly from Nogales through Guaymas and Culiacán to Mazatlán.

Don't forget to purchase Mexican insurance for your car at the border or online before leaving home. For more information on driving in Mexico, see "Driving," page 26.

BY FERRY

An interesting but more expensive and time-consuming alternative is to make the three-day drive from the California border to La Paz and take a ferry from there to Mazatlán. SEMATUR ferries make the eighteen-hour trip between La Paz and Mazatlán twice a week. Information is shown on at least one website, www.trybaja.com/ferry.html, but it might be outdated. The best way to get current schedules and fares and make reservations is through a Mexican travel agent in La Paz, or by calling SEMA-TUR directly in Mexico: 52 612-125-3833. Another company, Baja Ferries, makes the much shorter eight-hour trip fro La Paz to Topolobampo, 250 miles north of Mazatlán. For fares and schedules, visit www.bajaferries.com.mx. Reservations may be made through Baja Ferries' U.S. affiliate, Native Trails: www.nativetrails.com/Baja-Ferry/ferry.htm. The SEMA-TUR ferries are somewhat older and more dilapidated than the ship owned by Baja Ferries, which was built in 2001. To see pictures of the SEMA-TUR ferries, visit the Britis website www.simplonpc.co.uk/SEMATUR.html. Always get information on the condition of the Baja highway before committing to this route. For road conditions and more information on the ferries, check www.math.ucr.edu/ftm/baja.html.

ACTIVE SPANISH / ACTIVE ENGLISH

AT A GLANCE

Location: ✲✲
Facilities: ✲✲
Programs: ✲✲
Overall Rating: ✲✲
Cost: $ 7.50–$15/hour
Maximum number of students per class: two
Street address:
   Avenida Camarón Sábalo 333-D
   Mazatlán, Sinaloa, México

Tel: 52 669-916-7223 or 52 669-913-0423
Email: activeenglish@mzt.megared.net.mx
Director: Mónica Rodríguez

Active Spanish/Active English is right in the heart of the *Zona Dorada,* the main tourist area of Mazatlán. It's close to the beach and many of the major hotels, restaurants, and shops that appeal to tourists. The facilities consist of several small classrooms in a converted office building. There's a tree-shaded patio adjacent to the school where students may study or snack between classes.

CREDIT

Active Spanish is certified by the Secretaria de Educación Pública (SEP), but has no vehicle for granting credit. Independent community college credit may be arranged through Seattle Central Community College. *See "Getting College Credit," page 8.*

COSTS

Tuition is charged in pesos.

Private classes: 150 pesos/hour (about $15)

Shared classes (two persons): 75 pesos/person/hour (about $7.50)

LODGING

HOME STAY

This school serves the hotel zone and does not advertise its programs as "total immersion." Most students do not stay with a family; however, the school will arrange a home stay for students who request it. The cost depends on the accommodations.

OTHER OPTIONS

The school maintains a list of rentals, including apartments and rooms.

PROGRAMS AND SCHEDULES

Students may begin classes on any weekday.

SPANISH CONVERSATION

Beginning, intermediate, and advanced levels of conversational Spanish are offered.

MEDICAL AND BUSINESS SPANISH

Students may request instruction in medical or business Spanish. These programs are tailored to the needs of each student.

EXTRAS

BEACH ACTIVITIES. Active Spanish is close to the beach for swimming, surfing, and parasailing.

EXCURSIONS. The school does not offer excursions. However, the offices of local tour agencies are nearby and offer trips to interesting sites around Mazatlán.

INTERNET ACCESS. Active Spanish does not offer Internet access to its students. There are several Internet cafés within walking distance.

WHAT DISTINGUISHES THIS SCHOOL?

SMALL AND PERSONAL. Active Spanish specializes in individualized instruction. Most classes are one-on-one private instruction.

LOCATION. The school is in the *Zona Dorada* or Golden Zone, Mazatlán's tourist strip. It's convenient to hotels, and Spanish instruction can be easily combined with tourist activities.

CENTRO DE IDIOMAS DE MAZATLÁN

AT A GLANCE

Location: ☆☆☆☆
Facilities: ☆☆☆
Programs: ☆☆☆½
Overall Rating: ☆☆☆½
Cost: $160/week (four hours/day)
Maximum number of students per class: five
Street address
    Belisario Domínguez 1908
    Mazatlán, Sinaloa, México 82000

Tel: 52 669-985-5606
Fax: 52 669-982-2052
Email: centro@spanishlink.org
Website: www.spanishlink.org
Director: Dixie Davis

Centro de Idiomas de Mazatlán occupies the upper floors of an elegant old building in the historic district of downtown Mazatlán, not far from the cathedral. The atmosphere of the school is typical of Old Mazatlán. The classrooms are spacious and have very high ceilings. Students gather between classes in a common area with comfortable chairs and a small library of paperbacks, or on an upstairs patio that affords rooftop views of the city. The school is close to cultural activities in Old Mazatlán, including theater performances, concerts, and art exhibits. It's also within walking distance of the beach and harbor.

ACADEMIC BACKGROUND

Director Dixie Davis is originally from the U.S. but has lived in Mazatlán for the past twenty-seven years. She specializes in translations. All teachers have a university degree and in-house training.

CREDIT

U.S. university credit is available from University of Southern Mississippi or National Registration Center for Study Abroad (NRCSA). Community college credit may be arranged through Seattle Central Community College. *See "Getting College Credit," page 8.*

University of Minnesota at Mankato offers a twelve-week semester program held in part at this school. Students are accompanied by a professor from University of Minnesota.

Centro de Idiomas Mazatlán has also been approved for salary point credits by the Los Angeles Unified School District.

COSTS

REGISTRATION FEES

Reservations made at least 45 days prior to starting date: $100

Reservations made at least 30 days prior to starting date: $120

Reservations made fewer than 30 days prior to starting date: $140

TUITION (INCLUDING ROOM AND BOARD WITH A MEXICAN FAMILY)

Semi-Intensive Group - two hours/day: $130/week

Intensive Group - four hours/day: $160/week

Private instruction–two hours/day: $180/week

Private instruction–four hours/day: $360/week

Discounts: For participants in group courses only, there is a 10 percent discount on course fees and home stay costs for enrollment periods of four to seven weeks and a 20 percent discount for eight weeks or more. Two or more students who enroll together for a minimum of two weeks receive a 10 percent discount.

Lodging

Home Stay

Private room with three meals a day: $160/week

Shared room with three meals a day: $142/week

Other options

Hotel lodging is also available upon request. A hotel within walking distance of the school and recommended by the director charges $28 – $30/night.

Near the school there are simple apartments that are clean and safe; prices begin at around $500/month.

Programs and Schedules

Semi-Intensive Group Program

The Semi-Intensive Program includes two hours/day of structured Spanish study in a group setting, Monday through Friday. Classes are scheduled in the morning.

Intensive Group Program

The Intensive Program consists of four and one-half hours daily of Spanish study, from 8:30 a.m. – 1:30 p.m. Classes consist of a pronunciation and listening workshop, grammar and oral exercises, vocabulary, and conversation.

Individual Spanish Conversation

The individualized program follows the same pattern as the group program, including four hours a day of private instruction plus a one-hour pronunciation workshop.

Semi-Intensive Tutor Program

Students in this program receive ten private lessons per week.

MEDICAL AND BUSINESS SPANISH

Private classes in Medical and Business Spanish may be arranged. The school provides opportunities for students to meet and converse with local business people and medical professionals.

METHODS

Centro de Idiomas uses the Conversational Method for Adults, which encourages active student participation with emphasis on speaking and listening-comprehension skills. The eventual goal is to be able to speak at the level of a native speaker.

EXTRAS

FREE DAILY WORKSHOP. The school offers all students a daily one-hour pronunciation and listening-comprehension workshop at no additional cost.

PERSON-TO-PERSON ACTIVITY. Students who request this activity are introduced to local people in their own profession or area of interest.

FRIDAY NIGHT CONVERSATION CLUB. This is a language interchange that allows students to converse with some of the Mexicans who study English at the Center.

SATURDAY MORNING ACTIVITIES. Visits to local places of interest such as the market, the cathedral, and historic buildings provide extra language practice.

STUDENT DISCOUNT CARD. Students who send the school a photo receive an identification card upon arrival in Mazatlán. This can be used for student discounts at local businesses.

OPTIONAL ACTIVITIES OUTSIDE THE SCHOOL. Optional activities include fishing, sailing, jet skiing, scuba diving, snorkeling, parasailing, water skiing, surfing, Tai Chi and yoga classes, dance classes, tennis, golf, and kayaking. Several local tour companies offer a variety of activities, including walking tours of the of the old city, natural history and bird-watching excursions, trips to mountain villages, boat rides along the coast, ferry boat trips to La Paz, and visits to Mazatlán's aquarium, which is the largest in Mexico. Centro de Idiomas does not sponsor these tours and activities, but the school will provide information to interested students.

WHAT DISTINGUISHES THIS SCHOOL?

AWARD WINNER. Centro de Idiomas de Mazatlán has twice won the International Committee of Quality and Prestige Award, given by the Mexican National Chamber of Commerce.

LOCATION. The school is located in downtown Mazatlán, away from the over-touristed beach areas. Students can enjoy the advantages of studying in a beach town and still absorb some Mexican culture.

ENGLISH AND SPANISH FOR ALL

AT A GLANCE

Location: ✶✶✶
Facilities: ✶✶
Programs: ✶✶✶✶
Overall Rating: ✶✶✶½
Cost: $300/week (twenty-five hours of instruction)
Maximum number of students per class: four
Street address:
   Eloy Cavazos #149
   Fracc. El Toreo 82120
   Mazatlán, Sinaloa, México

Tel: 52 669-986-2471
Fax: 52 669-986-2471
Email: spanish@prodigy.net.mx and mixapixa@hotmail.com
Website: www.mexonline.com/efa.htm
Director: Martha B. Armenta

In a converted home on a tree-shaded residential street, English and Spanish for All is near the Zona Dorada and Playa Norte (North Beach) area of Mazatlán. The building is small and contains only a couple of classrooms. This school specializes in individualized (one-on-one) instruction, but does accept groups. Larger group classes are held at a local university. Despite its small size, English and Spanish for All is a professional operation. The director and teachers are well qualified and dedicated to teaching Spanish as a Second Language.

ACADEMIC BACKGROUND

Director Martha Armenta has a bachelor's degree in education and is a former university professor. She is an official English and Spanish translator for the Mexican Ministry of National Security (Instituto Nacional de Migración). She has taught at Paradise Community College in Phoenix, Arizona, and has translated for several U.S. Government departments. The two other teachers hold master's degrees in education and teaching foreign languages. The school has connections with \UAS (Universidad Autónoma de Sinaloa) and UDO (Universidad del Occidente). Group classes are held at these facilities to provide a realistic university experience and allow for interchange between Mexican and foreign students.

CREDIT

The curricula at English and Spanish for All have been approved by the Secretaria de Educación Pública or SEP, the Mexican Department of Education. Prescott College (Arizona) and Aims College (Colorado) currently offer credit programs at this school. Students from other colleges and universities should make arrangements for credit with their home schools before registering for classes at English and Spanish for All.

Community college credit may be arranged through Seattle Central Community College. See "Getting College Credit," page 8.

COSTS

Nonrefundable registration fee: $125
(Includes materials, registration and the trip to and from the Mazatlán airport)
Individual Instruction (twenty-five hours): $300/week
Discount rates are available for groups.

LODGING

HOME STAY

A home stay is required as part of the immersion program.

Full room and board: $190/week

OTHER OPTIONS

The school will also arrange for accommodations in hotels or apartments.

PROGRAMS AND SCHEDULES

INDIVIDUAL AND SMALL GROUP PROGRAM

This program includes twenty hours per week of classroom instruction in basic or intermediate Spanish. Also included are at least five hours of field practice, during which students, accompanied by a teacher, visit interesting places in the city.

GROUP PROGRAMS

Customized group programs can be designed to meet special needs and may begin at any time.

LEGAL AND MEDICAL SPANISH

Special programs are also offered for professionals and students pursuing careers in medicine and law. Students in these programs typically combine studies at English and Spanish for All with classes at a university and practical experience in a law office, medical clinic, or hospital.

INTENSIVE MEDICAL SPANISH FOR CLINICIANS

This is a two-week intensive Spanish course for emergency-room physicians and medical students that combines Spanish, clinical practices, and cultural experiences. Classes are held at the Nursing School facilities of the Universidad Autónoma de Sinaloa campus in Mazatlán. For more information contact Martha Armenta at spanish@prodigy.net.mx.

COMMUNICACIÓN ES VIDA Y SALUD

This thirty-six-hour Spanish program is organized by Migrant Clinicians Network of Austin, Texas, in coordination with The Universidad Autónoma de Sinaloa and English & Spanish For All. The program is held only once a year. Health professionals must enroll through the Migrant Clinicians

Network and may receive credit for the program through Texas A & M University. For more information contact:

Jillian Hopewell or Kathleen Lowell
Migrant Clinicians Network
PO Box 164285, Austin, Texas 78716
Tel: 512-327-2017
Email:mcn@migrantclinician.org

METHODS

Teachers at English and Spanish for All use a conversational, communicative method, including TPR (Total Physical Response). Most classes are very small and individualized.

TEXTBOOKS

Textbooks are not used in the classes, but the school maintains a large library of language resource material that is used in teaching.

EXTRAS

AIRPORT TRANSPORTATION. Transportation to and from the Mazatlán airport is included in the tuition.

EXCURSIONS. The school sponsors trips to places of interest in and around Mazatlán. One interesting excursion visits San Ignacio, about sixty miles north of Mazatlán, where the people are so proud of their quaint colonial town that they often point out places of interest and give spontaneous talks on a variety of topics.

VISA ASSISTANCE. The school provides translation or assistance to foreigners who are applying for an FM3 Visa (a non-immigrant visa other than a tourist visa). For more information contact English and Spanish for All by email.

PAYPAL PAYMENTS. Payment for tuition and room and board may be made electronically through PayPal: www.paypal.com. See the English and Spanish for All website for instructions on how to pay by this method.

WHAT DISTINGUISHES THIS SCHOOL?

UNIVERSITY CONNECTIONS. Students can benefit from the faculty's close connection to two universities in Mazatlán by visiting those universities to experience academic Spanish. More advanced students can also take short-term classes at the Universidad Autónoma de Sinaloa.

MEDICAL PROGRAM. The school has partnered with the Migrant Clinicians Network from Texas A & M University to offer a program for healthcare professionals who treat migrant workers.

PRACTICAL CLASSES IN AUTHENTIC SITUATIONS. Visits to the market, shops, museums, schools, and the theater are an integral part of the program.

DIPLOMA. Students may get a diploma signed by the local secretary of education (SEP) upon completion of their study programs at English and Spanish for All. Prior registration, two passport pictures, and a birth certificate are required. Contact the school for more information.

PUERTO VALLARTA

In the 1960s, Puerto Vallarta was a small fishing village of about 10,000 residents. The town became world famous in 1964 when Elizabeth Taylor and Richard Burton stayed there during the filming of Tennessee Williams's *Night of the Iguana.* Today, Puerto Vallarta has about 300,000 residents and is a major tourist de-stination. The city sits at the base of the Sierra Madre mountains on the *"Bahia de Banderas"* or "Bay of Flags." It now spreads for several miles north and south of its original site, with luxurious hotels and condominiums fronting the beach. The area around the main plaza retains some of the charm of a colonial Mexican village with its cobblestone streets, traditional market, and picturesque church crowned by a huge "jewel."

Although Puerto Vallarta is best known for its beaches, it offers a wide variety of other attractions and activities, from golf and sailing to whale watching and horseback riding in the jungle. There's great shopping for everything from Mexican handicrafts to fine jewelry and furniture. South of the city are several quaint seaside villages accessible only by water taxi.

GETTING THERE

BY PLANE

Because of its popularity as a vacation destination, getting to Puerto Vallarta by air is easy and relatively inexpensive. Many airlines have direct flights from the U.S. and Canada, including Alaska Airlines, America West, Mexicana, Delta, Continental, United, and AeroMexico. Round-trip airfares from the West Coast of the U.S. begin at about $320. Special airfares and charters sometimes lower the cost to less than $200.

BY BUS

It's possible to get to Puerto Vallarta by bus from the U.S., but it's a long ride (about thirty hours) from the border, and the slightly lower cost isn't worth the discomfort. The most direct route is from Tucson through Nogales to Mazatlán and then on to Puerto Vallarta. Two bus lines go to Mazatlán. The Cruceros line leaves from the Tucson Greyhound station and makes the trip through Nogales to Mazatlán in about twenty hours for a fare of about $80 one way. The other, TBC, leaves for Mazatlán from its own station in Tucson. You can call TBC at 520-903-2801 for their current schedules and fares. In Mazatlán, you'll need to change to another bus line to reach Puerto Vallarta. The trip from Mazatlán to Puerto Vallarta will take an additional six to eight hours and may require yet another change of buses in Tepic.

By car

The drive to Puerto Vallarta from the U.S./Mexico border will take at least three days in addition to the time it takes you to drive from your home to the border. From California, take Mexico Highway 2 out of Mexicali to Highway 15, the main pacific route. From Arizona, take Mexico Highway 15 from Nogales through Guaymas, Culiacan, and Mazatlán. Don't forget to purchase Mexican insurance for your car at the border or online before leaving home. For more information on driving in Mexico, see "Driving," page 26.

ARTE LANGUAGE SCHOOL

AT A GLANCE

Location: ✯✯✯
Facilities: ✯✯✯
Programs: ✯✯✯
Overall Rating: ✯✯✯
Cost: $75/week (three hours/day)
Maximum number of students per class: five
Street Address:
   Estadios #9
   Bucerías, Nayarit

Tel: 52 329-298-1628
Email: penichec@prodigy.net.mx or teremilan@hotmail.com
Website: www.artels.com
Director: Teresa Peniche de Milan

This small school is located in the traditional Mexican beach town of Bucerías, Nayarit, about ten miles north of Puerto Vallarta. It offers a small-town environment that's very different from the hustle and bustle of Puerto Vallarta. Director Teresa Milan and her husband live part-time on the premises, creating a homey atmosphere. At certain times of the year, the Arte school offers Spanish courses in the city of Progreso in the state of Yucatán, or in Cancún, Quintana Roo. Students may also choose to study in Guadalajara.

ACADEMIC BACKGROUND

Director and principal teacher Teresa Peniche de Milan holds degrees in Spanish, English, Italian, and French. She has many years of language teaching experience at Universidad Autónoma de Guadalajara and Universidad Panamericana in Guadalajara. She has also taught at the Alliance Française.

CREDIT

This school does not offer credit directly. University students who need credit for their courses should check with their home institution before registering.

Community college credit may be arranged through Seattle Central Community College. See "Getting College Credit," page 8.

COSTS

Registration fee: $100

Intensive Spanish Language Course
Four weeks (sixty hours): $300

LODGING

In Bucerías, Progreso, or Cancún, ocean-view apartments with a pool are available to students for $750/month. In Bucerías, students also have the option of staying at the school. Meals aren't included, but there are kitchen facilities at the school and in the apartments.

PROGRAMS AND SCHEDULES

A placement test is given to determine each student's language level. The school offers four levels of instruction. Each includes sixty hours of classes in a four-week session. Sessions begin the first week of each month.

Classes are held from 9 a.m. to noon daily. The first part of each instructional day includes grammar and exercises; the second part is devoted to culture and history, including songs, stories, and videos.

METHODS

Classes are based on a practical method, which covers all four language-learning skills—reading, writing, listening, and speaking.

TEXTBOOKS

Tesesa Milan is currently writing *Un paseo por México (A Tour Through Mexico),* a textbook that will be used as the text for all Arte Language School courses.

EXTRAS

CULTURAL CLASSES. Classes in dance and Mexican cooking are available on request.

EXCURSIONS. The school offers excursions to points of interest around Puerto Vallarta for students at the Bucerías campus. In Progreso, excursions to Mayan archeological sites may be arranged. All excursions are at extra cost to the student.

SCHOLARSHIPS. The school offers a special promotion in which prospective students can win a 50 percent or full scholarship by scoring high on a Mayan culture and history questionnaire. For more information, go to the school's website, www.artels.com, click on *Tuitions and Fees* and look for *Special Promotion.*

WHAT DISTINGUISHES THIS SCHOOL?

PERSONAL ATTENTION. Teresa Peniche de Milan personally directs and teaches in both schools. She and her husband live on the premises and are available to students outside of the classroom. Classes tend to be very small, often with one or two students.

MULTIPLE LOCATIONS. Students at Arte Language School have the option of living and studying near the popular beaches of Puerto Vallarta, or in Cancún, or Progreso, on the Yucatán Peninsula, which offers visits to Mayan ruins and a chance to experience an entirely different part of Mexico. Students may split their studies between locations; however, because of the distance between Puerto Vallarta and Progreso or Cancún, the additional transportation costs are substantial.

CEPE (CENTRO DE ESTUDIOS PARA EXTRANJEROS)

UNIVERSITY OF GUADALAJARA – PUERTO VALLARTA BRANCH

AT A GLANCE

Location: ★★★★
Facilities: ★★★
Programs: ★★★★
Overall Rating: ★★★★
Cost: $431/two- or four-week session (fifty hours total)
Maximum number of students per class: fifteen
Street address:
    Libertad 105-1 • Colonia Centro
    48300 Puerto Vallarta • Jalisco, México

Tel: 52 322-223-2082 • Fax: 52 322-223-2982
Email: cepv@prodigy.net.mx • Website: www.cepe.udg.mx
Director: José Luís Bravo

This school offers students a chance to study Spanish while enjoying one of Mexico's principal tourist destinations. Located in the more traditional downtown area of Puerto Vallarta, across the street from the crafts market and not far from the main plaza, the school is in an area removed from the hustle and bustle of the beaches. The environment is also traditional, with ten classrooms around a typical Mexican central patio. A branch campus of the University of Guadalajara, this school offers the same basic program as its larger sister campus, CEPE Guadalajara.

ACADEMIC BACKGROUND

The director, José Luís Bravo, has an MBA from the University of Guadalajara. Each of the teachers has at least a bachelor's degree and has been certified to teach Spanish by the University of Guadalajara.

CREDIT

Credit is available through the University of Guadalajara. Check with the counseling department of your home institution to see whether they'll accept UDG credits. CEPE issues an official certificate of study that includes all the courses you have taken, the number of hours you attended, and the grades you received.

U.S. University credit is available by registering for this program through National Registration Center for Study Abroad (NRCSA). Community college credit may be arranged through Seattle Central Community College. *See "Getting College Credit," page 8.*

COSTS

Nonrefundable registration fee: $35

Intensive Course (four-week session): $453
Two and a half hours/day, fifty hours total, three credits

Super Intensive Course (two-week session): $453
Five hours/day, fifty hours total, three credits

Supplementary Spanish Language Courses (two-week session): $453

Conversation I & II, Writing I & II, Grammar I & II
Five hours/day, fifty hours total, three credits

Content Courses (two-week session): $196

Mexican Culture and Mexican History
Two hours/day, twenty hours total, one credit

Basic Skills for Tourists (one-week session): $98
  Two hours/day, ten hours total, noncredit

Spanish for Kids (summer only) four-week session: $331
  Two hours activities and two hours Spanish/day, noncredit
  Two levels: lower elementary and upper elementary

One-on-one Private Instruction: $22/hour

Workbooks: $16–$26

LODGING

HOME STAY

	Two weeks	Four weeks	Extra day
Single (private) room	$426	$823	$30
Double (shared) room	$397	$794	$28

OTHER OPTIONS

A fully furnished two-bedroom apartment in the hotel zone is also available to CEPE students. It has all amenities, including a pool and laundry room, as well as weekly maid service.

ROOM PRICES

One person: $42/night

Two persons sharing bed: $50/night

Three persons (one single and two sharing bed): $60/night

NOTE: *There's a minimum stay of fourteen nights, and the apartment may be shared with one or two other students.*

PROGRAMS AND SCHEDULES

A placement test is required, except for basic skills courses.

Classes run from 8 a.m. to 4 p.m., Monday through Friday. Classes begin on specific dates every four to six weeks throughout the year. To determine the start dates, see the academic calendar in the Puerto Vallarta section of CEPE's website: www.cepe.udg.mx.

BASIC COURSE (THREE LEVELS OF INSTRUCTION)

LEVEL I, BEGINNING. For students who have had no previous experience with Spanish, this course includes simple forms of communication used in greeting people, introducing oneself, communicating in family situations, in stores and restaurants, and many other useful situations. Beginning students also learn basic grammar and verbs in the present tense.

LEVEL II, BEGINNING II. For students who already know some Spanish, this course focuses on learning to describe things, express opinions, and make suggestions in various situations. Students learn to use the past tenses as well as the present and informal future tenses.

LEVEL III, INTERMEDIATE. Intermediate students learn to express opinions and emotions, give advice, and make suggestions in various situations. They also learn to use the formal future tense and reflexive verbs.

SUPPLEMENTARY SPANISH COURSES

CONVERSATION I. (For students who have tested into Level II). This course provides conversational practice in various situations relating to the family, the city, leisure activities, and daily life.

CONVERSATION II. (for students who have tested into Level III). This course allows students to develop the ability to communicate in daily life in Mexico and in social situations. Students participate in activities that promote the expression of ideas and opinions, such as discussions, debates, group problem solving, panels, and interviews.

WRITING I & II. These writing workshops are adapted to the needs of the student, but require knowledge of Spanish grammar.

GRAMMAR I & II. This course concentrates on reviewing all the grammar that students should know up to their level and also covers some of the finer points.

CONTENT COURSES

Two-week content courses on Mexican culture and history are offered in Spanish.

THE HISTORY OF MODERN MEXICO. Students attend lectures on the history of Mexico from the War of Independence, through the Revolution, and on to the inductrialization of the 1940s. The course also provides an overview of the political scene in Mexico, focusing on popular movements, political parties, and the unions.

MEXICAN CULTURE. This course presents Mexican culture from an anthropological standpoint, including religion and national values within the Mexican context.

BASIC SKILLS FOR TOURISTS. This one-week class meets two hours per day, ten hours total, and is noncredit. Students learn a series of useful phrases and common vocabulary for traveling in Mexico.

SPANISH FOR CHILDREN. Four-week session, summer only. This noncredit course includes two hours of activities and two hours of Spanish instruction daily. The program is divided into two levels: lower elementary and upper elementary. Children learn survival Spanish and grammar, including the conjugation of some useful verbs.

METHODS

Learning is based on the communicative approach, with attention to grammatical accuracy. All courses are taught in Spanish.

TEXTBOOKS

There is one workbook per level. Workbooks are developed by the CEPE faculty and published by the school.

EXTRAS

MEDICAL SERVICE. Students have free medical consultation in the event of an accident or illness. CEPE will pay for the physician's fees, but students must pay for medication, lab tests, and other costs.

FRIENDSHIP PROGRAM. The school offers a cultural interchange and language program that gives foreign students the opportunity to practice Spanish with Mexican students.

EXCURSIONS. CEPE works with a tour company that offers tours and excursions varying in cost from $60–$300.

WHAT DISTINGUISHES THIS SCHOOL?

LOCATION. Puerto Vallarta is a major resort and tourist destination. Students can study at CEPE while enjoying beach activities, nightlife, and shopping. Because the school is located in the old town, students also have opportunities to experience Mexican culture and practice their Spanish; however, more English is spoken in this resort city than in more traditional inland cities.

CREDIT THROUGH UNIVERSITY OF GUADALAJARA. CEPE is a department of the University of Guadalajara, which allows the school to issue UDG transcripts and award direct credit for its programs.

Mountain Cities

㎝㎝㎝㎝㎝㎝㎝㎝㎝㎝㎝

Cuernavaca

A modern city with ancient roots, Cuernavaca has been occupied since pre-Columbian times. Its name is a Spanish version of Cuauhanáhuac, a word in Nahuatl, which was the language of the Aztecs. Cuernavaca's original name is said to mean "close to the trees," a description that still fits today because of the many natural refuges within the city. Built around a series of barrancas or ravines, Cuernavaca retains a rural flavor enhanced by its numerous parks and gardens. There is even an impressive natural waterfall known as the "Salto de San Anton" not far from the center of the city.

Cuernavaca was the base of Spanish conquistador Hernán Cortés, whose son later operated a vast sugar plantation nearby. Today the city offers many interesting colonial sites, among them the *Palacio de Cortés*, an interesting stone structure built like a castle. It is now a museum featuring interesting artifacts from all periods of Mexico's history as well as works by the famous muralists, Diego Rivera, David Alfaro Siquieros, and Rufino Tamayo. The city's lofty cathedral dates from the 16th century and is surrounded by ancient walls.

Ever since the Habsburg Emperor Maximilian established his summer residence in Cuernavaca in the mid-19th century, it has been a favorite vacation place for wealthy Mexicans.

It is also a university town and the home of many artists and intellectuals, which may account for the fact that Cuernavaca has evolved as the center of Spanish-language study in Mexico. There are more language schools in Cuernavaca than in any other Mexican city. The intellectual atmosphere also promotes cultural events such as poetry readings, concerts, ballet and theater performances, and art exhibitions. In the evenings, the sidewalk cafés turn into lively bars as the city's thriving nightlife begins. Cuernavaca's modern side can be seen in its suburbs, where there are shopping malls, fast-food restaurants, spas, gyms, and spectacular movie complexes.

With Mexico City close by, students can take advantage of the many historical and cultural benefits of the capital without the inconveniences of living in a huge metropolis. Cuernavaca is also well located for touring. The Pacific Coast resort city of Acapulco is just three hours away, the silver city of Taxco is even closer, and many archeological sites are near enough for day trips.

If you're interested in an intimate small-town experience, Cuernavaca may not be the best place for you, but if you're looking for a sophisticated city with opportunities to participate in myriad activities, this is the place!

CLIMATE

Mexicans often call Cuernavaca the City of Eternal Spring. At an altitude of just over 5,000 feet, this city of about 500,000 has an ideal climate with year-round high temperatures of 75 to 85 degrees.

GETTING THERE

Although there are no direct flights to Cuernavaca, it's easily accessible from Mexico City. Pullman de Morelos operates buses directly to Cuernavaca from inside the Mexico City Airport. The buses leave about every forty minutes and cost about $10 one way. By using this unique service, you can avoid taking a taxi across the city to a distant bus station, a risky and time-consuming process.

To catch the Pullman de Morelos bus after arriving in the Mexico City airport, turn to the right after passing through the sliding glass doors as you leave the customs area. Take the escalators up to the food court, walk past all the restaurants, and take a right at the last one. This should bring you to the bus-ticket counter in *Sala D* (National Gate D), where you can purchase a ticket to Cuernavaca. For departure times, go to www.cuernavacainfo.com, then scroll down and click on "Mexico City/Cuernavaca Airport Commuter Bus." The bus takes about an hour and forty-five minutes to arrive at Cuernavaca's Casino de la Selva bus station, where you can get a taxi to your host family's residence at a fare of about $5.

CUAUHNÁHUAC SPANISH LANGUAGE INSTITUTE

AT A GLANCE

Location: ✫✫✫✫
Facilities: ✫✫✫✫
Programs: ✫✫✫✫½
Overall Rating: ✫✫✫✫½
Cost: $65/week (two hrs./day) to $120/week (six hrs./day)
Maximum number of students per class: five
Mailing Address:
   Apartado Postal 5-26
   Cuernavaca, Morelos 62051, México

Street Address:
   Avenida Morelos Sur 123, Colonia Chipitlán
   62070 Cuernavaca, Morelos, México

Tel: 52 777-312-3673 or 52 777-318-9275
Fax: 52 777-318-2693
Email: marketing@cuauhnahuac.edu.mx or
inform@cuauhnahuac.edu.mx
Website: www.cuauhnahuac.edu.mx
Director: Dr. José Daniel Camacho

International Relations & Marketing Director: L. I. David Cano M.
Student Development Director: Josué Peña Macip
U.S. Contact: Judi González
12500 Edgewater Drive, Lakewood, OH 44107
U.S. Tel: 216-227-9273
Email: j52585@aol.com

Cuauhnáhuac was founded in 1972 and given the original Indian name for Cuernavaca. Just off busy Avenida Morelos, one of the main thoroughfares in Cuernavaca, the campus is a converted villa overlooking a peaceful garden and pool area surrounded by small, rustic classrooms. In the main building, there is a computer lab, a library, and a large lecture hall. An outdoor café offers typical Mexican food and drink. The spacious campus also offers a swimming pool, basketball and volleyball courts, and as Ping-Pong and billiard tables.

ACADEMIC BACKGROUND

Director Dr. José Daniel Camacho holds a master's degree and doctorate in higher education. Most teachers have bachelor's degrees in fields such as communication, linguistics, or tourism. All have previous teaching experience and have been trained in the Cuauhnáhuac method.

CREDIT

Cuauhnáhuac provides final evaluations and transcripts to students from various universities that grant credit for its programs. Any student who completes four weeks of study may qualify for six units of credit from the University of LaVerne in California. Teachers can earn one semester unit of graduate credit for each week of study at Cuauhnáhuac from Ashland University in Ohio. Community college credit may be arranged through Seattle Central Community College. *See "Getting College Credit," page 8.*

COSTS

Nonrefundable registration fee: $70

NORMAL INTENSIVE LANGUAGE PROGRAM *(thirty hours/week)*

	Regular tuition	*Off-season tuition*
One Week	$300	$230
Two Weeks	$480	$420
Three Weeks	$700	$570
Four Weeks	$800	$690
Super-Intensive Program	$520/week	$460/week
Individual Program	$20/hour	$20/hour

Off-season tuition is effective in March, April, September, October, and November.

CUSTOMIZED PROGRAMS

Customized programs with specialized vocabulary for professionals are offered for a 30 percent increase in the prices shown above.

LODGING

HOME STAY (INCLUDING THREE MEALS)

Shared room: $22/night

Private room: $35/night

PROGRAMS AND SCHEDULES

NORMAL INTENSIVE LANGUAGE PROGRAM

Intensive Spanish-language classes meet from 8 a.m. to 2:20 p.m. Monday through Friday. Extra-curricular activities are held from 4 p.m. to 7 p.m.

Students in this program spend three hours daily learning and practicing grammar using the school's original textbooks, which cover nine levels of instruction, from beginning to advanced. An additional three hours of instruction are equally divided between conversation and situational Spanish for beginners or cultural lectures on topics such as Mexican history, culture, literature and art.

LATINO PROGRAM

This program is for students who have been exposed to spoken Spanish at home but have very little formal grammatical background. Classes emphasize pronunciation, spelling, and grammar. The tuition rates and hours are the same as the Normal Intensive Language Program.

SUPER-INTENSIVE LANGUAGE PROGRAM

Designed for students who want to learn as much Spanish as possible in a short time, this program consists of six hours of private classes daily, structured to meet each student's specific needs.

SEMESTER PROGRAM

The fall and spring semester programs offer thirty hours of instruction weekly in Spanish language, conversation, history, literature, linguistics, culture, and Latin American studies. Internship programs in law, medicine, business, and education are also available to students in the semester program.

INDIVIDUAL LANGUAGE PROGRAM

Individualized one-on-one classes may be scheduled at the convenience of the student. Course content is structured to meet each student's needs

CUSTOMIZED PROGRAMS

Cuauhnáhuac also offers customized programs for business executives, healthcare professionals, bilingual teachers, diplomats, legal professionals and people planning to work, retire, or travel in Spanish-speaking countries.

METHODS

The school uses its own method based on The Silent Way and techniques employed by the Foreign Service Institute.

TEXTBOOKS

Cuauhnáhuac has published its own four-book series of Spanish-language texts, which is used in its classes as well as at other Spanish schools in Mexico. Additional teaching materials are drawn from various sources, including *Curso Intensivo de Español,* published by the Mexican-American Cultural Institute in Mexico City.

EXTRAS

CULTURAL ACTIVITIES. Cooking classes, arts and crafts workshops, and Spanish-language films are presented on a regular basis. The school also organizes a Mexican fiesta from time to time.

LANGUAGE EXCHANGE. Two evenings a week, there are group language exchanges with Mexican students learning English. The school will also arrange individual language exchanges on request.

COMPUTER LAB. The school maintains a computer lab for student use. Word, Excel, Power Point, and Corel WordPerfect may be used free of charge.

INTERNET ACCESS. Internet access is available in the computer lab for about $2/hour. Internet Explorer, Eudora, and WS-FTP may be used offline at no charge.

POOL. There is a swimming pool on campus available for student use.

EXCURSIONS. Cuauhnáhuac offers a variety of optional day trips to more than thirty places of interest near Cuernavaca, including the ruins of Xochicalco, the silver city of Taxco, the pyramids of Teotihuacan, Mexico City museums, and the Ballet Folklórico. Special three- and four-day excursions take students to Acapulco, Oaxaca, and Veracruz.

VOLUNTEER PROGRAM. The school organizes a volunteer program in which students work with Mexican children from low-income families or orphanages. Students develop a relationship with the children and teach them basic English.

WHAT DISTINGUISHES THIS SCHOOL?

UNIVERSITY RELATIONSHIPS. Cuauhnáhuac has developed programs for students from a number of U.S. colleges and universities, including University of LaVerne, LaVerne, California; Ashland University in Ashland, Ohio; University of Wisconsin, Oshkosh, Wisconsin; Northwestern Illinois University; California Polytechnic University, San Luis Obispo, California; New Mexico State University, Las Cruces, New Mexico; and Pikes Peak Community College, Colorado Springs, Colorado.

CUAUHNÁHUAC METHOD. The school has its own method, which it has published in a series of four textbooks that are also used by other schools in different parts of Mexico.

LATINO PROGRAM. Cuauhnáhuac offers one of the few programs in Mexico designed especially for Latino students who already speak Spanish but need practice in grammar, reading, and writing.

WELL ESTABLISHED. Cuauhnáhuac Spanish Language Institute has been teaching Spanish as a Second Language for more than thirty years.

CEMANÁHUAC EDUCATIONAL COMMUNITY

AT A GLANCE

Location: ★★★★½
Facilities: ★★★★
Programs: ★★★★★
Overall Rating: ★★★★½
Cost: $230/week (five hours/day)
Maximum number of students per class: five
Street Address:
   San Juan 4, Apartado 5-21
   Colonia de las Palmas
   Cuernavaca, Morelos 62051, México

U.S. Address:
   1253 B Lake Shore Drive
   Columbus, OH 43204

Mexico Tel: 52 777-318-6407 or 52 777-318-6419
U.S. Tel: 614-487-0965
Mexico Fax: 52 777-312-5418 • U.S. Fax: 614-487-0964
Email: cemanáhuac1@cs.com
Website: www.cemanahuac.com

Director: Francisco Guerrero Garro
Language Program Director: Martha Magana
Educational Programs Coordinator: Vivian B. Harvey
Admissions Coordinator: Charles Goff
Registrar: Harriett Goff Guerrero
Rural Studies Program Coordinator: Maricruz Ramírez

A s you enter through a shady garden area dotted with palm-thatched *palapas*, Cemanáhuac looks small and compact. It's only when you walk through the lobby in the main building that the rest of this large school reveals itself. Several classroom buildings, a large pool area, and an open-air cafeteria are interspersed with patios and lawns. A small library contains an impressive collection of books on Mexican history, culture and art, pre-Columbian civilizations, and Spanish language and literature. In addition to the Cuernavaca campus, Cemanáhuac maintains a rural-studies program in the village of Buenavista, where social workers and other interested students can experience firsthand the problems faced by Mexican families.

ACADEMIC QUALIFICATIONS

Director Francisco Guerrero Garro has a degree in history from Universidad Nacional Autónoma de México and three years of medical studies at the same university. He also studied art in France and has an impressive list of accomplishments, including directing the UN program on indigenous art in the state of Oaxaca, conducting anthropological research for the Oaxaca exhibit at the Museum of Anthropology in Mexico City, and directing the Indian migration program for Mexico City. The language-program director, Martha Magana, holds a master's degree in education from the University of Morelos and has taken a wide range of courses in teaching Spanish as a Second Language. Vivian Harvey, the educational programs coordinator, is a former child-development teacher and assistant dean of students at Ohio State University. She has an MA in education and an MS in family studies. More information on the educational background of Cemanáhuac's primary staff is posted on their website: www.Cemanáhuac.com.

CREDIT

Several U.S. universities grant credit for study at Cemanáhuac. They include the State University of New York (SUNY), West Virginia University, and University of Southern Mississippi. The state of California grants continuing education credit to nurses who study at Cemanáhuac, and graduate students may receive credit through the University of California at Santa Barbara.

Community college credit may be arranged through Seattle Central Community College. *See "Getting College Credit," page 8.*

Costs

Nonrefundable registration fee: $95

Intensive Spanish: $230/week

Business Program: $230/week

Social Work Program: $230/week

Medical Program: $230/week, plus $50/week for hospital experience

Children's Program: $230/week

Developmental Child-care Program: $75/week

Lodging

Home Stay

(paid to the school; includes three meals a day):

Double (shared) room $21/night

Single (private) room $30/night

Programs and Schedules

Intensive Spanish Language

Intensive Spanish classes begin on Mondays all year and are held from 9 a.m. to 1 p.m., Monday through Friday. Students in this program work on both grammar and communication skills, beginning at a level appropriate to their knowledge of Spanish.

Business Program

Cemanáhuac offers an intensive, forty-hour-per-week tutorial program in Business Spanish. There is also a language-immersion weekend program for foreign business people who live in Mexico.

MEDICAL PROGRAM

This program is designed for medical students, nurses, doctors, and medical therapists of all types. Cemanáhuac works closely with the Hospital del Niño Morelense (Morelos Children's Hospital) to offer medical terminology in Spanish, clinical observations, and language practice. Students in this program also learn about the prevailing concepts of health and medicine in Mexico by attending seminars on topics such as "Traditional Medicine in Mexico" and visiting rural health clinics and natural healers.

CALIFORNIA NURSING CEUs FOR SPANISH-LANGUAGE STUDY

California nurses may earn continuing education credit at the rate of ten hours per CEU for the Intensive Spanish Language program. Cemanáhuac is a California Board of Registered Nursing approved provider. Their provider number is CEP 13423.

SOCIAL WORK PROGRAM

Students in this program attend regular Spanish-language classes each morning, and special conversation and vocabulary classes for social workers in the afternoon. They also participate in professional seminars and take field trips. Visits to an orphanage, a children's hospital, a rural health clinic, and some of the many social service program offices in Cuernavaca can be included in a group program.

VOLUNTEER PROGRAM

Volunteer opportunities are available for groups or individuals in study programs of four weeks or more. Cemanáhuac works with a social service program called VAMOS!, which serves about 2,500 lunches per week to poor children in the state of Morelos. Students at Cemanáhuac have volunteered their time to this program and donated more than 4,000 bottles of vitamins.

CHILDREN'S PROGRAMS

The school offers a children's Spanish-language program from 9 a.m. to 1 p.m. daily in the summer. Classes are conducted in Spanish. This program is for children under age fourteen; tuition is the same as the regular adult Spanish classes.

Cemanáhuac also offers developmental child-care for children ages five to eleven in July and August. The primary objective of this program is to help children learn about Mexico, but not to learn Spanish.

LATIN AMERICAN STUDIES

Latin American studies classes are taught in Spanish. Topics include "Current Events in Mexico," "Mexico in the Twentieth Century," "Folk medicine and Traditional Healing," "Literature of the Revolution," and "Mesoamerican Religion." The staff at Cemanáhuac will also individualize a program of Latin American studies to meet the needs of a group.

SUMMER WORKSHOPS FOR EDUCATORS (GROUP PROGRAMS)

Each summer, Cemanáhuac offers seminars for educators on a variety of topics of interest to teachers who want to bring the culture of Mexico into their classrooms and improve their Spanish. The following seminars are available for graduate academic credit:

PROFESSIONAL DEVELOPMENT SEMINARS FOR SPANISH LANGUAGE TEACHERS

This program integrates lectures, discussions, readings, and projects, along with methodology and assessment correlated to the U.S. National Standards.

"CONNECTIONS" WORKSHOP

This forty-hour workshop focuses on writing and organizing lesson plans and course objectives and correlating them to the U.S. National Standards. Included are twenty to twenty-four hours of language classes, field-study excursions, lectures in English and Spanish, and other educational activities.

MESOAMERICA IN THE CLASSROOM

In this self-paced independent study class, teachers concentrate on including cultural elements in their classroom activities.

SPANISH FOR ADVANCED SPEAKERS OF SPANISH

A special class for advanced speakers of Spanish who want to refine and polish their Spanish speaking and writing.

SCHOLARSHIPS

Cemanáhuac offers two-week scholarships for educators enrolling in the summer program. Scholarships include registration, two weeks' tuition, housing, all meals, one field-study trip, and a certificate of participation. Each scholarship has a value of about $860.

TRAVEL SEMINARS

Each year, Cemanáhuac sponsors a number of travel seminars in which participants study the culture and history of Mesoamerica. Information on currently scheduled trips is available on the school's website: www.Cemanáhuac.com. The following trips were offered in 2005:

Peoples and Places in the Caribbean: Indigenous Cultures and Contemporary Questions

The Maya, Pre-Hispanic and Contemporary: Folk Art and Fiestas in Mexico

Intensive Study of the Culture of Guatemala

Magnificent Markets and the Maya: Holy Week in Guatemala

The Maya: Pre-Hispanic Cultures and Contemporary Questions

The Guelaguetza Festival and the Valley of Oaxaca

Women, Work, and Weaving in Guatemala

The Days of the Dead, a Most Mexican Celebration

RURAL-STUDIES PROGRAM

Cemanáhuac's rural-studies program operates in the village of Buenavista, in the mountains of Morelos about ninety miles from Cuernavaca. This program is appropriate for social workers, agricultural professionals, or healthcare workers who work with Spanish-speaking immigrants. Spanish-language classes meet for four hours each weekday, and the textbooks used are the same Pido la Palabra series used at Cemanáhuac in Cuernavaca.

RURAL-STUDIES WORKSHOPS. A series of workshops are held at the school in Buena Vista or in the homes and shops of local craftspeople. Workshop activities include Mexican cooking, basket weaving, embroidery, herbal medicine, and a variety of other arts and crafts. Students may also participate in activities such as horseback riding, folk dancing, and singing Mexican folk songs.

METHODS

Cemanáhuac emphasizes oral competency. The teachers have been trained using the Oral Proficiency Guidelines of the American Council on the Teaching of Foreign Languages (ACTFL). Many "out-of-the-classroom exercises" are included, with teachers frequently escorting students to the post office, a grocery store, or a restaurant for the purpose of vocabulary building and learning situation-appropriate behaviors and language. The language classes emphasize the development of communicative skills, stressing speaking and listening, with grammar embedded in the exercises.

TEXTBOOKS

The *Pido la Palabra* series, published by Universidad Autónoma de México is used in all Spanish-language classes.

EXTRAS

FREE GRAMMAR AND CONVERSATION WORKSHOPS. In addition to four hours of language study each day, Cemanáhuac offers an extra hour to review grammar, practice conversation, or learn special vocabulary.

BILINGUAL SCHOOL FOR CHILDREN. During the school year, Cemanáhuac will assist parents who wish to enroll their children in the bilingual International School of Cuernavaca.

CHILD-CARE. Children under the age of five may be cared for in family homes. In the summer, the school offers a daycare program for children ages five to eleven.

EXCURSIONS. The school offers weekend field-study trips to places of historic and cultural interest around Cuernavaca and in the Mexico City area, including the ruins of Teotihuacán, the Museum of Anthropology, the Templo Mayor, and the Ballet Folklórico.

LIBRARY AND MEDIA CENTER. Cemanáhuac has a catalogued library, which can be searched by computer. The library also includes a variety of audio and video materials.

WHAT DISTINGUISHES THIS SCHOOL?

FACILITIES FOR LARGE GROUPS. Cemanáhuac can accommodate large groups, and they host programs from many U.S. Universities.

RURAL-STUDIES PROGRAM. The rural studies program in Buenavista is unique in providing students an understanding of life in rural Mexico.

SCHOLARSHIPS FOR FOREIGN-LANGUAGE TEACHERS. Cemanáhuac offers ACT-FL scholarships to foreign-language teachers.

NURSING CEUs. Nurses from California can earn CEUs for Spanish-language study.

TRAVEL-STUDY PROGRAM. The school sponsors a variety of one-to-two-week travel seminars with historical and cultural themes.

ENCUENTROS

AT A GLANCE

Location: ★★★★
Facilities: ★★★★
Programs: ★★★★
Overall Rating: ★★★★
Cost: $200/week (five hours/day)
Maximum number of students per class: four
Street Address:
    Calle Morelos 36
    Colonia Acapantzingo CP 62440
    Cuernavaca, Morelos, México

Tel: 52 777-312-9800
Fax: 52 777-312-5088
Email: encuentros@learnspanishinmexico.com
Website: www.learnspanishinmexico.com
Director: Jean K. Andersen

As you walk down a narrow passageway just off a quiet residential street in Cuernavaca, there's little hint of the world you're about to enter. The double doors open into the school's two-story atrium and reveal its spectacular natural setting on a ravine or *barranca*. The atmosphere at Encuentros is home-like, with a kitchen, living room, and patio area where students can relax during breaks. Classes are often held on balconies or small patios overlooking the *barranca*. The school specializes in personal attention and will design a program especially for an individual, a couple, or a small group. Students may attend for periods of one week to several months.

ACADEMIC BACKGROUND

Director Jean Andersen has a BA in American Studies from Reed College and an MA in International Relations from Johns Hopkins University. She taught English to Mexicans for several years before founding Encuentros. Most teachers have bachelor's degrees, but some have only a high school diploma. Many of the teachers have taken an eight-month training course in teaching Spanish as a Second Language offered by the department of education at the University of the state of Morelos

CREDIT

U.S. University credit is available from Austin Peay State University in Clarksville, Tennessee. Community college credit may be arranged through Seattle Central Community College. *See "Getting College Credit," page 8.*

Encuentros also administers proficiency exams if required for credit by a student's home university. Upon request, the Secretaría de Educación Pública (SEP) of the state of Morelos will provide documentation verifying studies of more than four weeks at Encuentros.

COSTS

Registration fee: $100

Regular Program: $200/week

Encuentros for Professionals: $250/week

Encuentros for Executives: Tuition varies

Private Classes: $18/hour

LODGING

HOME STAY

Room and board with a family includes three meals a day.

Shared room: $18/night

Single room: $28/night

PROGRAMS AND SCHEDULES

INTENSIVE SPANISH PROGRAM

Classes begin every Monday throughout the year and meet from 9 a.m. to 2:30 p.m. daily, Monday through Friday. Instruction includes three hours in the classroom and two hours of other activities, including discussion groups, conferences, and "living" communication.

ENCUENTROS FOR PROFESSIONALS

This program is designed for students who need Spanish to communicate with clients, customers, students, and patients. Special "Survival Spanish" classes and "charlas" (chats) provide them with functional language and cultural information. The school arranges visits with its Mexican counterparts, as well as volunteer internships in the Cuernavaca community.

ENCUENTROS FOR EXECUTIVES

Featuring one-on-one instruction for all levels of Spanish proficiency, this program is tailored to the particular needs of executives and the firms they represent. Beginning students learn to use Spanish correctly in practical situations such as phone calls and meetings. More advanced students concentrate on writing letters and reports, giving presentations in Spanish, and discussing current economic issues in Latin America. Betty Ramos, founder of the Geo-Cultural Group, teaches these classes; Ms. Ramos has consulted with multinational corporations in the U.S., Mexico, and Canada for fifteen years.

METHODS

The school uses the communicative approach, which emphasizes natural verbal interaction.

TEXTBOOKS

The following textbooks are used in classes, but students do not need to purchase them:

Pido la Palabra, Estoy Listo, and Lotería, volumes 1–6. *The Encuentros Manual* and *Survival Spanish,* both published by the school, are also used.

EXTRAS

FREE GUIDED VISITS. Encuentros organizes and hosts weekly guided visits to cultural and recreational sites of interest in the Cuernavaca area. The tours are organized around themes such as Mexican Independence, Pre-Hispanic Cultures, and Animals of Mexico.

LIBRARY AND MEDIA CENTER. The school has an informal library with books in Spanish and English. There's also a media center where students can watch instructional videos in Spanish.

ACTIVITIES. Mexican cooking classes, films, and salsa dancing are included in the tuition.

SHORT COURSES. For additional fees, the school offers short courses taught by local residents, including Mexican crafts and alternative medicine.

EXCURSIONS. Weekend excursions to areas outside of Cuernavaca are offered at a cost of $20–$30.

WHAT DISTINGUISHES THIS SCHOOL?

SPANISH OUTSIDE THE CLASSROOM. Encuentros means "Encounters." True to its name, this school provides encounters with Mexicans by incorporating visits with local people and language exchanges into the daily schedule.

PERSONAL ATTENTION. The school emphasizes personal attention and small groups (a maximum of four students).

CUSTOMIZED PROGRAMS FOR INDIVIDUALS. Encuentros will customize programs for individuals as well as for groups.

HOME-LIKE ATMOSPHERE. Classes are held in a spacious home, complete with kitchen, dining area, and living room/library. Free coffee is available all morning in the kitchen.

EXPERIENCIA

AT A GLANCE

Location: ★★★½
Facilities: ★★★★
Programs: ★★★
Overall Rating ★★★½
Cost: Cuernavaca: $190/week (five hours/day)
Tepoztlán: $160/week (five hours/day)
Maximum number of students per class: five
Mailing Address:
    Apartado Postal 5-96
    Cuernavaca, Morelos, México

Street Address:
    Leyva #200, Colonia Las Palmas
    Cuernavaca, Morelos, México

Tel: **52 777-312-6579 or 52 777-310-0374**
Fax: **52 777-318-5209**
Email: **info@experienciaspanish.com**
Website: **www.experiencia.com.mx**
Director: **Arturo Ballinas**

Set in a spectacular mansion in a residential area of Cuernavaca, Experiencia offers a pool, gardens, and dorms on its campus. Most classes are held outside or on balconies overlooking the garden and pool area. Experiencia also has a second campus in the nearby town of Tepoztlán. It is recommended that prospective students communicate by email to determine the status of the Cuernavaca campus. In a recent conversation, Experiencia's former U.S. representative revealed that the Cuernavaca school may be in transition and not as active as the branch campus in Tepoztlán.

ACADEMIC BACKGROUND

This school has not provided information on the academic background of its director or teachers.

CREDIT

Experiencia does not grant credit directly, but community college credit may be arranged through Seattle Central Community College. *See "Getting College Credit," page 8.*

COSTS

One-time, nonrefundable registration fee: $100

SPANISH IMMERSION COURSE

	1 Week	4 Weeks
Group Study	$190	$700
One-on-one Study	$380	$1400
Children's Program	$75	
Text and workbook	$16	

LODGING

HOME STAY

Accommodations with a Mexican family are available; however, many students stay in the on-campus dormitory.

There are nine dorm rooms on the Cuernavaca campus, both shared and private, some with their own private bathrooms. Breakfast is the only meal provided, but there is a kitchen where you can prepare your own meals.

HOME STAY OR DORM RATES PER PERSON PER DAY

	Two meals Home stay	Breakfast only Home or Dorm	No meals Home or Dorm
Double room, shared bath	$20	$16	$13
Double room, private bath	$22	$18	$15
Single room, shared bath	$24	$20	$17
Single room, private bath	$26	$22	$19

PROGRAMS AND SCHEDULES

THE SPANISH IMMERSION COURSE

All fifteen levels of Spanish instruction begin every Monday throughout the year. Each student's skill level is determined in a personal interview on the first day. Beginning-level classes include grammar, verbal communication, reading, and writing. In advanced-level classes, students consolidate their acquired skills and expand their vocabulary.

SPANISH IMMERSION PROGRAMS FOR PROFESSIONALS

Special programs are available for students with a specific learning objective, including teachers, flight attendants, medical staff or technicians, and business and legal professionals.

CHILDREN'S PROGRAM

The children's program consists of Spanish lessons and age-appropriate activities such as arts and crafts, sports, and games. Children may participate in activities with local Mexican children and take weekly excursions.

METHODS

Experiencia uses a traditional method, combining written grammar exercises with group discussions. Illustrated teaching materials are used as often as possible.

TEXTBOOKS

The school's own grammar book is the basis for all programs. Teaching materials are written by the school staff and adapted to the needs and knowledge of the students.

EXTRAS

CULTURE, HISTORY, AND GEOGRAPHY LECTURES. Weekly lectures are presented on topics such as Art in Mexico, pre-Columbian history, the Mexican Revolution, Mexican contemporary history, the myth of Quetzalcoatl, the political system in Mexico, and the role of women in Mexico.

BILINGUAL EXCHANGE PROGRAM. Experiencia also offers foreign-language classes for Mexican students. An *intercambio* or language exchange is held once a week for all students. The participants discuss topics of interest in small groups, one hour in Spanish and another in English, German, Italian, or French.

FILM AND VIDEO EVENING. Documentaries and movies about history, culture, politics, and life in Mexico are shown in the evenings.

EXCURSIONS. Experiencia offers optional day trips to many interesting sites near Cuernavaca, including Xochichicalco, a ceremonial center of the Toltecs, and Malinalco, a fish hatchery and village.

There are longer trips to the pyramids of Teotihuacán, the silver city of Taxco, Mexico City's Museum of Anthropology and Ballet Folklórico, and the Pyramids of Tula, the center of the mighty Toltec empire. Two- or three-day guided excursions are available to the colonial cities of Puebla, Querétaro, Guanajuato, and Oaxaca, as well as the resort city of Acapulco.

WHAT DISTINGUISHES THIS SCHOOL?

BEAUTIFUL CAMPUS. The Cuernavaca campus occupies a spectacular villa. Classrooms are on many levels arranged around a garden and pool.

SECOND CAMPUS IN TEPOZTLÁN. The school in Tepoztlán offers instruction in both Spanish and Nahuatl (the indigenous language of the Valley of Mexico).

VOLUNTEER PROGRAM IN AGRICULTURE. In Tepoztlán, students may volunteer to work with farmers who still use pre-Hispanic agricultural methods.

EXPERIENCIA TEPOZTLÁN

Street address
   Cuauhtemotzin No. 8, Barrio de San Miguel
   Tepoztlán, Morelos, Mexico

U.S. Contact: Sherry Howell
Toll-free U.S. and Canada 888-397-8363
Fax: 530-626-4272

Spanish and Nahuatl classes are offered in Tepoztlán, a traditional indigenous village about half an hour's drive from Cuernavaca. Experiencia Tepoztlán has a swimming pool, kitchen, and dorm rooms, and is located close to an Internet café, gym, hospital, grocery stores, restaurants, and shopping.

TEPOZTLÁN LODGING

HOME STAY, TWO MEALS INCLUDED

Shared room: $16/day

Private room with shared bathroom: $24/day

HOME STAY OR DORM ROOM WITHOUT MEALS

Shared room: $11/day

Private room with bathroom: $15/day

There are several dorm rooms at Experiencia Tepoztlán, both shared and private, all with private baths. No meals are offered at the dorms, but there is a kitchen where students can prepare their own meals.

DISCOUNTS: Students who begin a two-week session in September or October receive free dorm housing when available.

TEPOZTLÁN CLASSES AND SCHEDULES

All levels of Spanish-language instruction begin every Monday throughout the year. Regular classes meet 9 a.m. to 12:20 p.m., Monday through Friday. Workshops and field trips are held from 2:30 to 4:30 p.m. A bilingual exchange program meets three days a week from 4:30 to 6 p.m.

Private one-on-one classes are available seven days a week between the hours of 9 a.m. and 8 p.m.

Nonrefundable registration fee: $100 (except for children)

TUITION RATES

	Per hour	Per day (25 hours)	Per week (100 hours)	Four weeks
Group Class	$30	$160	$600	
One-on-one Classes	$15	$60	$300	$1000
Children three to twelve	$75	$300		

EXTRAS

BILINGUAL EXCHANGE (ACOMPAÑANTES). Members of the Tepoztlán community join with students for a bilingual exchange three afternoons a week.

VOLUNTEER SERVICE. Students may volunteer for agricultural work with farmers of the area, growing corn, beans, squash, potatoes, and other crops, using pre-Hispanic techniques. Social-work experience may also be arranged for qualified students.

Ideal Latinoamericana

At a Glance

Location: ★★★★½
Facilities: ★★★★½
Programs: ★★★★
Overall Rating ★★★★½
Cost: $195/week (six hours/day)
Maximum number of students per class: five
Street Address:
    Privado Narciso Mendoza 107
    Colonia Pradera, C.P. 62170
    Cuernavaca, Morelos, México

Tel: 52 777-311-7551 or 52 777-311-9935
Fax: 52 777-311-5910
Email: ideal@ideal-l.com
Website: www.ideal-l.com
Director: Hermilo Brito
Assistant Director: Carlos A. Brito

Ideal Latinoamericana occupies a large suburban house and gardens in Colonia Pradera, a residential zone ten minutes from the center of Cuernavaca. The school is on a quiet cul-de-sac and has a tranquil, relaxing atmosphere. In addition to several classrooms and an inviting open-air cafeteria, there's a small auditorium for group presentations and movies. Ideal Latinoamericana was originally established twenty-seven years ago as Instituto Ideal. Hermilo Brito, the director, founded the Association for the Teaching of Spanish in Cuernavaca, (AIPEC), which is a consortium of ten Spanish-language schools dedicated to offering their students a quality learning experience.

ACADEMIC BACKGROUND

Hermilo Brito and his son, Carlos Brito, have a combined total of more than fifty years' experience teaching Spanish. María Estela Barrera, the academic coordinator, has a degree in journalism from the National University of Mexico and a certificate in teaching Spanish as a Second Language. She has eighteen years' experience teaching Spanish and trains new teachers at Ideal. Teacher Karina Tafolla is certified to teach Spanish at the high school level and has taught for Ideal for six years. Teacher Andrea González has more than twenty years' experience teaching Spanish as a Second Language.

CREDIT

Several colleges and universities have offered credit programs at Ideal, including Santa Barbara City College, Eastern Washington University, and Johns Hopkins University. Community college credit may be arranged through Seattle Central Community College. *See "Getting College Credit," page 8.*

COSTS

Nonrefundable registration fee: $100

Intensive Course in Spanish Language and Culture: $195/week

Professional Spanish: $230/week

Spanish for Children: $100/week

Private classes: $18/hour

Books and materials: $5–$30

LODGING

HOME STAY

Lodging with a Mexican family is strongly recommended.

Ideal Plan (private or shared lodging and three meals a day):
$18–$25/day

European Plan (private or shared lodging, breakfast only):
$16–$20/day,

Economic Plan (private or shared lodging, no meals):
$14–$16/day

OTHER OPTIONS

For students who prefer not to stay with a family, the school will
provide information about hotels in Cuernavaca.

PROGRAMS AND SCHEDULES

INTENSIVE COURSE IN SPANISH LANGUAGE AND CULTURE

This program consists of nine levels of study, ranging from beginning
to advanced. Based on personal interviews, new students are placed in
an appropriate level of Spanish instruction. Classes meet from 8 a.m. to
2 p.m., Monday through Friday. Grammar explanations and review are
presented in the morning, followed by language practice through games,
videos, or guided city tours. The afternoons are dedicated to optional activities such as private lessons, lectures, and discussions.

SPANISH FOR PROFESSIONALS

Special classes are offered for groups and individuals with specific academic interests or certain professions, such as teachers, doctors, nurses, social workers, business people, diplomats, flight attendants, travel
agents, and clergy. Students in these programs spend twenty hours/week
in group classes and five hours/week in private classes adapted to the
needs of their professions.

CHILDREN'S PROGRAM

For children, Ideal offers special courses that meet five hours/day or
twenty-five hours/week. Through games, exercises, group dynamics, and
sports children learn Spanish while having fun and staying active. This
program is for ages five and older and is available only during the months
of January, February, June, July, and August.

METHODS

Ideal Latinoamericana uses a communicative approach, encouraging students to practice their Spanish in real situations while in Cuernavaca.

TEXTBOOKS

The school publishes its own Spanish workbooks, which correspond to the nine levels of study they offer. The following textbooks are used as auxiliary texts: *Dos Mundos,* published by McGraw Hill, *Español para Extranjeros,* published by UNAM (Universidad Autónoma de México), and *Horizontes Gramaticales,* Published by Harper & Row.

EXTRAS

ADDITIONAL FACILITIES. The school has an open-air cafeteria, an auditorium for group functions, and a library. There's also a multimedia room, where students can view films in Spanish or watch Mexican TV programs.

COMMUNICATIONS. Fax service and local telephone calls are available to students. The school also provides mail service.

INTERNET AND EMAIL. Students may send and receive email at the school, and free Internet access is provided.

FREE ACTIVITIES. Ideal offers a variety of optional activities at no extra cost, including conferences and lectures on Mexican history, culture, and politics. Students may also attend sports events and plays.

EXCURSIONS. Every weekend the school organizes one-day guided visits to interesting places near Cuernavaca. Students learn about the main characteristics of the area beforehand, and a teacher guides the visit. The most commonly visited sites are Taxco, Toluca, Acapulco, the ruins of Teotihuacán and Xochicalco, and the historic Center of Mexico City, where students can attend a performance of the Ballet Folklórico or visit the National Museum of Anthropology. These excursions cost between $12 and $40.

WHAT DISTINGUISHES THIS SCHOOL?

FRIENDLY ATMOSPHERE. The school is small enough that everyone knows each other. The students and staff get together during breaks and participate in extracurricular activities.

Quiet location. In bustling Cuernavaca, it's difficult to find a quiet spot in which to locate a school, but Ideal Latinoamericana is on a cul-de-sac in a very quiet upscale neighborhood.

Respected director. Directors and faculty members of schools in other parts of Mexico often asked me if I had visited Ideal. Hermilo Brito is highly respected in the educational community in Cuernavaca and elsewhere. He is the former president and founder of the Association for the Teaching of Spanish in Cuernavaca, or AIPEC.

Instituto Chac-Mool

At a Glance

Location: ★★★★
Facilities: ★★★★½
Programs: ★★★★
Overall Rating ★★★★
Cost: $180 to $195/week (five hours/day)
Maximum number of students per class: five
Street address:
 Privada de la Pradera #108, Colonia Pradera
 Cuernavaca, Morelos, México 62170
 Mexico: 52 777-317-1163

U.S. Representative: Sherry Howell
Tel: (toll-free) U.S. & Canada 888-397-8363
Fax: 530-626-4272
Email: spanish@chac-mool.com
Website: www.chac-mool.com
Owners and Directors: Deana and Julio Najera

Instituto Chac-Mool occupies a large house and gardens in La Pradera, a residential area of Cuernavaca. Classes are held in the main building or in small palm-thatched shelters (*palapas*) around the swimming pool. The school was named for Chac-Mool, the Mayan messenger to the gods. The institute began as a summer school in 1996 and started to offer year-round classes in 2001.

ACADEMIC BACKGROUND

Instituto Chac-Mool's owners are educators in Southern California during the academic year and spend summers in Cuernavaca. All of the teachers have been trained in Stephen Krashen's Theory of Language Acquisition and the Seven Intelligences.

CREDIT

Instituto Chac-Mool cannot grant academic credit directly; however, some California schools and universities have offered credit programs at the institute, including Cuesta Community College, California State University San Marcos, and Ventura Community College. Ventura College and Cuesta College offer four-week credit courses each summer. For more information on these programs, email Instituto Chac-Mool at spanish@chac-mool.com.

California teachers may receive extension credit through California Lutheran University. Community college credit may also be arranged through Seattle Central Community College. *See "Getting College Credit," page 8.*

COSTS

Nonrefundable registration fee: $100 (Children: $50)

Group Classes	One to four weeks	Five + weeks
June through August	$215/week	$200/week
January to May & September to December	$199/week	$185/week

Children's Group Classes		
Ages four to seven; eight to twelve	$130/week	$125/week

Private Lessons: $17/hour or $375/week ($400 in summer)
Weekend excursions: $20–$35

MEDICAL SPANISH AND SPANISH FOR LAW ENFORCEMENT

GROUP INSTRUCTION (25 HOURS / WEEK): $275/week ($300 in summer)

SPANISH FOR BUSINESS

GROUP INSTRUCTION (25 HOURS / WEEK): $275/week ($300 in summer)

DISCOUNTS: There are discounts for extended stays, groups, and special programs.

PROGRAMS AND SCHEDULES

INTENSIVE SPANISH

New Spanish immersion classes begin each week. The program offers ten different levels of instruction. If a student's language ability falls between two levels, Instituto Chac-Mool offers free private instruction to bring the student up to the next level.

The regular program, which runs from 8:50 a.m. to 1:50 p.m., includes review and introduction of new grammatical points and vocabulary, plus discussion and interactive learning activities, followed by conversation. Students also study Mexican culture and its relationship to the language.

In the afternoons, there are optional lectures by faculty or guest speakers, excursion orientations, and other activities. Workshops are held to prepare California teachers for the BCLAD test (Bilingual Crosscultural, Language and Academic Development test). "Daily tune-ups" with grammar discussions and twenty-five-minute one-on-one tutoring sessions are available to students who need extra help. From 5 to 7 p.m., students can participate in the *Cotocafé* (chatting in Spanish), and other activities, such as cooking classes, dance and aerobics classes, movies, and arts and crafts.

CHILDREN'S PROGRAM

Instituto Chac-Mool offers a Spanish program for children who have at least one parent studying at the school. Hours are the same as the adult program, and the children may join weekend excursions with their parents. Children's classes start with basic Spanish, advancing with age and skill level. Teachers incorporate greetings, numbers, colors, actions, alphabet, animals, and other themes into activities such as writing a story, acting in a play, making a piñata, dancing, and cooking.

MEDICAL SPANISH

This course includes medical history, patient examination, terminology for internal and external anatomy, diseases and treatment options. Medical personnel may volunteer at the Dispensario program, housed in a church near Instituto Chac-Mool. There are also opportunities to observe techniques and methods at two public hospitals and one that provides emergency medical services for the freeway system.

SPANISH FOR LAW ENFORCEMENT PERSONNEL

This program focuses on basic Spanish phrases and questions necessary to carry out specific law enforcement protocols: interrogating, arresting, Mirandizing, and booking a suspect, as well as gathering intake data, reading probation orders, and conducting various types of drug tests.

BUSINESS SPANISH

This course covers making appointments and introductions, writing business letters, reading Spanish business documents, negotiating and selling in Spanish, giving a presentation in Spanish, and understanding customs in Latin America.

Students in the Medical, Business, and Law Enforcement programs attend regular classes in the morning and study their specialty for two hours in the afternoon. A private course is available for advanced Spanish speakers who need only the specialized portions of these programs.

SPANISH FOR TEACHERS

Instituto Chac-Mool offers a series of workshops especially designed for bilingual teachers. Topics include translations, writing parent letters, family customs, and relating to a school environment. Bilingual teachers can prepare for the California BCLAD certification. They may also have an opportunity to visit a public or private school to compare and contrast the educational systems of Mexico and the United States.

SPANISH FOR NATIVE SPEAKERS

This course is designed for students who have learned Spanish at home but may not be able to read or write the language. Students focus on reading selections from Mexican and Latin American literature as well as Spanish-language newspapers and magazines. They also learn to write and use proper grammar.

METHODS

Instituto Chac-Mool uses Sheltered Instruction and the Natural Approach. Learning is both active and interactive. Students are not just spoken to; they actively participate in all learning activities.

EXTRAS

STUDENT SERVICES. A reference library, postal service, telephone, and fax machine are available for student use.

FREE SNACKS. The school provides daily snacks and beverages prepared by their in-house cook.

MEDICAL CARE. A doctor is available during the summer months.

FREE TUTORING. Students have the option of signing up for additional one-on-one instruction for twenty-five-minute periods, four days a week, free of charge.

EXCURSIONS. Destinations include Taxco, Mexico City, the ruins of Teotihuacan and Xochicalco, Puebla, Tlayacapan, and Huitzilac. A special excursion to Mexico City focuses on Mexican Art and Architecture.

WHAT DISTINGUISHES THIS SCHOOL?

DAILY TUNE-UPS. An optional thirty-minute group session to explain a different grammatical point is available to all students who feel they would benefit from the additional instruction.

COTOCAFÉ. Students are invited to come to school in the afternoon to *cotorrear* (chat) with others. A teacher is on campus Tuesdays and Thursdays from 5–5:45 p.m. to converse with students over coffee and cookies, providing a relaxed, low-anxiety environment in which to practice their Spanish.

EXCEPTIONAL CULTURAL PROGRAM. Instituto Chac-Mool has completely computerized its culture program to include wide-screen projection of images and state-of-the-art technology. To reinforce classroom presentations, the culture and history teacher also accompanies students on excursions to places of interest around Cuernavaca.

MEANINGFUL EXCURSIONS. Each weekend excursion is a focused learning experience. The school's culture and history teacher accompanies the group. Students answer written questions about the destination and turn them in at the next class.

NATIVE SPEAKER CLASSES. This is one of the few schools that offers a course for students who've learned Spanish at home, but may not be able to read or write it or use proper grammar.

IMEC – Instituto Mexicano de Español y Cultura

At a Glance

Location: ★★★★
Facilities: ★★★
Programs: ★★★½
Overall Rating ★★★½
Cost: $190/week (six hours/day)
Maximum number of students per class: five
Street Address:
Piñanonas #26
Colonia Jacarandas
Cuernavaca, Morelos, México 62420

Tel/Fax: 52 777-315-7953
Email: pregunta@imeccuernavaca.com.mx and dalcortes@prodigy.net.mx
Website: www.imeccuernavaca.com.mx
Director: Mrs. Dalel Cortés

Although its location in a modern house in a quiet, upper-middle-class neighborhood of Cuernavaca presents a rather plain first impression, this school offers professional academic instruction in a warm and friendly atmosphere. Because of its small size, IMEC can offer flexibility in its programs and give students lots of personal attention. IMEC emphasizes the importance of the home stay in Spanish-language immersion programs, and the director is very particular about the families with whom she places students. She is considered the local expert on home stays and gives seminars for current and prospective host families under the auspices of the Association of Spanish Language Institutes of Cuernavaca.

ACADEMIC QUALIFICATIONS

Director and principal teacher Dalel Cortés has twenty-five years' experience teaching Spanish to foreigners. She has diplomas in both education and teaching Spanish as a Second Language.

CREDIT

Although the school has no vehicle for granting credit, the following colleges have offered credit programs using IMEC's facilities and teachers: State University of West Georgia, Carrollton, Georgia; Tarrant County College, Fort Worth, Texas; Coastal Bend College, Beeville, Texas; and East Texas State A & M University, Commerce, Texas.

Community college credit may be arranged through Seattle Central Community College. *See "Getting College Credit," page 8.*

COSTS

Nonrefundable registration fee: $100

INTENSIVE SPANISH (30 HOURS / WEEK)
Regular, university, and high school programs: $190/week
Business Program: $450/week
Children's Program: $90/week
Private classes: $25/hour

LODGING

Home Stay (paid to the school):
The school offers three different home-stay plans. The Luxurious plan and the Regular plan include three meals a day. The Luxurious plan also

guarantees that the home will have a pool. The Simple Plan does not include meals.

	Shared room	Private room
Luxurious Plan	$154	$210
Regular Plan	$140	$190
Simple Plan	$98	$119

PROGRAMS AND SCHEDULES

REGULAR, UNIVERSITY, AND HIGH SCHOOL PROGRAMS

These programs include six hours of instruction per day. Three hours are focused on functions, communicative skills, and supporting grammar; three more are devoted to reinforcing and developing communicative skills through conversation, short courses, lectures, and discussions on a wide variety of topics, including arts and crafts, cooking, dancing, and Mexican songs. There are six levels of instruction, and students take a placement test to determine the appropriate level at which to start.

A high school program has been developed especially for younger students. IMEC teachers are familiar with current texts, videos, and CDs used in teaching Spanish to high school students in the U.S. They are therefore able to correlate their instruction with what students might be learning at home.

BUSINESS PROGRAM

The business program is for professionals who wish to lean Spanish with vocabulary related to their work. It includes three hours daily of one-on-one instruction with occupation-specific vocabulary plus three hours of group classes to improve communication skills.

In the afternoon and evening students may participate in interviews and social activities with professionals in many fields. Students may also take part in daily and weekend excursions.

Former participants in the business program have included accountants, airline personnel, diplomats, engineers, attorneys, medical personnel, and social workers.

Some of the institutions whose personnel have participated in the business program at IMEC are Burlington, Inc., Cisco Systems, Excel Logistics, Trident Corporation, Export & Development Company of Canada, Medical Missionaries of Mary of Ireland, and the U.S. State Department.

CHILDREN'S PROGRAM

A children's program is offered for the children of adult students. It runs separately from the adult program and is adapted to the children's ages and knowledge of Spanish.

METHODS

IMEC uses the communicative method, focusing on conversation, but incorporating grammar and language structure.

TEXTBOOKS

Pido la Palabra, published by UNAM, the National University of Mexico, is used along with other textbooks, depending upon the needs of the student or group. Students may borrow textbooks at no extra cost.

EXTRAS

FREE FIELD TRIPS. IMEC offers free afternoon and evening field trips to places of interest in Cuernavaca.

EXCURSIONS. Longer trips are offered for $20–$40. Destinations include the pyramids of Teotihuacán, the ruins of Xochicalco, the silver city of Taxco, the traditional town of Tepoztlan, and the caves at Cacahuamilpa. There are also trips to Mexico City to visit the cathedral, the Shrine of Guadalupe, the Museums of History and Anthropology, Coyocán, and Xochimilco.

OPTIONAL ACTIVITIES. The school provides opportunities to attend movies, sports clubs, and café socials.

WHAT DISTINGUISHES THIS SCHOOL?

LOCATION. IMEC is located in an area of tree-lined residential streets away from the hustle and bustle of Cuernavaca's main avenues.

PERSONAL ATTENTION. The school is very small and provides personal attention to all its students.

EMPHASIS ON HOME STAY. The director carefully selects all host families for their ability to provide a safe, warm, and nurturing environment.

Spanish Language Institute (SLI)

Center for Latin American Studies

At a Glance

Location: ✫✫✫✫
Facilities: ✫✫✫✫½
Programs: ✫✫✫✫
Overall Rating ✫✫✫✫
Cost: $175/week (six hours/day)
Maximum number of students per class: five (at least 50 percent of the time)
Street Address:
   Bajada de La Pradera #208
   Colonia Pradera
   Cuernavaca, Morelos 62170, México

Tel: 52 777-311-0063
Fax: 52 777-317-5294
Email: sli@infosel.net.mx
Website: www.asli.com.mx/
Director: Francisco Ramos
Academic Director: Maria Ramos

Four attractive colonial-style bungalows in a residential area of Cuernavaca provide a tranquil setting for the Spanish Language Institute. The classrooms open onto a garden and pool area. The facilities also include a small cafeteria, a bookstore, several regular classrooms, and two larger multipurpose classrooms used for group presentations. This school prides itself on its international flavor, teaching the Spanish language and the culture of Latin America to students from all over the world. SLI is a medium-sized school that deliberately limits its size to a maximum of one hundred students to ensure the quality of instruction.

ACADEMIC BACKGROUND

All teachers have at least a bachelor's degree and advanced training in teaching Spanish as a Second Language. Members of the faculty have between ten and thirty-five years' teaching experience and are current on the research in language development and instructional methods.

CREDIT

University credit is available through Nicholls State University in Thiodaux, Louisiana.

Community college credit may be arranged through Seattle Central Community College. See "Getting College Credit," page 8.

COSTS

Nonrefundable registration fee: $100

Regular Program: $175/week

Semiprivate Program: $450/week

Executive Program: $2400/week

Materials (books and cassettes when required): $15–$25

NOTE: SLI publishes its own textbooks.

Excursions: Half day $20–$22: full day $20–$27

Weekend (one or two nights): $80–$130

Airport Transfer, Mexico City-Cuernavaca (one way): $70

Two people traveling together: $90

LODGING

HOME STAY (PAID DIRECTLY TO THE FAMILY)

Plan "A" (private room): $22/day

Couples (private room): $44/day

Plan "B" (shared room & bath): $15/day

NOTE: *These prices include three meals daily as well as transportation to and from the institute at 8 a.m. and 2 p.m. Room and board is paid directly to the family.*

PROGRAMS AND SCHEDULES

Classes meet from 8 a.m. to 2 p.m. Each program may be taken in one of the following formats:

REGULAR PROGRAM

Group classes (three to five students per group)

SEMIPRIVATE PROGRAM

Three hours of private classes and three hours of group classes

EXECUTIVE PROGRAM

Six hours of private instruction, specialized vocabulary, and cross-cultural training. Cost includes tuition, registration fee, family stay, books, airport transportation, and laundry services.

SPANISH LANGUAGE PROGRAM

The basic program includes three hours of grammar, drills and conversation, one hour of situational Spanish, and two hours of conversation. The following optional activities are available from 5 to 6 p.m. at no additional cost (except for the cooking class):

Mexican Contemporary Literature

Roundtable Discussions

Grammar Clinics

Videos on Latin America

Mexican Cooking

SPANISH FOR TEENS

This is a total-immersion language and cultural program for high school students (ages thirteen to seventeen). It is held at a separate "teen campus" near the main Institute, and combines serious study and leisure activities such as arts and crafts, soccer, swimming, fiestas, movies, bowling, salsa dancing, guitar lessons, ceramics, and visits to the market. Students may also take part in a variety of excursions and field trips.

SPANISH FOR HISPANICS

Especially designed for Hispanics who have learned the language in a non-academic setting, this program provides a review of Spanish grammar with special emphasis on false cognates, colloquial Spanish, and written accents. The course also includes a panoramic view of Mexican history and culture.

SPANISH FOR MEDICINE

For nurses, physicians, physician's assistants, social workers, or any student majoring in a medical field, this program develops skills for communicating with Hispanic patients. The curriculum includes terminology and Spanish vocabulary specific to the student's professional area. Practical experience is provided through visiting and volunteering in hospitals, clinics, orphanages, and other healthcare facilities, to expose students to the healthcare system in Mexico.

SPANISH FOR TEACHERS

This program is for teachers and school employees who work with Spanish speakers. It combines language instruction in Spanish with cultural information in English. SLI is accredited to prepare students for the ACTFL (American Council on the Teaching of Foreign Languages) oral proficiency interview. The sessions consist of six hours of instruction per day, five days a week, divided into forty-five-minute sessions, concentrating on specialized vocabularies and school-related activities. Courses begin on the first Monday of every month, but may be adapted to blocks of two, three, or four weeks.

The Spanish for Teachers program covers the following topics:

- Instructions and directions
- Meeting and talking with parents
- Using the telephone and communicating effectively

- Vocabulary and expressions for the classroom
- Discussing time, schedules, and cultural situations
- Motivation and value systems
- Mexican customs and traditions
- The family and social relations
- Mexican urban middle class vs. rural
- Machismo and territorialism

BUSINESS PROGRAM

This specialized program is conducted in English or Spanish, as required. Sessions typically consist of six hours per day, five days a week. Besides Spanish-language instruction, topics covered in the business program include:

- Understanding the Mexican mystique
- Politeness vs. submission
- Social and business protocols
- Cultural blunders ("the do's and don'ts")
- The concepts of time and work in Mexico
- Mexican customs and traditions
- Doing business and Mexican law

SPECIAL PROGRAMS

SLI also offers the following special programs; descriptions of these are available on the school's website: www.asli.com.mx.

- Spanish for Senior Citizens
- Spanish for Airline Personnel
- Survival Spanish
- Technical Spanish

METHODS

All teachers have received special training in the institute's teaching methods, which are based on the Natural Approach. The teachers involve students at all levels in cooperative activities to develop oral proficiency in Spanish.

TEXTBOOKS

The textbooks and cassettes used are written and produced by SLI faculty and staff.

EXTRAS

FREE INTERNET ACCESS. The school reserves two computers for student Internet access.

POOL. The swimming pool on the campus is available for student use.

EXCURSIONS. The institute offers guided excursions in private transport both after classes and on weekends. Excursions are optional and cost extra. Typical destinations include the Xochicalco Archeological Zone, Santiago Tianguistenco (a mountain wool market near Cuernavaca), the silver city of Taxco, and the pyramids of Teotihuacan. In Mexico City students may visit the Museum of Anthropology, Bazaar Sábado, or the Frida Kahlo Museum. Weekend trips are offered to Acapulco, Puebla, and Cholula.

WHAT DISTINGUISHES THIS SCHOOL?

WELL-DEVELOPED EXECUTIVE PROGRAM. The executive program is a specialty here. It is well developed and defined, but flexible enough to accommodate executives from many different types of organizations. SLI has, for example, provided language instruction and cross-cultural training for employees of Caterpillar, International Paper, The World Wildlife Fund, The Interamerican Development Bank, and the American Embassy in Mexico.

TRANSPORTATION INCLUDED. Daily transportation to and from the school is included in the home-stay prices.

HOME-STAY FAMILIES PAY NO COMMISSION. Since students pay the family directly, and no commission is charged to the families as in other schools, SLI's families are very loyal to the school and provide an exceptional home-stay experience.

UNIVERSAL

CENTRO DE LENGUA Y COMUNICACIÓN SOCIAL

AT A GLANCE

Location: ★★★★
Facilities: ★★★★½
Programs: ★★★★
Overall Rating ★★★★½
Cost: $180/week (five hours/day)
Maximum number of students per class: five
Street Address:
   J.H. Preciado 171
   Colonia San Antón, C.P. 62020
   Cuernavaca, Morelos, México

Tel: 52 777-318-2904 and 777-312-4902
Fax: 52 777-318-2910
Email: students@universal-spanish.com
Website: www.universal-spanish.com
Director: Ramiro Cuéllar Hernández
Spanish Department Director: Irma Salazar

On the edge of a ravine or *barranca* in a pleasant residential area of Cuernavaca, Universal seems more rural than it actually is. The facilities include twenty classrooms, and some of them occupy a rustic pavilion overlooking the pool and gardens. There is also an indoor-outdoor cafeteria that serves breakfast and Mexican food. Student activities often take place in the spacious lawn area.

ACADEMIC BACKGROUND

Spanish Department Director Irma Salazar has a bachelor's degree in communication services and a master's degree in educational administration, as well as twenty-five years' teaching experience. She was recently invited to teach for a year at Gettysburg College in Pennsylvania. Director Ramiro Cuéllar Hernández has a bachelor's degree in architecture and more than twenty years' experience as a professor of Spanish. Each language instructor has at least a bachelor's degree.

CREDIT

Universal does not have the ability to grant credit directly; however, the school has ongoing credit programs with the following colleges and universities: Indiana University and Brethren Colleges Abroad in Indiana; The Center for Global Education of Augsburg College and Gustavus Adolphus College in Minnesota; Elgin Community College in Illinois; Gettysburg College in Pennsylvania; Plymouth State College in New Hampshire; Rhode Island College; the University of Massachusetts; and Arizona State University. Universal will provide contact information for students interested in participating in one of these programs.

U.S. University credit is also available by registering for this program through National Registration Center for Study Abroad (NRCSA). Community college credit may be arranged through Seattle Central Community College. *See "Getting College Credit," page 8.*

COSTS

Nonrefundable registration fee: $100

INTENSIVE SPANISH (TWENTY-FIVE HOURS / WEEK)

Regular Spanish Program: $180/week
Advanced Spanish Program: $220/week
Spanish For Professionals: $260/week

Traveler's Spanish U.S.: $180/week

Individual Tutorial Classes U.S.: $18/hour

Universal Textbooks U.S.: $15/book

DISCOUNTS: Seasonal discounts are offered during April, May, October, and November for groups of ten or more students.

LODGING

HOME STAY (PAID TO THE SCHOOL)

Private room with private bath: $28/day

Private room with shared bath: $24/day

Shared room with shared bath: $18/day

Home stays include three meals a day, towels, and linens.

PROGRAMS AND SCHEDULES

Student placement is determined by a proficiency test. Classes are held Monday through Friday, from 8 a.m. to 1:10 p.m.

REGULAR SPANISH PROGRAM

Made up of sixty modules teaching basic grammar, this program covers all aspects of the structure of Spanish and can be completed in sixteen to twenty weeks.

ADVANCED SPANISH PROGRAM

Tailored to the individual's needs, this program could include a detailed grammatical review, development of oral and written fluency, improvement of composition skills, or expansion of vocabulary.

TRAVELER'S SPANISH

A two-to-four-week course in "survival Spanish," including vocabulary for travel, eating in restaurants, and shopping. The emphasis is on expressions and usage particular to Mexico and Latin America.

SPANISH FOR PROFESSIONALS

These courses for professionals in the fields of business, diplomacy, law, medicine, religion, and social work include intensive grammatical study and practical vocabulary needed for each specific profession.

OPTIONAL LECTURES

An optional lecture series allows students to improve their understanding of more formal Spanish. The lectures also provide concise introductions to many different aspects of Mexican culture such as history, education, art, sociopolitical issues, and women's issues.

METHODS

The program director and the instructors at Universal develop an individualized course of study in collaboration with each student before classes start. Student progress is evaluated weekly, and adjustments are made as necessary. The Intensive Spanish Program has four components: grammar, conversation, reading comprehension, and composition. Instruction focuses on mastery of the grammatical structure of Spanish through exercises from Universal's textbooks. Students develop their speaking ability in discussions of Mexican politics, history, and culture, and improve their reading comprehension by reading a variety of materials that also broaden their knowledge of Mexican and Latin American literature. They also develop vocabulary and writing ability through directed composition, dictation, and other exercises.

TEXTBOOKS

Español Universal 1, 2, and 3 (Ediciones Universal A.C., México, 1996, 2000). Written by the Universal faculty, these textbooks are used as the basis for all programs. Supplementary exercises are taken from the following textbooks: *Dos Mundos: A Communicative Approach* (Random House, New York) and *Modern Spanish Grammar, A Practical Guide* by Juan Kattan-Ibarra and Christopher J. Pountain.

EXTRAS

INTERNET ACCESS AND OTHER SERVICES. The school offers its students free Internet access, local Internet connections for laptop computers, mail service, telephones (including long-distance), a fax machine, laundry service, money-changing, stamps, and an airport shuttle.

POOL, VOLLEYBALL, AND RACQUETBALL COURTS. A swimming pool, as well as volleyball and racquetball courts, are available on campus for student use.

EXCURSIONS. Each weekend, Universal offers day excursions to nearby places of historical, archeological, or recreational interest. These trips take place either on Saturday or Sunday and cost $12 – $25. Destinations include places of interest in Cuernavaca, the ruins of Xochicalco, the caves at Cacahuamilpa, Acapulco, Taxco, Oaxaca, Mexico City, Teotihuacán, and Tepoztlán.

WHAT DISTINGUISHES THIS SCHOOL?

SETTING. Universal's campus is located in the city of Cuernavaca, but there is a distinct rural, even rustic, atmosphere.

EMPHASIS ON NEEDS OF COLLEGE AND UNIVERSITY STUDENTS. Universal's program is directed toward college and university students majoring in fields that require Spanish-language ability.

INDIVIDUALIZED APPROACH. Each student's course of study is adapted to his or her aptitude, previous experiences, personal interests, and rate of progress.

ACADEMIC QUALIFICATIONS OF INSTRUCTORS. Each language instructor has at least a bachelor's degree, and most have fifteen to thirty years' teaching experience. The school will provide a description of each instructor's preparation and experience upon request.

GUEST SPEAKERS AND VISITING PROFESSORS. An impressive list of local professionals and visiting professors participate in Universal's programs.

ADVISORY BOARD. This school maintains an advisory board composed of professors and administrators from various U.S. colleges and universities.

Universidad International (Uninter)

The Center for Bilingual and Multicultural Studies

At a Glance

Location: ★★★★½
Facilities: ★★★★★
Programs: ★★★★★
Overall Rating ★★★★★
Cost: $200/week (eight hours/day)
Maximum number of students per class: five (applies only to the Intensive Spanish program)
Mailing Address:
    Apartado Postal 1520
    Cuernavaca, Morelos , México C.P. 62000

Street Address:
    Calle San Jerónimo # 304
    Colonia Tlaltenango
    Cuernavaca, Morelos, México C.P. 62179

Tel: 52 777-317-1087 • Toll-free: 800-932-2068 from U.S.A.
877-463-9428 from Canada

800-770-UNIN (8646) from Mexico • Fax: 52 777-317-0533
Email: admission@bilingual-center.com
Website: www.uninter.com.mx
President: Francisco Javier Espinosa Romero
International Promotion Director: Teresa Molina
Spanish Department Director: Alvaro Vergara
Group Coordinator: Francisco Cisneros

Universidad Internacional was founded in 1980 as the Center for Bilingual Multicultural Studies. In 1994, the school received approval from the Mexican government to operate as an institution of higher learning and changed its name to Universidad Internacional (Uninter). Uninter is the only school in Cuernavaca that grants university credit and offers associate, bachelor's, and master's degrees. Located on its expansive, park-like campus are several classroom buildings, administrative offices, a large computer lab, a cafeteria, a bookstore, and a library. Universidad Internacional has the facilities and atmosphere of a small college.

ACADEMIC BACKGROUND

Alvaro Vergara, the director of the Spanish department, has a degree in pedagogy (education). There are thirty faculty members at Universidad Internacional. Two have doctorates, four have master's degrees, and the rest have bachelor's degrees or their equivalent. Most of the teachers have at least five years' experience teaching Spanish. A complete list of faculty and their qualifications is available by contacting Group Coordinator Francisco Cisneros.

CREDIT

Credits granted by Universidad Internacional through the Center for Bilingual Multicultural Studies are transferable to institutions abroad. If your home university has no agreement with Universidad Internacional, make sure that credits earned there will be accepted. Students in the Intensive Spanish Program can earn one credit for every fifteen contact hours.

U.S. University credit is also available by registering for this program through National Registration Center for Study Abroad (NRCSA). Community college credit may be arranged through Seattle Central Community College. *See "Getting College Credit," page 8.*

COSTS

Nonrefundable registration fee: $100

Intensive Spanish Program*: $200/week

Intensive Spanish Semester Program: $1,800 for twelve weeks

Intensive Spanish Program for Nurses: $200/week

Intensive Spanish Program for Bilingual Teachers: $200/week

Diplomatic Program: $250/week

High School Program: $200/week

Health Care Program: $200/week

Airlines and Travel Agencies: $180/week

Executive Program Option A: $650

Executive Program Option B: $950

Executive Program Option C: $1,250

Tutorial Sessions: $25/hour

Weekend Classes: $30/hour

No registration fee is required for tutorials and weekend classes.

Books and materials: $30 to $50

Children's Program (ages four to twelve):
 Registration fee: $50   Weekly tuition: $150

Daycare Center (ages one to three), five blocks from school:
 Weekly rate: $50

Excursions:
 Half day: $15–$25   One day: $20–$30

Full Weekend (three days/two nights): $130

TRANSPORTATION

Private Taxi: Mexico City to Cuernavaca (1 person): $70; (2 persons, same address): $80

Private Van: Mexico City to Cuernavaca (3 to 7 persons, same address): $110

---

* Upon request, special rates are extended to former students, seniors, travel agents, and airline employees.

Public Bus (Pullman de Morelos): Mexico City Airport to Cuernavaca: $10

Return transportation is also available from Cuernavaca to Mexico City at the same cost.

LODGING

HOME STAY

Plan "AA" (Luxury): $32/night

Plan "A" (Superior): $24/night

Plan "B" (Economic): $19/night

OTHER OPTIONS

Guest Residence (limited availability): $25–$40/night

Bed & Breakfast Plan: Private Room: $21/night

Universidad Internacional will assist students in finding hotels and apartments.

PROGRAMS AND SCHEDULES

INTENSIVE SPANISH PROGRAM

New classes begin every Monday. Students may enroll for any number of weeks.

Classes run from 8 a.m. to 2 p.m., Monday through Friday. Optional sessions, such as conversation and pronunciation workshops, dance and cooking classes, and tutoring in grammar, are held from 2 to 4 p.m.

A typical daily schedule in the Intensive Spanish program includes three hours of Spanish classes, two hours of Latin American studies, and one hour of lectures (*conferencias*).

INTENSIVE SPANISH SEMESTER PROGRAM

In a period of twelve weeks, students may earn up to eighteen semester credits in intensive Spanish-language and Latin American culture classes. This program follows an academic calendar. Spring semester classes begin the last week in January and end the last week in April. Fall classes begin the first week in September and end the first week in December.

For students in the semester program, Universidad Internacional offers a long list of Spanish-language classes:

SPN 101 – Introduction to Spanish Grammar

SPN 102 – Introduction to Spanish Grammar

SPN 111 – Beginning Spanish I

SPN 112 – Beginning Spanish II

SPN 211 – Intermediate Spanish I

SPN 212 – Intermediate Spanish II

SPN 222 – Communicative Strategies

SPN 294 – History of Mexico

SPN 301 – Advanced Grammar

SPN 305 – Readings in Spanish*

SPN 306 – Introduction to Literature*

SPN 308 – Mexico Today

SPN 309 – Latin American Studies*

SPN 311 – Spanish Civilization*

SPN 312 – Spanish American Civilization

SPN 320 – Spanish for Spanish Speakers

SPN 322 – Spanish Conversation I

SPN 323 – Spanish Composition I

SPN 324 – Spanish Stylistics I*

SPN 346 – Mexican Culture

SPN 371 – Spanish for Business

SPN 405 – Spanish American Literature I

SPN 406 – Spanish American Literature II

SPN 407 – Spanish American Story

SPN 408 – Mexican Literature*

SPN 409 – Chicano Literature*

SPN 420 – Spanish for Spanish Speakers I

SPN 421 – Phonetics and Phonology

SPN 422 – Spanish Conversation II

SPN 423 – Spanish Composition II

SPN 424 – Spanish Stylistics II*

SPN 434 – Psychology of the Mexican*

SPN 581 – Educational Aspects of Mexico

Courses marked with an asterisk (*) are offered only in conjunction with the twelve-week semester program. The school also offers a variety of other classes, principally in sociology, history, and literature. A complete listing with course descriptions is available on their website: www.uninter.com.mx

INTERNSHIP PROGRAM

Internships are available in the following fields: medical and social work, business and economics, education, hotel and restaurant management, and criminal justice.

CERTIFICATE PROGRAMS

Universidad Internacional offers certificate programs in a variety of areas, including Teaching Spanish and Hispanic Literature, International Relations, Foreign Trade, Tourism, and may more. Although these programs are designed for local Spanish-speaking students, foreign students with advanced Spanish skills may enroll.

DEGREE PROGRAMS

Universidad Internacional also offers many different associate, bachelor's, and master's degrees. Of particular interest to foreigners are the bachelor's degrees in Latin American Literature and History, International Relations, Foreign Trade, and Tourist Business Administration. For Spanish teachers, the university offers a bachelor's degree in teaching Spanish Language and Literature, and a master's degree in teaching Spanish as a Foreign Language.

BINATIONAL DEGREE PROGRAM

In association with the State University of New York at Cortland (USA), Universidad Internacional offers a Spanish Bachelor's Degree Program in International Business with a concentration on Mexican History and Literature. Students in this program study for the first two years (freshman and sophomore) at SUNY and the following two years (junior and senior) at Universidad Internacional.

METHODS

Universidad International follows a traditional method for teaching Spanish. Classes consist of regular drills in grammar with practice in conversation, composition, and listening. Board games and role-playing exercises are used to review and expand vocabulary.

TEXTBOOKS

The school publishes its own textbooks, which can be purchased in the on-campus bookstore.

EXTRAS

INTERNET ACCESS. Students have free email and Internet access in the computer lab.

CAMPUS FACILITIES. Facilities on this large campus include a library, bookstore, money exchange office, copy center, bookstore, and cafeteria.

COMPUTER LAB. A special feature of the campus is the large, well-equipped computer lab that is available to all students.

MEDICAL SERVICE. Basic medical service is available on campus free of charge Monday through Friday, 8 a.m. to 2 p.m.

THE AMIGO PROGRAM. Foreign students in university and high school programs meet with local Spanish-speaking students twice a week to exchange language skills, culture, traditions, hobbies, and interests.

EXCURSIONS. The school offers mini-excursions to places of interest around Cuernavaca, such as Indian markets, hot springs, haciendas, the ruins of Xochicalco, and the village of Tepoztlán. Weekend excursions are offered to Mexico City, Taxco, Teotihuacán, the volcano of Popocatepetl, Acapulco, Puebla, Oaxaca, San Miguel de Allende, and Guanajuato. Fees for these excursions range from $15 for a day trip, to $130 for a three-day trip.

WHAT DISTINGUISHES THIS SCHOOL?

TRANSFERABLE CREDITS. Universidad International may be the only private language school in Mexico whose credits are routinely transferred to U.S. colleges and universities. National Registration Center for Study Abroad (NRCSA) rates credits from this school as the most likely Mexican private school credits to be accepted by U.S. universities.

DEGREE PROGRAMS. Universidad Internacional is the only private language school that offers associate, bachelor's, and master's degree programs to foreigners.

LARGE CAMPUS. The school's facilities are designed to accommodate large groups, and there is a university atmosphere on campus.

AFFILIATIONS WITH COLLEGES AND UNIVERSITIES. Universidad International has affiliations with an impressive list of colleges and universities in the U.S., Canada, and Europe, which are shown under "Affiliated Universities" on the school's website.

GUADALAJARA

Guadalajara, the capital of the state of Jalisco, is Mexico's second largest city. It has a population of about 5 million, most of whom live in the suburbs. Known as the most Mexican of cities, Guadalajara is the birthplace of Mariachi bands and the home of the Mexican cowboys known as *Charros*.

The twin-towered cathedral, surrounded by five plazas with gardens, fountains, and colonial architecture, dominates the historic center of the city. The main plaza (*Plaza de Armas*) is the site of the Government Palace, which dates from the 1700s and contains impressive murals painted by one of Mexico's most famous artists, Jose Clemente Orozco. In front of the Government Palace is a small plaza planted with roses and featuring an ornate French bandstand. Free concerts are often held there in the evenings. At one end of the huge *Plaza de la Liberación* is the neoclassical *Teatro Degollado*, where world-class performances are held. The *Plaza Tapatía* is an oasis of fountains and shade trees in an area of shops and restaurants. The word *tapatía (or tapatío)*, which you will likely hear many times while in Guadalajara, is used to describe anything or anyone who is distinctly Guadalajaran.

Just east of the historic center of Guadalajara is its largest market, the three-story *Mercado Libertad*, also known *as Mercado San Juan de Díos*. The array of goods sold in this market is incredible: everything from fruits, vegetables, and flowers, to pottery, weavings, clothing, furniture, and even supplies for witch doctors.

The area around Guadalajara provides some interesting day trips. The nearby artisan towns of Tonalá and Tlaquepaque produce handcrafted ceramics, textiles, wood, and glassware. The city of Zapopan is known for its Shrine of the Blessed Virgin of Zapopan, which was established in the 1600s. Also in Zapopan is the colorful Huichol Indian Museum. You can take a longer excursion to Tequila, the town that produces the major ingredient in Margaritas, or Lake Chapala, where there is a large American colony at Ajijic.

GETTING THERE

BY PLANE

Major U.S. and Mexican airlines fly into Guadalajara, including American, United, Continental, Delta, Alaska, Aeromexico, Mexicana, and Aviacsa. Guadalajara's international airport is a thirty- to forty-five-minute taxi ride from the city. Taxi fares vary by zone from $12 to $20, and tickets are sold just outside the baggage area. Minivans, called combis, may be less expensive, especially if you share one with another passenger.

BY BUS

Guadalajara is the hub of bus transportation in North-central Mexico. If you take a bus into Mexico from the U.S. border region, and wind up in Mazatlán, Durango, or even Monterrey, you should have no trouble finding a bus to Guadalajara, but expect a very long ride. For example, it will take you more than thirty hours to get from Tucson to Guadalajara, not counting the time needed to transfer bus lines in Mazatlán. Also, the fare is about $100 each way. Autobuses Crucero (www.autobusescrucero. com) offers transportation to Mexico from many western U.S. cities, including Tucson, Phoenix, Los Angeles, Stockton, Las Vegas, Santa Barbara, Fresno, Portland, and Yakima, Washington. Crucero buses are allied with Greyhound Mexico and usually leave from a Greyhound terminal. Greyhound also has alliances with Autobuses Americanos, which serves the area south of Texas to Monterrey, and Autobuses Amigos, which serves the Gulf Coast. For more information, call Greyhound at 800-229-9424.

BY CAR

After crossing the border in California or Arizona, all-weather highways make it possible to reach Guadalajara in three or four days. From California, take Mexico Highway 2 out of Mexicali to Highway 15, the main Pacific route in Mexico. From Arizona, take Highway 15 directly from Nogales through Guaymas and Mazatlán to Guadalajara.

Don't forget to purchase Mexican insurance for your car at the border or online before leaving home. For more information on driving in Mexico, see "Driving," page 25.

CLIMATE

Guadalajara's climate is mild year-round, probably due to its altitude of more than 5,000 feet. In winter the high temperatures are often in the 70s, with cool evenings; summers are a little warmer, but generally comfortable. It usually rains every afternoon from June through October.

Cepe (Centro de Español Para Extranjeros)

University of Guadalajara

At a Glance

Location: ★★★★½
Facilities: ★★★★★
Programs: ★★★★★
Overall Rating ★★★★★
Cost: $338/two- or five-week session (fifty hours total)
$675/two- or five-week session (one hundred hours total)
Maximum number of students per class: fifteen
Mailing Address:
  Apartado Postal 1-2130
  44100 Guadalajara, Jalisco, México

Street Address:
  Tomás V. Gómez 125
  Col. Ladrón de Guevara
  44600 Guadlajara, Jalisco, México

Tel: 52 333-616-4399 • Fax: 52 333-616-4013
Email: cepe@corp.udg.mx • Website: www.cepe.udg.mx
Director: Ismael A. Crôtte
Marketing Director: Ana Leticia Gutiérrez

CEPE is the University of Guadalajara's Spanish-language center for foreigners. Although the school is in a residential area of Guadalajara and not on the university campus, there is definitely a university atmosphere. The most striking feature of the impressive modern building is a colorful semicircular mural in the entrance lobby. The twenty-three light, airy classrooms are located on several levels, and there is a central patio and garden near the café where students congregate between classes. The school also has a library and an auditorium for large gatherings.

ACADEMIC BACKGROUND

Since CEPE is a department of the University of Guadalajara, all language teachers are required to have degrees in areas like literature, modern language studies, and philosophy of arts. Before beginning to teach at CEPE, they must take a hundred-hour course in grammar and instructional theory and observe classes for an additional thirty hours. At the end of this course, they must also pass an exam before being accepted to teach at CEPE. Teachers of content courses have a master's degree or doctorate in the specific area to be covered, such as history, literature, culture, or the arts.

CREDIT

University of Guadalajara awards credit for courses taken at CEPE. See the school's website for details on earning credit and a list of colleges and universities that have accepted CEPE's courses for credit. Check with the counseling department of your home institution to determine whether they'll accept UDG credits. CEPE issues an official certificate of study that includes all the courses you've taken, the number of hours you attended, and the grades you received.

U.S. University credit is also available by registering for this program through National Registration Center for Study Abroad (NRCSA). Community college credit may be arranged through Seattle Central Community College. *See "Getting College Credit," page 8.*

Costs

Nonrefundable registration fee: $100

INTENSIVE PROGRAM (FIVE-WEEK SESSION – TUITION ONLY)

One course (two hours daily, three credits): $338

Two courses (four hours daily, six credits): $675

Super-intensive program (two-week session–tuition only)

One course (five hours daily, three credits) $338

FULL-IMMERSION PROGRAM (FIVE-WEEK SESSION, INCLUDING HOME STAY)

One course (two hours daily, three credits): $1017 (double room); $1165 (private room)

Two courses (four hours daily, six credits) $1354 (double room); $1502 (private room)

FULL-IMMERSION SUPER-INTENSIVE PROGRAM (TWO-WEEK SESSION, INCLUDING HOME STAY)

One course (five hours daily, three credits): $610 (double room); $669 (private room)

One-on-one private instruction: $23/hour

Textbooks and cassettes: $26–$44/level

Lodging

HOME STAY

A home stay with three meals daily is included in the cost of the "Full Immersion" programs.

OTHER OPTIONS

Casa Internacional, the University of Guadalajara guesthouse, is available to CEPE students at the following rates:

Two-week session: $146 (double room); $205 (private room)

Five-week session: $363 (shared double room); $513 (private room)

Casa Internacional has a private bathroom in each room, all utilities, and daily maid service. There is also a TV lounge, dining room, and kitchen facilities for student use. Internet access and a self-service laundry are available at extra charge.

PROGRAMS AND SCHEDULES

Most classes meet in the mornings, but there are afternoon sessions as well. Students may enter classes only at the beginning of a scheduled session, shown in the calendar section of the school's website, www.cepe.udg.mx

SPANISH LANGUAGE PROGRAM

Students may choose either a two- or five-week session. A written placement exam is given to determine each student's Spanish-language ability. Ten levels of classes are taught in the five-week sessions at CEPE:

Spanish for Beginners: Levels 1, 2, 3, and 4

Intermediate Spanish: Levels 5, 6, 7, and 8

Advanced Spanish: Levels 9 and 10

Only three levels are taught in the two-week sessions: Beginning, Intermediate, and Advanced.

Students in the five-week session may choose from the following additional courses. Each course requires fifty hours and carries three university credits.

Advanced Grammar I and II

Grammar for Bilingual Students I and II

Conversation I, II, and III

Written Spanish I and II

Writing for Bilingual Students I and II

Contemporary Mexican literature

Latin American literature

Hispanic American literature

A General History of Mexico I (up to 1872)

A General History of Mexico II (contemporary)

The history of relations between Mexico and the United States

Economic and political history of Mexico (1880–1994)

Economic and political history of Latin America

The Mexican political system

Mexico and international trade

Mexican culture (separate courses in Spanish or English)

History of Mexican art

Mexican civilization and culture

Pre-Hispanic cultures: culture, society and myth

Mass media in Mexico

Mexican cinema

SPECIAL PROGRAMS

Spanish for Teachers in Bilingual Education Programs
Two weeks, five hours of instruction per day, fifty hours total, three credits

Spanish Language and Culture Course for International Educators and Administrators
Two weeks, seven hours of instruction per day, sixty-six hours total, four credits

Program for Teachers of Spanish as a Foreign Language
Five weeks, six hours of instruction per day, 150 hours total, nine credits

Spanish for Chicanos
Ten weeks, six hours of instruction per day, 300 hours total, eighteen credits

Spanish for Business Purposes
Two weeks, five hours of instruction per day, fifty hours total, three credits

Graduate Spanish Program in International Business Administration
Ten weeks, five hours of instruction per day, 250 hours total; credit awarded by UCLA This program is offered in conjunction with the Anderson Graduate School of Management at the University of California, Los Angeles.

Societal, Political, and Economic Impacts of NAFTA in Mexico
A ten-day seminar, including twenty hours of lectures. In addition to attending lectures, students visit maquiladoras *and multinational corporations, and take excursions within Guadalajara and surrounding towns. This seminar is offered upon request at any time of year, with a minimum of ten students.*

NON-CREDIT WORKSHOPS

NOTE: *There is a five-student minimum for most of these classes.*

Pottery (ten students minimum)

Mexican songs and guitar accompaniment

Folk dancing

Contemporary Latin dancing

Mexican cookery

METHODS

Learning is based on the communicative approach, with attention to grammatical accuracy. All Spanish-language courses are taught in Spanish.

TEXTBOOKS

Students at CEPE use different textbooks according to their level. *Estoy Listo* (with cassette) is used for Levels 1 and 2. *Pido la Palabra,* Levels I through V is used for Levels 3 through 10. *¡Que te cuento!* is used in the conversation classes. CEPE has also published its own workbooks for Levels 3 through 10.

EXTRAS

MOVIE CLUB. Spanish movies are shown throughout the year, including selections from the Guadalajara International Film Festival.

INTERNET ACCESS. Students have access to the Internet and other applications in the computer lab for a $25 fee for the five-week session.

MEDICAL SERVICE. Free medical consultation is available in the event of an accident or illness. CEPE will pay physicians' fees, but the patient pays for medication, lab tests, and other costs.

IMMIGRATION. The Student Services Coordinator will provide assistance with visas.

CAFETERIA. A cafeteria on the CEPE campus provides breakfast, lunch, and snacks.

FRIENDSHIP PROGRAM. The school offers a cultural and language-exchange program so that foreign students can practice Spanish with Mexican students.

VOLUNTEER PROGRAM. Students at CEPE may volunteer at an orphanage, a school for blind girls, a center for children with AIDS, and a senior citizen home.

INTERNSHIPS. Student internships may be arranged in a variety of professional areas, including marketing, ecology, finance, hospitality, travel, import and export, international business, and publishing.

FOREIGN CURRENCY EXCHANGE. The school will change foreign currency or traveler's checks without charging a commission.

MAIL AND FAX. Students can send and receive mail and receive faxes for a fee.

SHOP. The school shop sells T-shirts, souvenirs, phone cards, pencils, pens, maps, and stamps. It also provides a photocopying service.

TOURIST INFORMATION. CEPE provides up-to-date tourist information for the city of Guadalajara and surrounding areas.

EXCURSIONS. The school offers one-day excursions to places of interest in the Guadalajara area, Lake Chapala, and the town of Tequila at an extra cost of $20–$33. Weekend excursions, which require a minimum of fifteen students, can be arranged by the Student Services Coordinator and cost $190 including bus transportation, lodging in a four- or five-star hotel, continental breakfast, tours, museums, and other activities. Typical destinations are Guanajuato, Zacatecas, Michoacan, and Puerto Vallarta.

WHAT DISTINGUISHES THIS SCHOOL?

TRANSFERABLE CREDITS. Because CEPE is a department of the University of Guadalajara, all courses earn credit from that institution that are accepted by many colleges and universities in the U.S.

ACCESS TO UNIVERSITY ACTIVITIES. Many university activities are available to CEPE students. For example, renowned authors come to the school to present their books, and conferences on a variety of topics are presented throughout the year.

NUMBER AND VARIETY OF COURSES. In addition to Spanish grammar and conversation, CEPE offers a large number of university-level-content courses in literature, history, economics, and Mexican cultural topics.

GRADUATE AND PROFESSIONAL PROGRAMS. The school offers credit programs for teachers and administrators, as well as a graduate Spanish program in international business administration through UCLA.

MULTIMEDIA LANGUAGE LAB. CEPE is one of the few Spanish-language schools in Mexico to have a multimedia language lab. Students work on controlled-practice exercises corresponding with material presented in their classes.

STUDENT ID CARD. Students are given an identification card that can be used within the university as well as for access to libraries, discounts in cinemas, theaters, gyms, and on long-distance bus routes.

INSTITUTO MEXICO AMERICANO DE CULTURA (IMAC)

AT A GLANCE

Location: ✫✫✫✫
Facilities: ✫✫✫½
Programs: ✫✫✫✫½
Overall Rating ✫✫✫✫
Cost: $194/week (four hours/day); $336 for two weeks
Maximum number of students per class: six
Street Address:
   Donato Guerra No.180
   Historic Downtown Area
   Guadalajara, Jalisco 44100, México
Tel: 52 333-613-1080

Fax: 52 333-613-4621
Email: spanish-imac@imac-ac.edu.mx
Website: www.spanish-school.com.mx
Director: Juan Tamayo
Academic Director: Reginaldo Ramos
Course Director: Eugenio Avila
Placement Exams Coordinator: Jesús Arredondo
Coordinator of Student Services: Alberto García

Instituto Mexico Americano de Cultura, better known as IMAC, was established in 1977 and is located in the downtown Guadalajara historic district. The cathedral, plazas, museums, and historic monuments are within walking distance. The school is housed in a converted colonial building that offers somewhat cramped quarters, balanced by its nearness to stores, restaurants, and many of the principal tourist attractions. The classrooms occupy multilevel balconies surrounding a small, enclosed central courtyard. There is a café where students can get drinks and snacks, and a computer lab equipped with software for practicing Spanish. English is the main language taught at IMAC, but the English program seems to complement rather than overshadow the Spanish program.

ACADEMIC BACKGROUND

Juan Tamayo, director of the school, has an MBA from the University of Guadalajara and fifteen years of university teaching experience. Academic Director Reginaldo Ramos has a diploma in language teaching and twenty-five years of teaching experience. The course director, Eugenio Avila, has been certified in the teaching of languages by the Mexican Secretary of Education. The placement exams coordinator has a BA in the teaching of languages from the University of Guadalajara. Most instructors have bachelor's degrees.

CREDIT

IMAC is accredited by the Mexican Department of Education (SEP) and has the authority to grant credit for its courses. Check with your college or university to determine whether they'll accept IMAC credits.

For community college students, credit for IMAC courses can be arranged through Seattle Central Community College. *See "Getting College Credit," page 8.*

COSTS

Application deposit (applied to tuition): $150

Lifetime registration fee: $50

INTENSIVE SPANISH (GROUP CLASSES)

Tuition includes four hours of instruction per day and use of the computer lab.

   One week: $194; two weeks: $336; three weeks: $426; four weeks: $517

Discounted weekly tuition rate (for more than four weeks):

   From four to fifteen weeks: $129.25/week

   From sixteen to thirty-one weeks: $110.00/week

   From thirty-two to fifty-two weeks: $104.00/week

Private Tutoring (tuition includes use of the computer lab)

   One hour of instruction daily: $100/week

   Two hours of instruction daily: $167/week

   Three hours of instruction daily: $245/week

   Four hours of instruction daily: $320/week

NOTE:*There are significant discounts for more than four weeks of tutoring.*

   TEFL/TESL teacher training (four weeks, 140 hours): $1400

Optional Extracurricular activities

   Guitar class: $45

   Mexican folk dance class: $45

   Airport reception fee (optional): $22

LODGING

HOME STAY (STUDENTS PAY THE HOST FAMILY DIRECTLY)
One week (including three meals a day): $98

OTHER OPTIONS
IMAC can arrange lodging at a variety of inns and hotels for about $10 to $50/night. For longer stays, guesthouse rooms with access to kitchen and laundry facilities are available for about $350/month.

PROGRAMS AND SCHEDULES

Classes are in session from 9 a.m. to 1 p.m. daily, Monday–Friday.

Students may also practice their skills in IMAC's multimedia language lab for an additional hour daily from 1 to 2 p.m.

INTENSIVE SPANISH

Six levels of Intensive Spanish classes are offered in three categories: Beginning, Intermediate, and Advanced.

SPANISH FOR SPECIFIC PURPOSES
(INDIVIDUAL TUTORING OR PRIVATE GROUP CLASSES)

Spanish for Business and Finance

Spanish for Medical Personnel

Spanish for Social Services

Spanish for Teachers

Spanish for Law Enforcement

Spanish for Household Management

COURSES OFFERED TO GROUPS OR ON A PRIVATE TUTORING BASIS

Getting Along in Spanish (Survival Spanish)

All Basic to Intermediate Points of Spanish Grammar

Communicative Grammar Review

Comprehensive Grammar Review

Writing

Conversation

Introduction to the Appreciation of Authentic Literary Pieces

Historia de Hispanoamérica

Literatura Hispanoamericana

TEFL/TESL teacher training

Course descriptions are shown on the school's website: www.spanish-school.com.mx.

METHODS

IMAC uses an integrated four-skill approach (listening, speaking, reading, and writing), which prepares students to use Spanish in real-life situations by emphasizing oral communication while developing the other basic language skills.

TEXTBOOKS

Beginning levels: *Spanish Now* 1 and 2

Intermediate levels: *¡Continuemos!,* 6th Edition

Other texts may be used for advanced levels and special classes, depending on the specific course and student needs.

EXTRAS

FREE MULTIMEDIA LANGUAGE LAB. Students have unlimited access to IMAC's multimedia lab, which provides Internet access, email, and interactive Spanish programs.

CULTURAL EXCHANGE GROUP. Language practice with native Spanish speakers is provided in a daily instructor-supervised session at no extra cost.

VARIETY OF FREE OPTIONAL ACTIVITIES. Students may participate in a variety of cultural activities at IMAC and around the city of Guadalajara. There are free lectures using videos, CDs, and slide shows, with discussions in Spanish afterward. Topics include History and Culture of Mexico and Guadalajara, Guadalajara Now, La Quinceañera, Mexican Holidays, Los Aztecas, and Celebrating the Day of the Dead. Some additional free activities offered are Salsa lessons, a karaoke club, guitar lessons, Mexican cooking classes, and a ceramics class.

FIELD TRIPS. Free city walking tours are offered in the summer. The following tours are available at extra cost: Lake Chapala, $20; Tequila, $20; Tlaquepaque, $15.

WHAT DISTINGUISHES THIS SCHOOL?

LOCATION. This is the only Spanish-language school in the historic center of Guadalajara. The location allows students access to shopping, restaurants, museums, activities in the five plazas, and much more.

LANGUAGE LAB. The computer lab is well equipped; interactive software and microphones allow it to serve as a language lab.

VARIETY OF COURSES OFFERED. IMAC offers a huge variety of courses, from Intensive Spanish to literature, history, and cultural classes. On an individualized basis, there are courses for teachers, medical personnel, business people, law-enforcement personnel, social workers, and household managers.

TEFL / TESL TRAINING. Students can become qualified to teach English as a Second Language and receive TESL or TEFL certification at IMAC through the school's association with the International Teacher Training Organization (ITTO).

Se Habla Guadalajara

At a Glance

Location: ☆☆☆☆
Facilities: ☆☆☆☆
Programs: ☆☆☆
Overall Rating ☆☆☆½
Cost: $220/week (four hours/day)
Maximum number of students per class: five
Street Address:
   Lázaro Cárdenas #3022 at Avenida Chapilita
   Guadalajara, Jalisco, México

Tel/Fax: 52 612-122-7763
Website: www.sehablalapaz.com
Email: info@sehablalapaz.com
Director: Juli Goff
Director of Education: Antonio Reynoso

A branch of Se Habla La Paz, this school is located in a converted home in a residential section of Guadalajara, convenient to public transportation. The school has three indoor classrooms and one outdoor classroom, all decorated in traditional Mexican style with rustic leather furniture and local handicrafts. Although the school has local faculty, Directors Juli Goff and Antonio Reynoso split their time between the original Se Habla La Paz and the new school in Guadalajara.

Academic Background

Director Julie Goff has a degree in physical therapy from the University of Kansas. She has worked in hospitals and public schools, and has fourteen years' experience in hospital administration, managing programs and personnel from all medical disciplines. Director of Education Antonio Reynoso has a degree in teaching Spanish and English; he is also qualified in detecting and treating learning problems in children. He is the author of Se Habla's general and medical teaching materials.

Credit

Community college credit may be arranged through Seattle Central Community College. *See "Getting College Credit," page 8.*

Continuing education credit for healthcare professionals is available through the Arizona State Nurses Association.

Costs

General/Conversational Program (twenty hours/week), all materials included.

Registration fee: $75

Weekly rates

One week: $220 group (twenty hours) or private (ten hours)

Hourly Rates

Individual – Private: $22.00/hour

Couples – person: $16.50/hour

Group – person: $11.00/hour

Healthcare Program (forty hours / week)

One week: $550   Four weeks: $2090

LODGING

HOME STAY (INCLUDING TWO MEALS A DAY)

Private room, $120/week

NOTE: *Home-stay fees are paid directly to the host family. Most families can accommodate couples or small families. Home-stay matching is done well in advance of arrival, and students have prior information about their families.*

PROGRAMS AND SCHEDULES

GENERAL CONVERSATIONAL PROGRAM. The conversational Spanish classes meet for twenty hours/week. Students take a placement exam to determine the level of their language proficiency before beginning classes. Individualized language programs may be designed for specific interests and for any length of time needed to successfully accomplish a student's language goals.

HEALTHCARE PROGRAM. Students attend Spanish-language classes for twenty hours weekly and spend up to twenty hours in clinical environments with their medical counterparts. The program is designed for the student to be present, observe, listen, converse, and relate to the professionals and their patients in local hospitals, private offices, clinics, and community-based outreach programs. Instruction can be tailored for a variety of healthcare workers: nurses, doctors, therapists, social workers, religious associates, psychologists, psychiatrists, administrators, and volunteers.

METHODS

Se Habla uses an individualized communicative approach. After each student's language level is assessed to determine the most appropriate study program, educational materials are compiled.

TEXTBOOKS

Se Habla compiles each student's materials depending upon their particular needs, both in levels of proficiency and professional areas of interest. All educational materials are produced at the school and are included in the tuition. Students are expected to have an adequate Spanish-English bilingual dictionary.

EXTRAS

AIRPORT PICKUP. The school will arrange to pick you up at the Guadalajara airport pickup and deliver you to your accommodation for an additional charge of $35.

FREE ACTIVITIES. Se Habla organizes weekly cultural activities and fiestas and screens Spanish-language films.

LIBRARY. There is a small library of Spanish-language books that students can borrow.

FREE SNACKS. There is a snack break each day with coffee and other beverages and typical Mexican food.

PAYPAL PAYMENTS. The school accepts payment through the online service PayPal. For more information on how to pay with this method, visit www.paypal.com.

WHAT DISTINGUISHES THIS SCHOOL?

HEALTHCARE PROGRAM. In addition to attending Spanish classes, healthcare professionals have the opportunity to observe and practice the language in a clinical setting for up to twenty additional hours weekly.

CUSTOMIZED PROGRAMS. Your individual language program can be designed for your specific interests and for any length of time you need to successfully accomplish your language goals.

TWO LOCATIONS. By arranging a study program that includes both Se Habla schools, students have the opportunity to experience a small, coastal city in Baja California (La Paz) as well as a very large metropolitan area (Guadalajara).

Vancouver Language Centre (VLC)

At a Glance

Location: ✮✮✮✮
Facilities: ✮✮✮½
Programs: ✮✮✮
Overall Rating ✮✮✮½
Cost: $108/week (four hours/day)
Maximum number of students per class: seven
Street Address:
  Avenida Vallarta #1151
  Colonia Americana
  CP 44100 Guadalajara, Jalisco, México

Tel: 52 333-826-0944 or 52 333-825-4271
Fax: 52 333-825-2051
Email: vlc@study-mexico.com or info@study-mexico.com
Website: www.study-mexico.com
Director: Patricia Moir
Director of Student Services: Adriana Gamboa Soto
Spanish Coordinator: Juan Carlos Herrera Maza

Vancouver Language Centre is a branch of Vancouver English Centre in Vancouver, Canada. Although their principal function seems to be to teach English to local children and adults, VLC also has a well-established Spanish-language program. The school is located in a modern building on a tree-lined street in a residential area of Guadalajara. The four Spanish classrooms are comfortable and air-conditioned. In addition to Spanish, the school offers preparatory courses for teachers of English as a Foreign Language.

ACADEMIC BACKGROUND

Juan Carlos Herrera Maza, the Spanish Coordinator, has a degree in communications. All the instructors have university degrees; most hold bachelor's degrees in communication, literature, or business.

CREDIT

VLC is accredited by the Mexican Secretaria de Educación Pública (Federal Department of Education). Upon completion of their courses, students receive a diploma and a letter confirming the number of hours of study in grammar and conversation. Check with your home university to determine whether courses at VLC will be accepted for credit.

Community college credit may be arranged through Seattle Central Community College. *See "Getting College Credit," page 8.*

COSTS

First-time nonrefundable registration fee: $75

Re-registration fee: $40

Note: Registration fees are nonrefundable and are not applied to tuition.

SPANISH COURSES

Four-week Spanish Intensive (ten hours/week): $430

Four-week Spanish Grammar (ten hours/week): $250

Four-week Spanish Conversation (ten hours/week): $250

Private Instruction in Spanish: $15/hour

ENGLISH TEACHER PREPARATION

Four-week TEFL Certificate Course (thirty hours/week): $1095

Text and materials fee (Spanish programs, per level): $20–$30

Materials fee (TEFL): $35

Airport reception fee: $50

LODGING

HOME STAY

Home-stay placement fee: $65

Room and board (includes three meals a day): $15/night

NOTE: *Home-stay fees are paid directly to the host family.*

PROGRAMS AND SCHEDULES

Classes start every four weeks; for exact dates, see VLC's website: www. study-spanish.com.

Six levels are offered in both grammar and conversation courses, from beginner to advanced.

Spanish Grammar: Monday–Friday 9:30–11:30 a.m.

Spanish Conversation: Monday–Friday, noon–2 p.m.

Students may choose either a grammar or a conversation class, or they may study both components simultaneously.

BUSINESS SPANISH COURSE

This course focuses on business terminology, report writing, and public speaking for advanced Spanish speakers. Elective courses are available in both grammar and conversation formats.

COMBINED PROGRAM

Students who wish to learn both Spanish and English may do so simultaneously by taking the combined Spanish/English program.

ENGLISH TEACHER PREPARATION

The TEFL certificate program is offered for students who wish to prepare to teach English as a Foreign Language. The school also offers the TEFL electives Teaching Business English (TBE) and the Teaching English to Children (TEC).

METHODS

In addition to traditional classroom instruction, Spanish teachers use videotapes and role-playing, encouraging group participation. Also, they often take students on short trips within the neighborhood in Guadalajara.

TEXTBOOKS

Teachers at Vancouver Language Centre have developed their own textbooks. They also use a variety of other materials to complement the program, including texts such as *Pido la Palabra, Lotería,* and others recognized by the Secretaria de Educación Pública (Mexican Secretary of Public Education).

EXTRAS

CONVERSATION CLUB. A twice-weekly language exchange is held at the school at no extra cost.

INTERNET ACCESS. Within the building there is an Internet café with low hourly rates.

SPORTS. The activities coordinator arranges opportunities for students to play soccer, basketball, and cricket with local residents.

EXCURSIONS. Local outings include tours of downtown Guadalajara, Tonalá, Tlaquepaque, Lake Chapala, and Zapopan. The school also organizes longer trips to the town of Tequila and the nearby Pacific coast of Jalisco and Colima.

WHAT DISTINGUISHES THIS SCHOOL?

SCHOLARSHIP PROGRAMS IN MEXICO AND CANADA. Along with its sister school in Vancouver, BC, Canada, Vancouver Language Centre offers scholarships for combined study programs at both centers. For more information see the school's website: www.study-mexico.com.

TEFL CERTIFICATION. A benefit of teaching both English and Spanish in the same facility is that English-speaking students can receive certification for teaching English as a Foreign Language.

Guanajuato

Guanajuato is a virtual treasure-trove of Mexican colonial history. It was once the seat of the Spanish colonial government, and is known as the "Cradle of Independence" because the movement for Mexico's independence from Spain started here. Situated in a narrow canyon, the city has only a few streets that carry traffic, and some of those are underground. Narrow, cobblestone pedestrian-only streets called *callejones* ascend the steep slopes on either side of the canyon, making it an ideal place for those who love to walk. From the Valenciana silver mine high above the city, to the plaza with its neoclassical Teatro Alcalá and up the Paseo de la Presa to the picturesque lake, Guanajuato never ceases to delight the eye, offering surprises around every corner.

As the location of the University of Guanajuato, the city has long been a center of learning and culture. Students can attend plays, symphonies, concerts, lectures, and the many festivals that are held throughout the year. The Cervantes Festival (*Festival Cervantino*) in October celebrates the work of Spain's most famous author with indoor and outdoor performances, music, and art exhibits. A year-round favorite pastime is visiting the city's many restaurants and sidewalk cafés and enjoying its lively nightlife.

Climate

Because of its high altitude (about 7,000 feet), Guanajuato is cooler in winter than many other cities of the central plateau. It has the same dry season (November through April) and rainy season (May through October) as other parts of Mexico. In the summer, you can expect afternoon showers and some rainy days. It seldom gets cold, except sometimes in December or January, when you might need warm clothing and an extra blanket.

Getting There

Flying into León / Bajío Airport. The closest airport is León / Bajío near the city of León, which is about thirty-five minutes by car from Guanajuato. Taxis from León / Bajío airport to Guanajuato charge about $25.

Flying into Mexico City or Guadalajara. Flying to one of these cities may be considerably cheaper than flying directly to León / Bajío Airport.

Guanajuato is more or less equidistant from Mexico City on the south and Guadalajara on the north.

BY BUS

FROM MEXICO CITY. There are a couple of ways to get from Mexico City to Guanajuato by bus. Of the two described below, Option 1 is the safest way; Option 2 may be less expensive, but it is less secure because you need to cross Mexico City in a taxi.

OPTION 1: Take the AeroPlus bus (tel. 52 555-786-9357), which leaves the Mexico City airport for Querétaro about every hour and costs about $17. From Querétaro, you can travel to Guanajuato through Irapuato. You'll find the AeroPlus buses just outside the doors in front of *Sala D* (National Gate D). To get to the bus-ticket counter, leave the international customs area and take the escalator to the second floor. Proceed directly through the food court into a windowed hallway and look for the AeroPlus counter. After buying your ticket, make your way down the staircase to the right and look for the boarding area marked "Querétaro." The bus takes about three hours to get to Querétaro. When you arrive there, you'll be in Terminal A. Go out the door, turn right, and walk to Terminal B. Primera Plus/Flecha Amarilla buses for Irapuato leave from Terminal B and cost about $4. In Irapuato, you can purchase a ticket to Guanajuato on one of the same bus lines for another $4. You may be able to buy a ticket to Guanajuato while in Querétaro, but you'll probably need to change buses in Irapuato.

OPTION 2: Take a taxi from the airport to the North Bus Station, (*Central de Autobuses del Norte*).

Always buy a ticket for an authorized taxi at the booth in the baggage area of the airport. Under no circumstances should you hail a taxi in the street in Mexico City—unauthorized or pirate taxis have been involved in robberies and kidnappings.

Allow about twenty minutes by taxi from the airport to the *Central de Autobuses del Norte*, where you can take one of the frequent buses to Guanajuato.

FROM THE GUADALAJARA AIRPORT. Take a taxi to that city's main bus station (*Central de Autobuses*). Be sure to buy ticket for an authorized taxi, and let the driver know that you are going to Guanajuato so that you will be dropped off in the right section of Guadalajara's enormous bus station.

First-class buses depart every hour or two for Guanajuato and take a little over four hours. Fares are between $11 and $15. For a shorter ride, take *"Directo"* service to avoid stopping in the smaller towns along the way. Some of the better and fastest bus lines are Primera Plus/Flecha Amarilla, Futura/EstrellaBlanca/Turistar and ETN (Enlaces Terrestres Nacionales). Primera Plus/Flecha Amarilla allows you to see schedules and fares (*tarifas*) online at www.primeraplus.com.mx. Prices and comfort vary depending on which service you choose. ETN, Turistar, and Primera Plus are the most luxurious.

ACADEMIA FALCÓN

AT A GLANCE

Location: ★★★★½
Facilities: ★★★★
Programs: ★★★★★
Overall Rating ★★★★½
Cost: $65/week (two hours/day) to $120/week (six hours/day)
Maximum number of students per class: five (up to twelve in the semester program)
Street address:
  Paseo de la Presa #80
  Guanajuato, Guanajuato CP36000 México

Tel: 52 473-731-1084 • Fax: 52 473-731-0745
Email:infalcon@academiafalcon.com.
Website: www.academiafalcon.com
President and founder: Jorge Barroso
Director: Erika Gutierrez Tejada
Sub-director: Leticia Barajas Ramirez

As you walk up the street in Guanajuato looking for Academia Falcón, you may not expect to find it in a chalet. Surprisingly, the entrance to this school is just that—a large house built in the chalet style favored by wealthy Europeans in Mexico during the latter half of the 19th century. Taking advantage of the spaciousness of the grounds, the school has expanded into a new building containing several classrooms, a library, and a few dormitory rooms. Between the modern building and the chalet, there is a garden area, an indoor-outdoor cafeteria, a lecture hall, and a covered patio where dance classes are held.

ACADEMIC BACKGROUND

President Jorge Barroso holds degrees in languages, philosophy, and humanities. He is a former professor at the University of Guanajuato, and taught for several years at Academia Hispano-Americana in San Miguel de Allende. All instructors at Academia Falcón have university degrees and are trained in language instruction. The school holds methodology workshops every three weeks to maintain the quality of instruction.

CREDIT

The University of Arizona offers credit for their summer program at Academia Falcón. For more information, see the UA website: www.universityofarizona.com or call 305-666-8838.

Academia Falcón will prepare students to take the CLEP (College Level Examination Program) in order to receive academic credit from a U.S. university. Check with your home institution to find out if credit may be awarded for studies at Academia Falcón. The school will provide course descriptions, transcripts, and other materials required by the university.

Community college credit may be arranged through Seattle Central Community College. *See "Getting College Credit," page 8.* For additional information or questions about credit, email the school: questionscredit@academiafalcon.com.

COSTS

One-time nonrefundable registration fee: $75

SMALL GROUP CLASSES
Two sessions daily: $65/week
Three sessions daily: $85/week
Four sessions daily: $100/week

Five sessions daily: $110/week

Six sessions daily $120/week

ONE-ON-ONE CLASSES

One session daily: $70/week

Two sessions daily: $140/week

Three sessions daily: $210/week

Semester Program: $595/semester

The semester program includes sixteen weeks of instruction with three sessions daily.

Book deposit: $25

Discounts are available September through April. If you attend group classes during this time, you will receive a 10 percent discount on tuition. For parents traveling with children, a 15 percent family discount is available.

LODGING

HOME STAY (INCLUDING THREE MEALS DAILY, PAID DIRECTLY TO THE FAMILY)

Private room: $20/day   Shared room: $17/day

On-campus dormitory rooms are available for 80 to 220 pesos/night (about $8–$22), depending on the size of the room and whether it has a private or shared bath. Located in the classroom building, these rooms are spartan but comfortable.

PROGRAMS AND SCHEDULES

All classes are held Monday through Friday in fifty-five-minute sessions.

INTENSIVE SPANISH-LANGUAGE PROGRAM

Students may choose from a wide variety of Spanish-language classes, including:

Grammar (three levels)

Basic Communication

Vocabulary

Pronunciation

Conversation

Reading Comprehension

Composition and Writing Skills

Special-Interest Classes

Intermediate and advanced students may take one or more of the following special-interest classes, which are taught in Spanish:

Mexican History

Mexican Politics

Mexican Culture

Latin American Literature

Local History and Legends

Mexican Business Culture

Mexican Cuisine

Latin American Dance

Muralism

Pre-Hispanic Art

Indigenous Peoples of Mexico

History of the Mexican Revolution

Mexican Music

Spanish Medical Terms

Spanish Law Vocabulary

Cinema Workshop

Women's Role in Mexican Society

Brief descriptions of all the classes offered at Academia Falcón are shown on their website: www.academiafalcon.com. More complete descriptions are available at the school and may be requested by mail, email, or fax.

Semester Program

Students who enroll for the sixteen-week semester program take both Spanish-language classes and classes in the special-interest areas listed above. This program starts at the end of January or the beginning of August and requires three hours of classes daily. There are five levels; different classes are offered for each level. Students in the semester program also receive discounts on family stays and excursions.

BILINGUAL TEACHERS' PROGRAM

This program is designed for bilingual teachers who need to improve their Spanish grammar, listening skills, oral competency, writing ability, or reading comprehension in preparation for certification exams.

LATINO PROGRAM

Especially for students who learned Spanish at home and may need to improve their grammar or writing ability, this program focuses on spelling, composition, and using correct grammar when speaking.

CHILDREN'S PROGRAM

For children from six to twelve years old, this program offers three hours daily of language learning using games, videos, and songs in Spanish. Two hours per week are dedicated to interacting with local Mexican children.

SENIOR CITIZENS' PACKAGE

Travelers sixty years and older pay no registration fee for this special program, which includes "Spanish for Travelers" and Mexican cooking, as well as visits to historical sites in Guanajuato.

METHODS

Academia Falcón's teaching method emphasizes all four language skills: speaking, listening, reading, and writing. Students learn grammar and practice their conversational skills by telling stories, discussing newspaper articles, and making short presentations. Teachers use a wide variety of visual aids to enhance the experience.

TEXTBOOKS

Beginning and advanced students do not use textbooks; *Schaum's Grammar* Series is used as a reference book in these levels. Intermediate students use the textbook created by Academia Falcón.

EXTRAS

STUDENT ID. A student identification card is given to all students who provide a photograph.

COMPUTER CENTER AND INTERNET ACCESS. Students have free Internet access as well as the use of Microsoft Office applications in the computer center.

CONVERSATION EXCHANGE WITH MEXICAN STUDENTS. This activity provides conversational practice with native Spanish speakers who are learning English.

LECTURES. Teachers or guest speakers give free weekly lectures on Mexican history, politics, literature, art, legends, traditions, and other topics of interest.

FILMS. A Spanish-language feature film is shown once a week.

PARTIES OR CALLEJONEADAS. On Fridays, there is usually a student party or *callejoneada*, which is a walk through the streets of Guanajuato while singing traditional songs accompanied by one of the musical groups called *Estudiantinas* or *Tunas*.

EXCURSIONS. Weekend excursions to places of interest and neighboring cities, such as San Miguel de Allende, Querétaro, Morelia, and León, are offered at extra cost.

WHAT DISTINGUISHES THIS SCHOOL?

SEMESTER PROGRAM. Academia Falcón is one of only a few immersion schools that provide a comprehensive semester program for serious students.

WIDE VARIETY OF COURSES. This school offers an impressive number of cultural, historical, and activity classes, as well as a complete Spanish-language program, including pronunciation, reading comprehension, vocabulary, and composition classes.

WELL-ROUNDED EXPERIENCE. Academia Falcón provides a winning combination of classroom instruction and activities such as guest lectures, films, dance classes, and excursions.

Escuela Mexicana

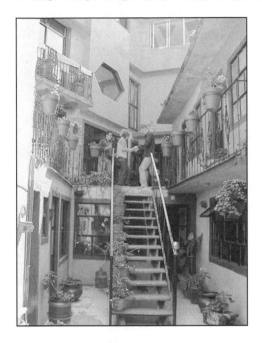

At a Glance

Location: ★★★½
Facilities: ★★★½
Programs: ★★★★
Overall Rating ★★★½
Cost: $50/week (two hours daily) to $115/week (five hours daily)
Maximum number of students per class: five
Street Address:
  Potrero 12, Zona Centro 36000
  Guanajuato, Guanajuato, México

Tel: 52 473-732-5005
Email: escuelamexicana@hotmail.com
Website: www.escuelamexicana.int.com.mx
Director: Hayde López
Curriculum Coordinator: Angel Rolando Rodríguez Lara
English Program Coordinator: Torsten Rufer

E scuela Mexicana occupies a beautiful colonial building right in the heart of Guanajuato and very near the main plaza or *Jardín de la Unión*. As you enter the building, the personality of this school is revealed. The airy patio surrounded by yellow and white walls and decorated with potted plants exudes Mexican charm. Language instruction is very personal and given in an intimate atmosphere enhanced by the typical Mexican décor.

ACADEMIC BACKGROUND

Director Hayde López holds bachelor's degrees in law and tourism administration and has five years' experience teaching Spanish as a Second Language. Most instructors have bachelor's degrees in language and literature and language-teaching experience. Curriculum coordinator and instructor Angel Rolando Rodríguez holds a degree in philosophy and letters and has five years' experience teaching Spanish. Torsten Rufer, who is originally from Germany, coordinates the English program. He also communicates by email and phone with prospective students who need information in English, German, or French.

CREDIT

Escuela Mexicana does not offer credit for its courses. Check with your home university to determine whether they can grant credit for courses at the school. Community college credit may be arranged through Seattle Central Community College. *See "Getting College Credit," page 8.*

COSTS
One-time registration fee: $30

GROUP CLASSES
Two classes daily: $50/week
Three classes daily: $75/week
Four classes daily: $100/week
Five classes daily: $115/week

ONE-ON-ONE CLASSES
One session daily: $65/week
Two sessions daily: $130/week
Three sessions daily: $195/week

INTENSIVE SPANISH FOR TRAVELERS

Four group classes daily: $150/week

Four private classes daily: $220/week

PLUS PROGRAM

Includes five hours of private instruction plus one hour of group instruction per day

June through September: $400/week

October through May: $350/week

TRIMESTER PROGRAM

Trimester programs begin in January, April, and September. Check the school's website for current starting dates.

Twelve weeks: $559   Children's Program: $4/class

DISCOUNTS: Winter Special (January through April), four classes daily: $87/week
There is a year-round discount for advance payment of tuition.

Senior Citizen Discount: Seniors receive a 15 percent discount on the trimester program year-round.

LODGING

Escuela Mexicana arranges home stays. Students also have the option of staying in the rooms at Casa Mexicana, the school's guesthouse.

HOME STAY

Private room and three meals a day: $21

Shared room and three meals a day: $18

ROOM AT CASA MEXICANA

(includes free cable TV and kitchen services):

With private bath: $16

With shared bath: $13

PROGRAMS AND SCHEDULES

Most classes start every Monday. The twelve-week trimester program starts in January, April, and September. Placement exams are given to students with some knowledge of Spanish.

STANDARD SPANISH PROGRAM

Students may take two to five classes per day in a private or group setting. This program comprises twenty different grammar courses, structured conversation courses, culture, literature, legends, politics, business, Mexican history, Mexican cooking, and dance.

PLUS PROGRAM

This is a three-week intensive Spanish-language and cultural immersion course. It includes five hours of one-on-one classes daily: two hours of grammar, two hours of conversation, and a one-hour guided visit to a market, a museum, or another local attraction. In addition, students have one group activity class per day, either dance or Mexican cooking. For more information, see the Plus Program FAQs on the school's website: www.escuelamexicana.int.com.mx.

TRIMESTER PROGRAM

Students may begin this twelve-week program in January, April or September. There are three hours of instruction daily and three different levels. A placement exam is given on the first day. The trimester program combines grammar, conversation, culture, history, and literature classes. There are no more than ten students per class, and all trimester students have the option of taking cooking or dance classes for two hours per week.

INTENSIVE SPANISH FOR TRAVELERS

This one- or two-week course focuses on survival skills for travelers who need to learn to communicate in various situations, such as in restaurants, hotels, shops, or bus stations. These classes meet for four hours per day, with a maximum of three students.

CHILDREN'S PROGRAM

The children's classes are divided into three groups by age: three to six, seven to nine, and ten and over. Classes meet for three to five hours per day. From July 15 to August 15 there's a special children's program at Casa de la Cultura, where the students meet Mexican children and participate in folk dance, theater, and art classes.

METHODS

Classes at Escuela Mexicana include activities that integrate reading, speaking, listening, and writing, including role-playing and dramatization.

The focus is on interaction and learning exchange among students and native speakers.

TEXTBOOKS

The school publishes its own workbooks, which cover four weeks of classes and cost $5.

EXTRAS

INTERCAMBIO. A weekly gathering allows students to practice conversing with local Spanish speakers in an informal social setting.

FREE MOVIES. One night a week, students watch a movie in Spanish and then discuss it.

TABLE GAMES. Pictionary, cards, bingo, and other games are available for student use.

FREE GUIDED ACTIVITIES AND TOURS. The school offers guided city tours and trips to local events such as concerts at no extra cost.

EXCURSIONS. Escuela Mexicana organizes tours to nearby destinations such as San Miguel de Allende, Pátzcuaro, Morelia, León, and Dolores Hidalgo. Students pay the cost of transportation and accommodations.

ADDITIONAL SERVICES. For additional fees, the school offers transportation from the León (Bajío) airport, laundry service, and Internet access.

WHAT DISTINGUISHES THIS SCHOOL?

FAMILY ATMOSPHERE. Because of the small number of students, there is a distinct family atmosphere.

SMALL CLASSES. Even though the maximum number of students per class is five, many classes at Escuela Mexicana have only two or three students.

TRADITIONAL MEXICAN DÉCOR. You really feel like you're in Mexico at this school.

VARIETY OF CLASSES. For a small school, Escuela Mexicana offers a very wide variety of classes. In addition to twenty different grammar classes, there are classes in Spanish conversation, Mexican culture, history, literature, legends, politics, and business. Mexican cooking and dance classes are offered as well.

Instituto Miguel de Cervantes

At a Glance

Location: ✯✯✯✯
Facilities: ✯✯✯✯½
Programs: ✯✯✯
Overall Rating ✯✯✯✯
Cost: $149/week (three hours/day)
Maximum number of students per class: five
Street Address:
  Cerro del Erizo #100
  Valenciana, Guanajuato 36000, México

Mailing Address:
  Apartado Postal #406
  Guanajuato, Gto. 36000, México

Tel: 52 473-732-8069
Fax: 52 473-732-3870
Email:info@spanish-immersion.com
Website:www.spanish-immersion.com
Director: Celi Martínez Tremblay

A school with a view, Instituto Miguel de Cervantes sits on a hill overlooking the city of Guanajuato. It's located near the village of Valenciana and very near the silver mine of the same name. As you travel up the winding road that leads to the institute, there are spectacular panoramas of Guanajuato, Valenciana, and the surrounding mountains. The institute occupies two buildings, which are surrounded by tree-shaded gardens and patios from which you can savor that magnificent view. In the summer, classes are also held in an adjoining building, which during the school year is a private school for local children. The institute has four nicely appointed apartments on campus that are especially convenient for students with families. Since most students stay with local families a few miles away in Guanajuato, the school provides transportation to and from classes in the morning and afternoon. For those who prefer to walk, a scenic trail skirts a canyon leading down to the city.

ACADEMIC BACKGROUND

Director Celi Martínez Tremblay, a former professor of languages, started this school in 1981. The teaching staff is made up of graduates of the University of Guanajuato.

CREDIT

The school does not offer credit for its courses; however, some U.S. universities have held credit summer programs at Instituto Miguel de Cervantes. Community college credit may be arranged through Seattle Central Community College. See "Getting College Credit," page 8.

COSTS

Nonrefundable deposit (applied to tuition): $100

Basic Program (fifteen hours/week)
   Initial Week: $149 without home stay; $299 with home stay
   Additional weeks: $109 without home stay; $229 with home stay

Basic Plus Program (twenty-one hours/week)
   Initial Week: $299 without home stay; $449 with home stay
   Additional weeks: $209 without home stay; $329 with home stay

Materials fee: $10

LODGING

HOME STAY

The school will arrange accommodations with a Mexican family and include the cost in the tuition.

OTHER OPTIONS

As an alternative to a home stay, families with children may consider renting one of the four on-campus apartments at the institute. Weekly rents start at $210 and there are discounts for multiple weeks. Detailed rental information is available on the school's website: www.spanish-immersion.com.

The school will also reserve hotel or apartment accommodations in Guanajuato for students who do not wish to stay with a family or on the campus.

NOTE: *Transportation to and from the Institute may cost extra for students not staying with a family.*

PROGRAMS AND SCHEDULES

Students are asked to take an online placement test to determine whether they will be in beginning, intermediate, or advanced classes. The level may be adjusted during the first week of class.

BEGINNING. The beginning level concentrates on development of basic communication skills such as listening comprehension, vocabulary development, pronunciation, and conversation.

INTERMEDIATE. The intermediate level classes help students advance their communication skills through vocabulary development and conversation practice with role-playing.

ADVANCED. This level focuses on continued vocabulary enhancement through conversation practice with a review of essential grammar structures for writing activities and authentic reading assignments

BASIC PROGRAM

Classes meet from 9 a.m. to 12:30 p.m. with a half-hour break at 10.

BASIC PLUS PROGRAM

Classes meet from 9 a.m. to 12:30 p.m. with a half-hour break at 10. There is also an additional session from 1 to 2:30 p.m., Monday through

Thursday, in which Basic Plus students receive individualized practice in the vocabulary and grammatical structures introduced in their morning classes.

PROFESSIONAL PROGRAMS

The institute can also plan customized professional programs for groups of five or more students. They have arranged programs for teachers in bilingual classrooms, doctors and other medical service personnel, lawyers, and social service professionals.

CHILDREN'S PROGRAM

The Institute has no formal children's program; however, during the school year, elementary school children may be able to register and attend Spanish classes at the adjacent Colegio Valenciana, a private elementary school.

METHODS

Instructors at Instituto Miguel de Cervantes use an integrated communicative approach that includes the four essential language skills—listening, speaking, reading, and writing—in a cumulative and measured curriculum. The emphasis is on developing the vocabulary, grammar skills, and pronunciation necessary for real-world communication. Instructors undergo intensive training, and their classroom performance is continually reviewed.

TEXTBOOKS

The faculty has assembled their own teaching materials and workbooks; the materials fee to cover reproduction costs for these is $10.

EXTRAS

FREE INTERNET ACCESS. Several computers are available for student use in the office / library area.

LIBRARY. There is a small library with a collection of Spanish-language reading material, guidebooks, and books on Mexican culture and history.

COMPLIMENTARY COFFEE. Coffee is available in the kitchen area, and snacks are served at a minimal cost.

FREE AIRPORT TRANSPORTATION. Students who have booked a home stay will be picked up at the Leon (Bajío) airport by their host family or someone from the institute. For those staying in an apartment or hotel, airport pickup costs $30 round-trip.

CULTURAL ACTIVITIES. Dance classes, cooking classes, local excursions, and films and lectures on Mexican history, art, and literature are offered free of charge after class hours. For an additional fee, students can participate in art and ceramic workshops. A weekly calendar of activities is posted every Monday.

OPTIONAL WEEKEND EXCURSIONS. The school offers day and overnight trips to places of interest in central Mexico, including Dolores Hidalgo, San Miguel de Allende, Querétaro, and parts of the state of Michoacán. Students pay the cost of transportation and accommodations.

SPORTS TOURS. The school offers mountain-bike and hiking tours in the mountains. Students may bring their own bikes or rent bikes. The guides are experienced and equipped with 1:50 000 topographic maps and GPS systems.

WHAT DISTINGUISHES THIS SCHOOL?

LOCATION. The school's location on a hill overlooking the city of Guanajuato and the historic mining town of Valenciana affords spectacular vistas. Surrounded by landscaped gardens with mature trees, flowering plants, and fountains, the outdoor terraces may be used for conversation or study.

ASSOCIATION WITH COLEGIO VALENCIANA. One of the best private elementary schools in Guanajuato, Colegio Valenciana is right next door to Instituto Miguel de Cervantes. During the school year, students at the institute may have the opportunity to interact with the children, and the elementary school facility is available for additional classes and activities during the summer.

FREE DAILY TRANSPORTATION. For students who are staying in Guanajuato, the school provides morning and afternoon transportation to and from their residences.

MORELIA

M orelia is a beautiful traditional Mexican city about 200 miles north-west of Mexico City. It is the capital of the state of Michoacán, which offers a wide variety of attractions, from the beaches of Zihuatene-jo and Ixtapa, to the Pre-Columbian site of Tingambato and the Paricutín volcano. West of Morelia is Lake Pátzcuaro, the most picturesque lake in Mexico, surrounded by Indian villages known for their handicrafts. The best guitars in Mexico are made in Paracho, and Santa Clara del Co-bre produces almost anything you could imagine in copper. The town of Pátzcuaro retains its rustic Spanish colonial atmosphere and has become a center for the arts and the study of nature.

The city of Morelia is the cultural center of the state of Michoacán. It offers a variety of events, such as theater productions, concerts, and folk-loric dances. Many of these activities are sponsored by the cultural cen-ter of the University of Michoacán.

Morelia has a long and interesting history. It was founded in 1541 un-der the name Valladolid. The name was changed about 300 years later to honor the revolutionary hero José María Morelos, who was born there. Originally intended to provide an example of Spanish culture for the re-gion's large population of Indians, Morelia shows traces of an aristocrat-ic past in the grand colonial architecture of some of its older buildings. The main plaza, with its manicured shrubs, is adjacent to the domed ca-thedral, which dates from 1745 and contains an impressive pipe organ. At the other end of *Calle Madero,* the city's main street, there is an ex-ceptionally beautiful fountain and an old aqueduct. Walking under the arches of the aqueduct, you pass through a small park and end up at one of the oldest and most beloved churches in the city. Despite its many attractions, Morelia is a decidedly "untouristy" city. Although it is of-ten visited by Mexicans on vacation, it is not a popular destination for foreign tourists.

CLIMATE

Because Morelia is at an altitude of about 6,000 feet, it seldom gets very hot, with high temperatures hovering between 70 and 80 degrees most of the year. As with all areas of the central plateau, there is a rainy season from May to October and a dry season from November through April. In the rainy season you can expect afternoon thundershowers and some overcast days. The warmest months are March and April, and the coldest November and December.

Getting There

By plane

Morelia's airport is about fifteen miles from the city center. Taxis meet each flight and charge about $20 to take you into town. The Mexican airlines Aviacsa and AeroMexico, as well as American and Continental, operate flights from San Francisco and Los Angeles to Morelia; fares begin at about $400 round-trip. Flights from the East Coast of the U.S. are available on Aeromexico and Continental at a cost of $600–$650 round-trip.

Since there are often special discounted fares to Mexico City, a less expensive option may be to fly to the capital and take a bus to Morelia.

By bus

Almost all buses to Morelia leave from Mexico City's Terminal Poniente, (Western Bus Station), which is also called Observatorio. There is no bus service directly from the Mexico City airport to Morelia, but you can take an authorized taxi from the airport to the bus terminal. Always buy a ticket for an authorized taxi at the booth in the baggage area of the airport. Under no circumstances should you hail a taxi in the street in Mexico City—unauthorized or pirate taxis have been involved in robberies and kidnappings. Allow twenty to thirty minutes for the taxi ride from the airport to the bus station. Several bus lines, including ETN, Pegaso, Primera Plus, and Autovías, travel from Mexico City to Morelia. There are usually three or four departures every hour. Make sure to request a "directo" or "via autopista" to ensure that the bus you take will not stop in every little town along the way. The trip takes four to five hours and costs between U.S. $10 and $15. ETN (Enlaces Terrestres Nacionales) generally offers the best service.

You'll arrive at the new *Central Camionera* in the far northwest side of Morelia, near the soccer stadium. From the *Central Camionera*, you can get a taxi into town for about $5.

BADEN-POWELL INSTITUTE

AT A GLANCE

Location: ✫✫✫✫
Facilities: ✫✫✫½
Programs: ✫✫✫✫
Overall Rating ✫✫✫✫
Cost: $165/week (four hours/day)
Maximum number of students per class: five
Street Address:
    Antonio Alzate No. 565
    Centro, C.P. 58000
    Morelia, Michoacán, México

Tel/Fax: 52 443-312-4070
Email: contacto@baden-powell.com
Website: www.baden-powell.com
Director: Eugenio Cortez

Founded in 1987, the Baden-Powell Institute was named after the founder of the Boy Scouts, but the school has no connection with that organization. The institute occupies a picturesque colonial-style building in the historic center of Morelia. Although the exterior is rather plain, the interior is very inviting, painted in bright contrasting colors of terra cotta, gold, and blue, and decorated with plants and statuary. The twenty-one classrooms, computer lab, and administrative offices are on several levels interspersed with patios and balconies. English is taught here, but the Spanish program is an integral part of the curriculum.

ACADEMIC BACKGROUND

Director Eugenio Cortés holds master's degrees in three different fields: Roman philology, Spanish literature, and applied linguistics. He has done postgraduate study and taught undergraduate classes at Fribourg Universität in Switzerland. All instructors are bilingual; each has at least a bachelor's degree, and one, Gabriela Pedraza, has a master's degree in Spanish. Before beginning to teach at the Baden-Powell Institute, each teacher is required to spend twelve months attending a 480-hour internal training course to prepare them to teach Spanish to foreign students.

CREDIT

The Baden-Powell Institute offers credit through the University of Southern Mississippi.

Community college credit may be arranged through Seattle Central Community College. *See "Getting College Credit," page 8.*

COSTS

Nonrefundable registration deposit: $50

Group instruction: $170/week

Private instruction: $14/hour

Additional Courses: (see list in Programs and Schedules) **$15–$17/lesson**

Spanish for high school students: $1900 for four weeks, all-inclusive

LODGING

HOME STAY

Housing with a Mexican middle-class family, including three meals a day; usually only one student is placed with a family, but double rooms are available on request.

Private room: $22/day

OTHER ACCOMMODATIONS

Double hotel rooms, no meals included.

Three-star hotel: $35 and up/night

Four-star hotel: $55 and up/night

PROGRAMS AND SCHEDULES

INTENSIVE SPANISH COURSE (GROUP INSTRUCTION)

This school specializes in individual instruction, but will provide group lessons for two or more students who are at the same level of language skill. The group course includes four hours of conversation, reading, and grammar exercises per day and is adapted for students in beginning, intermediate, advanced, and superior levels.

INTENSIVE SPANISH COURSE (PRIVATE INSTRUCTION)

This course includes four hours daily of private instruction consisting of conversation, reading, and grammar exercises. The instruction can be adapted to individual preferences.

SPANISH FOR HIGH SCHOOL STUDENTS

Baden-Powell Institute organizes a one-month stay in Mexico for groups of high school students age sixteen and up. The program includes travel preparation, tuition, accommodations with full board, transportation from Mexico City to Morelia and back, and two guided excursions. Instruction is adapted to students' previous knowledge of Spanish and to the syllabus of their next school year. Students spend four hours per day in classes: three hours of Spanish conversation, reading, and grammar, plus one hour of history, cooking, or arts and crafts.

Additional courses are available for an hourly fee of $15–$17/hour. Students with sufficiently advanced language skills may take Mexican and Latin American history and literature, medical, dental, and business terminology, and Mexican architecture, art, and muralism. All students may participate in Mexican cooking, folk dance, arts and crafts, computer courses, and watercolor painting. Guitar lessons are offered for students who bring their own guitars.

SPANISH FOR TRAVELERS

This is a special program for foreigners who would like to travel in Mexico but speak little Spanish or none at all. The program includes private or group lessons for four hours per day one or two weeks prior to a trip through Mexico. The tuition is the same as regular group or private lessons. While students are taking classes in Morelia, the school's in-house travel agent will organize their journeys.

The travel study program teaches expressions and phrases to enable students to communicate in Spanish at a basic level. The vocabulary is adapted to travel needs (transportation, sightseeing, menus, and accommodation, etc.). Mexican customs and traditions are also presented.

METHODS

The Baden-Powell Institute uses traditional methods to teach grammar, and uses the communicative method to teach conversation.

TEXTBOOKS

The school maintains a supply of textbooks for student use. Some examples: *Pasajes,* by Bretz, Dvorak and Kirschner (Random House); *Spanish 3 Years* (high school) by Levy and Nassy (AMSCO); and *Nuevo curso de conversación y redacción,* by Busquets and Bonzi, (published in Spain).

EXTRAS

FREE INTERNET ACCESS. The school maintains a computer lab with Internet access especially for student use.

FREE FAX. Students may send faxes from the school free of charge.

EASY CONTACT WITH THE DIRECTOR. The director gives every student a card with his personal telephone numbers, including his cell phone number, so that he can be contacted in case of a problem or emergency.

DOCTOR. A doctor is available to treat students' medical problems.

CONVERSATION GROUPS. Spanish and English students meet in conversation groups conducted partly in Spanish and partly in English; participation is free of charge.

Transportation. The school can arrange to pick you up at the Morelia bus station, the Morelia Airport, or the Mexico City airport. Charges for transportation vary. For more information, see the school's website: www.baden-powell.com.

What Distinguishes This School?

Individualized instruction. Individualized instruction seems to be the norm at this school. The $14/hour fee is very reasonable; schools in other areas charge $15–$25/hour for private instruction.

In-house travel agency. The institute's travel agency can answer questions and arrange travel for students, from bus tickets to airline tickets, hotels, and tours.

Computer lab. The computer lab has twelve computers available for student use. All computers are connected to the Internet and loaded with Microsoft Office. The computer lab is open all day and there's no charge for computer use.

Nursing program. Each year, the Baden-Powell Institute organizes a nursing program for the University of Portland in Oregon. In addition to Spanish-language courses, these students visit public and private hospitals, mental institutions, and nursing schools.

Centro Cultural de Lenguas (CCL)

At a Glance

Location: ✮✮✮
Facilities: ✮✮✮
Programs: ✮✮✮½
Overall Rating ✮✮✮½
Cost: $220/week (four hours/day)
Maximum number of students per class: six
Street Address:
    Avenida Madero Oriente 560
    Centro 58000
    Morelia, Michoacán, México

Tel: 52 443-317-4151
Fax: 52 443-312-0589
Email: edu@ccl.com.mx
Website: www.ccl.com.mx
Director: Alejandro Cerna Mier
Academic Coordinator: Husai Ching Pérez
Spanish Program Coordinator: Graciela Beltrán Cazares

Hidden behind the stone façade of a colonial building, Centro Cultural de Lenguas is right on Avenida Morelos, the main avenue in the historic center of Morelia. The entrance is through a courtyard surrounded by plants and dominated by the stained-glass window of the administrative office. All the classrooms open onto a second courtyard. There is also a small but well-equipped library and media center. This school teaches both Spanish and English.

ACADEMIC BACKGROUND

This school has not provided information on the academic background of its director and teachers.

CREDIT

The school does not offer credit; but some U.S. universities have offered credit for studies at CCL, most notably Western Washington University. Check with your home university to determine whether they can grant credit for courses taken at Centro Cultural de Lenguas.

Community college credit may be arranged through Seattle Central Community College. *See "Getting College Credit," page 8.*

COSTS

Deposit (applied to tuition): $100 (required four weeks prior the start of the course)

ONE-ON-ONE INSTRUCTION IN SPANISH LANGUAGE OR MEXICAN ART AND CULTURE

One week: $280

Two or three weeks: $250/week

Four weeks or more: $220/week

GROUP CLASSES

One week: $180

LODGING

HOME STAY (INCLUDES THREE MEALS)

Private room: $22/day

Shared room: $20/day

PROGRAMS AND SCHEDULES

Classes begin on Mondays throughout the year.

INTENSIVE SPANISH AND CONVERSATION

Basic, intermediate, and advanced Spanish classes are available. Besides grammar and vocabulary, students may choose topics from Mexican history, culture, or literature.

BASIC AND INTERMEDIATE LEVELS: Four hours daily, including two hours of grammar and vocabulary and two hours of conversational practice.

ADVANCED LEVELS: Three hours daily of grammar, vocabulary and conversation, plus one hour concentrating on one of the following subjects:

Contemporary Mexico

Mesoamerican cultures and modern Mexican Indian groups

Mexican History

Contemporary Mexican Literature

INTERNSHIPS

Centro Cultural de Lenguas and Patronato MESE, a private charity organization, offers advanced Spanish students the opportunity to work part-time with homeless Mexican children in an internship situation. Students attend Spanish classes an average of four hours daily and work in their internship for another four hours. Internships of up to ten weeks are available in the health and education fields. Students in the program pay their own costs and must register for credit with Oregon State University. Details on the program and the current fees are shown on Global Internship's website: http://ie3global.oregonstate.edu/mexic24.html.

VOLUNTEER WORK

Centro Cultural de Lenguas, Patronato MESE, and DIF (Desarrollo Integral de la Familia), a state office, also provide opportunities for students to do volunteer work with Mexican homeless children. DIF and MESE support about 350 boys and girls economically and psychologically. CCL Students participate in an informal manner by conversing with the children and participating in their activities. Volunteer work requires a high intermediate level of Spanish and a commitment of at least one month.

Methods

The method used at Centro Cultural de Lenguas focuses on oral fluency and precision, which the student achieves through practicing in real-life situations both inside and outside the classroom.

Textbooks

Several textbooks are used at CCL, as well as magazines, newspapers, and other relevant material.

Extras

Self-access Media Center. Students can practice their Spanish with videos and CDs of Mexican music, history and cultural traditions, audiobooks, and radio interviews. Games, newspapers, and magazines are also available.

Free Internet access. Free Internet access is available in the media center.

Excursions. Weekend excursions are offered to artisan villages and other places of interest in the state of Michoacán. Excursion prices range from $50–$70/person and may include two or three of the following towns or areas: Janitzio Island, Pátzcuaro, Uruapan, Zirahuén Lake, Santa Clara del Cobre, Paricutín volcano, Tupátaro, the Tingambato ruins, and the sanctuary of the Monarch butterfly. For more details and pictures of the various places, see the school's website: www.ccl.com.mx.

Cultural events. CCL provides opportunities for students to attend some of the many cultural events that are held frequently in Morelia, including concerts, art exhibits, plays, and dances.

What Distinguishes This School?

Emphasis on individual instruction or very small groups. Most classes have only two or three students.

Volunteer program. CCL's volunteer program gives students Spanish practice while providing a service to the community.

Internship Program. Internships give professionals and college students the opportunity to learn Spanish related to their chosen profession and gain an understanding of that profession in Mexico.

QUERÉTARO

Santiago de Querétaro is a charming Spanish colonial city often over-looked by tourists. Founded in 1531 on the site of a village of the Otomi Indians, the city is rich in history and colonial architecture. As you stroll through the downtown area, you'll see well-preserved baroque churches and mansions with graceful balconies and ornate façades. Nestled among these architectural masterpieces are well-tended plazas featuring fountains or statues paying homage to famous local sons and, in at least one case, a famous daughter. Some of the most important events of the Mexican Independence movement took place in this city between 1810 and 1821. One of the heroines of the insurrection against Spain was Doña Josefa Ortiz de Dominguez, who, as the wife of the *Corregidor* (magistrate) of Querétaro, was called *La Corregidora*. There is an impressive statue of *La Corregidora* in a small plaza, and her house still survives as the *Palacio de Gobierno* (Government Palace).

Two historic sites have gained national recognition as symbols of the city. Built of local sandstone between 1726 and 1735, the aqueduct of Querétaro rises to a height of seventy-five feet with dozens of arches extending about a mile. *El Cerro de las Campanas* (Hill of the Bells) was the site of the execution of the former Emperor Maximilian in 1867. It is now a large and beautiful park, its gardens leading up to hill topped by a huge statue of Benito Juarez, the president who returned from exile to depose Maximilian and order his execution.

Located in the heart of México about 130 miles north of Mexico City, Querétaro is not only a city steeped in history, but also an important center of industrial activity. Many international corporations have chosen to locate there instead of in overcrowded and polluted Mexico City. While the city has sprawled outward in recent years in response to its growth to some 600,000 inhabitants, in the center of the city the colonial flavor has been preserved.

CLIMATE

Querétaro's high plateau location moderates the climate, even though it is well south of the Tropic of Cancer. Daytime temperatures are usually in the 70s and 80s, except in the spring, when 90s are common. Nights are cool, especially in winter, when the climate is influenced by the near-by mountain areas where it sometimes snows.

GETTING THERE

BY PLANE

FLYING INTO QUERÉTARO. AcroMexico operates flights from the U.S. to Querétaro through either Mexico City or Guadalajara. Fares from Los Angeles are about $500. From New York, the ticket price is close to $700.

FLYING INTO MEXICO CITY OR GUADALAJARA. Fares to one of these cities may be considerably lower than flying directly to Querétaro, which is more or less equidistant from Mexico City on the south and Guadalajara on the north.

BY BUS

FROM MEXICO CITY. There are a couple of ways get to Querétaro by bus from the Mexico City Airport. Of the two options described below, Option 1 is the safest and fastest; Option 2 may be less expensive, but it takes longer and is less secure because of the long taxi ride across Mexico City.

OPTION 1. AeroPlus buses to Querétaro leave every hour from outside *Sala D* (National Gate D) in the Mexico City airport. To get to the Aero-Plus counter, leave the international customs area and take the escalator to the second floor. Proceed directly through the food court into a windowed hallway and look for the bus-ticket counter. After buying your ticket, make your way down the staircase to the right and look for the boarding area marked "Querétaro." The bus takes about three hours to get to Querétaro; the fare is about $17.

OPTION 2. If the AeroPlus bus is not available, you can take a taxi from the Mexico City airport to the North Bus Station (*Central de Autobuses del Norte*). *Always buy a ticket for an authorized taxi at the booth in the baggage area of the airport. Under no circumstances should you hail a taxi in the street in Mexico City—unauthorized or pirate taxis have been involved in robberies and kidnappings.* Allow about twenty minutes by taxi from the airport to the *Central de Autobuses del Norte*, where you can take one of the frequent buses to Querétaro. The trip takes about three hours, and the fare is about $18.

FROM GUADALAJARA. Take a taxi from the airport to the main bus station (*Central de Autobuses*). Be sure to buy a ticket for an authorized taxi, and let the taxi driver know that you are going to Querétaro so that you'll be dropped off in the right section of the enormous Guadalajara bus station. First-class buses depart every hour or two for Querétaro. The trip takes about five hours and costs $13–$15. For a shorter ride, take *"Directo"* service to avoid stopping in the smaller towns along the way. Some of the better and fastest bus lines are Primera Plus/Flecha Amarilla, Futura/EstrellaBlanca, Turistar, and ETN (Enlaces Terrestres Nacionales). Primera Plus/Flecha Amarilla allows you to see schedules and fares (*tarifas*) online at www.primeraplus.com.mx. Prices and comfort vary depending on which service you choose. ETN, Turistar, and Primera Plus are the most luxurious.

Olé Spanish Language School

At a Glance

Location: ☆☆☆☆
Facilities: ☆☆☆☆½
Programs: ☆☆☆☆
Overall Rating ☆☆☆☆½
Cost: $140/week (three hours/day)
Maximum number of students per class: five
Mailing Address:
Apartado Postal 446
C.P.76000 Querétaro
Querétaro, México
Street Address:
   Mariano Escobedo #32 (between Allende and Juárez streets)
   Colonia Centro C.P. 76000
   Querétaro, Querétaro. México

Tel/Fax: 52 442-214-40-23 or 52 442-214-2628
Email: info@ole.edu.mx
Website: www.ole.edu.mx
Director: Alejandra Gómez Sánchez
Spanish Program Director: Guadalupe Gómez Vázquez
Marketing Coordinator: Michelle Lases Pérez

ACADEMIC BACKGROUND

Director Alejandra Gómez Sánchez has a degree in business and tourism and marketing. Spanish Program Coordinator Guadalupe Gómez Vázquez has been teaching Spanish to foreigners for more than thirty years. Teacher Zoraida Alvarez has a bachelor's degree in education with a minor in Russian language. She has taught for thirty-four years and has written manuals for teaching Spanish as a Second Language. Victor M. Ayala teaches the culture and history classes. He has a civil engineering degree and has taught mathematics at the university level. He has lived in the U.S. and has a broad knowledge of Mexican history. All of the teachers have taken OLE's in-house workshops to be trained in the school's method of teaching.

OLÉ Spanish Language School is on a cobblestone street in the historic center of Querétaro. The school occupies an old estate, with classrooms around a large patio in the main building and an ample lawn and garden area in back. The ambiance at OLÉ is friendly and open, and it is within easy walking distance of the beautiful plazas, ancient churches, and monuments that make Querétaro one of the most interesting cities in Mexico.

CREDIT

U.S. university credit is available through National Registration Center for Study Abroad (NRCSA). Community college credit may be arranged through Seattle Central Community College. See "Getting College Credit," page 8.

COSTS

Nonrefundable registration fee: $60

Group Spanish Classes (fifteen hours/week): $140/week

Intensive Group Spanish Classes (twenty-five hours/week): $227/week

Cultural Group Spanish Classes (six hours/week): $50/week

NOTE: *There are significant discounts for multiple weeks of group classes. For example, a week of group instruction costs $140, two weeks $250, and three weeks $360.*

Intensive Private Spanish Classes (twenty-five hours) $350/week

Private lessons $14/hour

Two students studying together with the same tutor receive a 50 percent discount on the hourly rate.

Special Vocabularies: $25/hour

Executive Spanish (twenty-five hours/week): $276/week
(fifteen hours of group instruction plus ten hours with a tutor)

Intensive Executive Spanish (forty hours/week): $437/week
(twenty-five hours of group instruction plus fifteen hours with a tutor)

Weekend Intensive (ten hours total): $250
(six hours on Saturday and four hours on Sunday)

Spanish for Travelers (two weeks–thirty hours total): $300

Kids & Teen Program (fifteen hours/week): $160

Seniors Program (one week, all inclusive): $548;
(two weeks, all inclusive): $976

Books (one book per level): $25

Book copy for rent: $8

Internet & email use: $2/hour

Bank fee: $20 (Charged if you pay in U.S.-dollar checks or traveler's checks)

LODGING

HOME STAY

Private room with three meals: $150

Shared room with three meals: $130

The school has a one-student-per-family rule. Only students who travel together or have previously arranged for a roommate may share a room. For students who do not want to stay with a family, OLE will provide information on hotels and apartments.

PROGRAMS AND SCHEDULES

Classes start every Monday and generally run from 8 a.m. to 3 p.m.

Spanish group classes are held in the morning, and cultural classes in the afternoon.

Tutoring hours may be scheduled at any time from 8 a.m. to 7 p.m.

GROUP AND INTENSIVE GROUP SPANISH

There are ten levels of Spanish instruction, from complete beginner to post-advanced. A written and oral placement test is given to students who have previously studied Spanish.

PRIVATE LESSONS

Hourly lessons can be scheduled according to your instructional needs and the time you have available.

SENIOR PROGRAM

This program is especially designed for senior citizens. Each week of the program includes eight hours of Spanish lessons, four hours of cultural classes (in English), ten hours of cultural activities (in English), as well as home-stay accommodations. There is no registration fee for the senior program.

SPECIAL VOCABULARIES

These courses include technical and medical Spanish, and Spanish for engineers, lawyers, archeologists, architects, and other professionals. Students are given private lessons developed by professionals in each field.

METHODS

OLÉ uses a traditional method to present grammatical concepts, and the communicative method for conversational classes.

TEXTBOOKS

OLÉ uses the *Método de Español de Cuauhnáhuac.* This five-level course was developed by the Cuauhnáhuac Spanish Language Institute in Cuernavaca.

EXTRAS

INTERNET ACCESS. Internet access is available on campus for a $1.50 hourly fee.

CERTIFICATES. At the end of each block of instruction, students receive a certificate indicating the language level they have achieved.

FREE ACTIVITIES. Every Thursday from 4–6 p.m., a free activity is scheduled: workshops, games, movies, city tours, history classes, grammar workshops, or audio activities.

EXCURSIONS. Both day trips and weekend trips are offered to nearby cities and places of interest.

WEEKEND TRIPS

Guanajuato

Michoacán

Teotihuacán

Mexico City

Acapulco

DAY TRIPS

Sierra Gorda Queretana

Tequisquiápan

Bernal

San Miguel de Allende

San Joaquín

WHAT DISTINGUISHES THIS SCHOOL?

LOCATION. OLÉ is the only school in Querétaro that specializes in Spanish immersion courses. Querétaro is a gem of a city that is somewhat off the beaten path and sees fewer tourists than most of the other cities where schools are located.

A WIDE VARIETY OF PROGRAMS. OLÉ is a small school, but offers thirteen different programs plus private classes and special vocabularies.

FLEXIBILITY. You can sign up for just one week, several weeks, or a semester. Your study program can include from one to eight hours per day of instruction. You can choose whether to study grammar or conversation, reading, listening, spelling, composition, history, literature, or a combination of subjects.

OAXACA

Set in a mountain valley and surrounded by Indian villages, Oaxaca is known as Mexico's center of handicrafts (*artesanías*); it's a great place for shopping, but there's much more to this fascinating city. The Basilica de Santo Domingo is arguably the most elaborately decorated church in Latin America. Its gold-embellished decorations depict saints, flowers, and vines, and at the entrance, the family tree of the founder of the Dominican order. Oaxaca has a number of beautiful old churches, many museums, two huge markets, and many smaller ones. The church of La Soledad, which contains the figure of the city's patron saint, is well worth a visit, as is its small museum. The museum of the state of Oaxaca (next to Santo Domingo) contains the golden treasures of Monte Albán as well as ethnic salons representing the numerous indigenous cultures in the state.

The main plaza or *zocalo*, with its garden and decorative bandstand, is surrounded by sidewalk cafés. It connects with the *alameda*, a tree-shaded plaza in front of the cathedral where local artisans often set up their stands. Cars are prohibited from entering the *zócalo* and some nearby streets, creating pleasant walking for locals and visitors to enjoy the center of the city.

There are dozens of pre-Columbian ruins in the valley of Oaxaca. The largest and most spectacular is Monte Albán, situated on a mountain overlooking the city. It's accessible by bus, as is the ceremonial center of Mitla, farther down the valley.

Small towns in the valley of Oaxaca hold their markets on different days of the week, and each specializes in a specific handicraft. For example, Teotitlan del Valle is famous for weaving the best *sarapes* (woolen blankets) in Mexico. The colorful weavings resemble those produced by the Navajo in the U.S. Southwest. San Bártolo de Coyotepec is known for its unique black pottery, created for many years by the venerable and revered Doña Rosa, whose son continues the tradition. Fantastic carved wooden animals called *Alebrijes* are produced in the villages of San Martin Tilcajete, Arrazola, and La Unión Tejalapan.

The city of Oaxaca has everything except beaches, but the Pacific Coast will soon be only a three-hour bus ride away. A new *Super carretera* (superhighway) is being built to carry traffic from Oaxaca to the upscale

Pacific Coast resort town of Huatulco. If your tastes are more modest, you can take a bus north from Huatulco to the more pedestrian resorts of Puerto Angel or Puerto Escondido. There are also flights from Oaxaca to Huatulco and Puerto Escondido.

CLIMATE

Oaxaca is situated in the mountains at an altitude of about 5,500 feet. Because it is well below the Tropic of Cancer, it enjoys a moderate climate with two distinct seasons. The dry season extends roughly from November through April. During the rainy season, May through October, you can expect thundershowers in the late afternoon, usually clearing by evening. It seldom rains in the dry season, but it can get chilly at night, especially in December and January. High temperatures are usually in the 70s and 80s except during March and April, when temperatures often soar into the high 90s.

GETTING THERE

BY PLANE

Azteca, Aviacsa, and Aeromexico have daily flights to Oaxaca from Mexico City. The Oaxaca airport is small and easy to negotiate. To get into the city, look for the specially marked vans outside the terminal. Because of the high airfares between cities in Mexico, you may want to consider getting to Oaxaca from Mexico City by bus, which is considerably less expensive.

BY BUS

First-class and deluxe buses to and from Mexico City use the new superhighway toll road (autopista), which takes about six hours. Almost all buses to Oaxaca leave from Mexico City's TAPO bus station. There is no service directly from the Mexico City airport. To get to the TAPO bus station, take an authorized taxi from the airport. Always buy a ticket for an authorized taxi at the booth in the baggage area of the airport. Under no circumstances should you hail a taxi in the street in Mexico City—unauthorized or pirate taxis have been involved in robberies and kidnappings. Allow about twenty minutes by taxi from the airport to the TAPO, where you can take one of the frequent ADO buses to Oaxaca.

ADO (Autobuses del Oriente) and its affiliates handle most of the first-class and deluxe bus service from Mexico City to Oaxaca and throughout the southeastern portion of Mexico. *Primera clase* (first class) ADO buses depart about once an hour from the TAPO station; the one-way fare is $25. More legroom is available on the ADO GL, which offers seven or more departures per day for $34 one way. The best service is *ejecutivo*, which has more legroom and super-wide seats that recline almost into beds. Buses with *ejecutivo* service are called UNO and make five or more departures per day at $46 one way. During holidays, such as the Day of the Dead, Easter Week, and Christmas, all buses are full, and it's best to reserve a seat. It's possible to reserve on the Internet for the higher levels of service, ADO-GL and UNO. You can also check departure times and prices at either of ADO's websites: www.adogl.com.mx and www. uno.com.mx/.

In Oaxaca, the ADO station is on Calzada Niños Héroes, which is also the Pan American Highway. From the station, you should be able to get a taxi to your host family's home at a cost of $5–$7.

Instituto Amigos del Sol

At a Glance

Location: ★★★
Facilities: ★★★
Programs: ★★½
Overall Rating ★★★
Cost: $90/week (three hours/day) to $120/week (four hours/day)
Maximum number of students per class: five
Street Address:
    Libres #109, C.P. 68000
    Oaxaca, Oaxaca, México

Tel: 52 951-514-3484
Fax: 52 951-514-2046
Email amisol@oaxacanews.com or amisol1@prodigy.net.mx
Website: www.oaxacanews.com/amigosdelsol.htm
Director: Rogelio Ballesteros

A migos del Sol is a small school located in an older two-story building not far from the historic center of Oaxaca. Classrooms are arranged around a traditional patio, with balcony access to the upper story. The personable director, Rogelio Ballesteros, also works for a local newspaper, the *Oaxaca News*. Amigos del Sol specializes in individualized courses with a great deal of personal attention.

CREDIT

By pre-arrangement, the school will issue a certificate recording a student's attendance and grades. Check with your home university to determine whether they can grant credit for courses at Amigos del Sol. Community college credit may be arranged through Seattle Central Community College. *See "Getting College Credit," page 8.*

COSTS

Three hours/day, 9 a.m.–noon (fifteen hours/week): $90
Four hours/day, 9 a.m.–1 p.m. (twenty hours/week): $120
Additional class hours may be arranged at an extra charge.
Group classes: $6/hour   **Private lessons: $10/hour**

LODGING

HOME STAY

The Amigos del Sol website shows pictures of host families and their homes, along with a short description of the accommodations they offer.

Private room (no meals): $12/day
Private room and breakfast: $14/day
Private room and two meals: $17/day
Private room and three meals: $19/day

OTHER OPTIONS

The school recommends two bed & breakfast inns for students who would rather not stay with a family.

PROGRAMS AND SCHEDULES

INTENSIVE SPANISH

Classes begin on Mondays all year. Regular classes are held from 9 a.m. to

1:30 p.m., Monday through Friday. A late-afternoon schedule (4–7 p.m.) is also available. Intensive Spanish is offered in beginning, intermediate, and advanced levels. Daily instruction is divided into two sessions, each taught by a different instructor. The first session covers grammar, focusing on the structure and uses of the different verb tenses; the second teaches vocabulary and conversational use of the language.

METHODS

Teachers at Amigos del Sol use a conversational method and give written exercises as homework.

TEXTBOOKS

Amigos del Sol publishes its own textbook and instructional materials, which are given to students at no extra cost.

EXTRAS

INTERCAMBIO OR LANGUAGE EXCHANGE. Each student meets individually with a Mexican student to practice Spanish for thirty minutes and English for thirty minutes. There is no extra charge for this activity.

CULTURAL TOURS. The school arranges one visit per week to a place of interest in or around the city of Oaxaca. Each tour costs $5.

INFORMATIONAL SESSION. Amigos del Sol makes an effort to assist students by holding a casual informational session each day to answer questions about sightseeing and services in the Oaxaca area.

Salsa lessons and cooking classes. These special classes are offered at a small extra charge to enhance the language program.

WHAT DISTINGUISHES THIS SCHOOL?

INDIVIDUAL ATTENTION. Amigos del Sol offers Spanish instruction in a non-threatening environment with lots of individual attention.

LOW PRICES. The school's tuition cost is about half the tuition in other areas of Mexico.

NO REGISTRATION FEE. Unlike most Spanish-language schools, Amigos del Sol does not charge a registration fee.

ACADEMIA VINIGULAZA

AT A GLANCE

Location: ★★★★
Facilities: ★★★½
Programs: ★★★
Overall Rating ★★★½
Cost: $110/week (four hours/day)
Maximum number of students per class: five
Street Address:
   Abasolo 503
   Centro Historico, Oaxaca
   C.P. 68000, Oaxaca, México

Tel: 52 951-513-2763
Website: www.vinigulaza.com
Email: director@vinigulaza.com
Director: Catherine Kumar

Academia Vinigulaza is the Spanish-language department of "The Cambridge Academy," an English-language school, which is located in a recently remodeled colonial building a short walk from the historic center of Oaxaca. The classrooms are on two levels surrounding a traditional central courtyard. The director and teachers are vibrant and enthusiastic. Academia Vinigulaza is a good value: books, materials, and even excursions are included in the very reasonable tuition.

ACADEMIC BACKGROUND

Director Catherine Kumar is originally from England and has both a BA and an MA from Cambridge University. Most of the instructors have bachelor's degrees in education or teaching foreign language.

CREDIT

The school cannot grant college credit directly. However, they do issue a certificate that indicates the number of hours of class and workshops a student has attended and the grammar points they have covered. Check with your home university to determine whether they can grant credit for courses at Academia Vinigulaza. Community college credit may be arranged through Seattle Central Community College. *See "Getting College Credit," page 8.*.

COSTS

There is no enrollment fee.

Intensive Spanish Program

   Fifteen hours/week: $83   Twenty hours/week: $110

   Private Classes: $10/hour

Discounts are available for students who stay for more than one month and for groups of eight or more. There is also a 5 percent discount for pre-booking via the school's website.

The classes are complemented by a no-cost language exchange.

LODGING

HOME STAY

Breakfast only: $15
Breakfast and lunch: $19
Breakfast, lunch, and dinner: $20

OTHER OPTIONS Studio apartments and small fully equipped bungalows are available starting at 4,000 pesos/month (about $400).

PROGRAMS AND SCHEDULES

INTENSIVE SPANISH

Classes are held from 9 a.m. to 1 p.m., Monday through Friday. There are beginning to advanced levels. Students may attend classes from two to four hours per day with a small group or privately. The school will arrange a combination of group classes and private instruction for students who request it.

METHODS

Academia Vinigulaza emphasizes communicative skills directed toward holding simple conversations with native speakers. Grammar is presented through dynamic and productive exercises focused on using the language in practical situations.

TEXTBOOKS

The faculty at Academia Vinigúlaza is writing textbooks that will be published by the school. Currently, teachers often use the textbook *Pido la Palabra* in class. A variety of published materials are available to students and teachers in the school's resource library.

EXTRAS

FREE WORKSHOP. A Spanish slang workshop is offered free of charge.

FREE MATERIALS. Notebooks, pens, and course materials are included in the price.

FREE EXCURSIONS. Excursions to craft villages near Oaxaca are offered every Thursday.

CONVERSATION EXCHANGES OR INTERCAMBIOS. Mexican students learning English at the Cambridge Academy participate in weekly language exchanges with Academia Vinigúlaza students.

FREE AIRPORT PICKUP SERVICE. The school will pick up students at the Oaxaca airport upon their arrival.

FREE EMAIL AND INTERNET ACCESS. Internet access and email are available free of charge, but students must sign up to use the one available computer.

WHAT DISTINGUISHES THIS SCHOOL?

LOW PRICES. Academia Vinigúlaza's tuition is about half the cost of tuition in other areas of Mexico, and considerably less than some other schools in Oaxaca.

NO REGISTRATION FEE. The school does not charge a registration fee.

MONEY-BACK GUARANTEE. Academia Vinigúlaza offers the guarantee of a full refund if a student is unhappy after his or her first hour in class.

MANY FREE SERVICES AND EDUCATIONAL OPPORTUNITIES. Workshops, excursions, and even school supplies are included in the tuition.

BECARI LANGUAGE SCHOOL

AT A GLANCE

Location: ✫✫✫
Facilities: ✫✫✫½
Programs: ✫✫✫
Overall Rating ✫✫✫
Cost: $105/week (three hours/day) to $210/week (six hours/day)
Maximum number of students per class: five
Street Address:
   M. Bravo # 210
   Plaza San Cristobal
   Oaxaca, Oaxaca, México, 68000

Tel/Fax: 52 951-514-6076
Email: becarioax@prodigy.net.mx
Website: www.becari.com.mx
Directors: Martha Canseco Bennetts and
Sandra Rivera Bennetts

Becari Language School is located in a beautiful 200-year-old building a few blocks from Oaxaca's main square or *zócalo*. The sixteen classrooms surround a patio where students can sit and chat before and after class. The building also houses a restaurant and a café.

ACADEMIC BACKGROUND

Martha Canseco Bennetts holds a degree in dentistry from the Universidad Regional del Sureste and a British certificate for English teachers from the Universidad Autónoma Benito Juárez de Oaxaca. In addition to teaching Spanish at Becari, she has taught English to non-native speakers at the high school and university level. Sandra Rivera Bennetts holds a certificate in English as a Second Language from California, a British certificate for English teachers, as well as Food Engineering and Architecture certificates. In addition to teaching Spanish at Becari, She has taught English as a Second Language at the elementary level. Most of the teachers do not have degrees, but all have been trained in teaching Spanish as a Second Language.

CREDIT

Credit for Becari's programs is available through Austin Peay University in Clarksville, Tennessee, and Seattle Central Community College. *See "Getting College Credit," page 8.*

COSTS

Nonrefundable registration fee: $70

GROUP CLASSES

Regular program (fifteen hours/week): $105/week

Intensive program (twenty hours/week): $140/week

Super-intensive program (thirty hours/week): $210/week

Super-intensive workshop (thirty hours/week): $220/week

DISCOUNTS: Students who register for six or more weeks of group classes and pay the entire fee before their first class begins receive a 5 percent discount.

NOTE: *There is no reimbursement of prepaid tuition if a student cannot attend or must drop out for any reason.*

PRIVATE LESSONS

Regular program (fifteen hours/week): $225/week

Intensive program (twenty hours/week): $300/week

Super-intensive program (thirty hours/week): $450/week

Super-intensive workshop (thirty hours/week): $460/week

PROMOTIONAL PACKAGES

Spring (April and May), fall (August & September), and Christmas

These programs include twenty hours per week group intensive classes with maximum of five students. During these slow times of the year, tuition is discounted, there's no registration fee, and home-stay accommodations with two meals daily are included.

LODGING

HOME STAY (PAID TO THE SCHOOL)

One week (breakfast only): $105

One week (including two meals): $133

One week (including three meals): $147

Middle class hotel with bath: $20–$35/night

Two-room apartment with kitchen: $350–$500/month

PROGRAMS AND SCHEDULES

Classes begin every Monday. There is an orientation session on Monday at 1 p.m., including a short tour of the downtown area.

REGULAR PROGRAM

Three hours of classes, five days a week, are divided into two sessions, with a different teacher for each session. The first session includes a review of specific grammar points; in the second, students practice what they have learned through conversation and practical exercises. Classes run from 9 a.m. to 1 p.m. or 3 to 7 p.m., with a fifteen-minute break between sessions.

INTENSIVE PROGRAM

Four hours of classes, five days a week, are divided evenly between two teachers. Classes run from 9 a.m. to 1 p.m. or 3 to 7 p.m., with a fifteen-minute break between sessions.

SUPER-INTENSIVE PROGRAM

This program includes six hours of classes, five days a week, divided into three sessions, each with a different teacher. There's a fifteen-minute break between the first two sessions. The last session is held after the afternoon meal (between 4 and 5 p.m.).

SUPER-INTENSIVE WORKSHOPS

Four hours of regular Spanish classes, five days a week, divided into two sessions, each with a different teacher; and two more hours of workshops in the afternoon, 4 to 6 p.m. Students may choose to attend three different workshops per week. Cooking, weaving, ceramics, salsa, and folk dance are offered.

SPANISH FOR HEALTH PROFESSIONALS

Students in this program study Spanish in the mornings and work in a local hospital in the afternoon. Three of Becari's teachers have medical backgrounds, and one of the directors, Martha Canseco Bennetts, is a dentist.

SPECIAL PROGRAMS

Business Spanish

Spanish Literature Course

Spanish for Children

METHODS

A combination of communicative, cultural, and natural approaches is used at Becari. Subscribing to the theory that students can master Spanish if they understand the cultural and historical aspects of Latin America and Mexico, the school also provides opportunities to learn about pre-Hispanic culture, Latin American and Mexican history, literature, and politics.

TEXTBOOKS

Pido la palabra 1, 2, 3, 4, y 5, edited by the University of Mexico (UNAM)

Dos Mundos, by Terrell, Andrade, Egasse, and Muñoz

Pasajes, by Bretz, Dvorak, and Kirshener

Perspectivas, by Mary Ellen Kiddle and Brenda Wegmann

Intercambios, by Emily Spinnell and Carmen García

¡Eso es! by Joaquin Masoliver and Lila Hakanson

Spanish One, Two and Three Years, by Robert J. Nassi

Salsa y Salero, by Eduardo Neal-Silva

Español 1, 2 and 3 para extranjeros, by Ana María Maqueo

Becari's Workbook, edited by the Becari faculty

EXTRAS

MEXICAN UNIVERSITY LANGUAGE EXAM. Becari provides testing information for students who are interested in taking the exam "Posesión de la Lengua Española," which is recognized by the Universidad Autónoma de México.

FREE INTERNET ACCESS. The school has two computers with free Internet access for students.

GUEST LECTURE PROGRAM. Becari offers "cultural Wednesdays," a series of free lectures by well-known local artists, writers, politicians, and professors.

WEEKEND EXCURSIONS. The school offers an optional weekend on a farm where students can enjoy Mexican cooking and go horseback riding.

WEEKEND CLASSES. The school will arrange weekend Spanish classes upon request.

WHAT DISTINGUISHES THIS SCHOOL?

CREDIT OPTIONS. Credit is available through two different organizations.

TEACHERS' BACKGROUNDS. Curriculum vitae and personal information such as birthplace, nationality, and age of Becari's teachers are printed in the school's brochure.

DETAILED PROGRAM EXAMPLES. Also in the school brochure are detailed course outlines for the intermediate and advanced-level courses.

Instituto Cultural de Oaxaca

At a Glance

Location: ✭✭✭✭½
Facilities: ✭✭✭✭✭
Programs: ✭✭✭✭✭
Overall Rating ✭✭✭✭✭
Cost: $115/week (six hours/day)
Maximum number of students per class: ten
Street Address:
    Av. Juárez 909 C.P. 68000
    Oaxaca, Oaxaca, México

Tel: 52 951-515-3404
Fax: 52 951-515-3728
Email: inscuoax@prodigy.net.mx
Website: www.inscuoax.net
Director: Lucero Topete

S et in the spacious grounds of a 19th-century estate, Instituto Cultural exudes an atmosphere of elegance and gracious living. The expansive facility provides ample space for large groups. The various buildings,
including a grand mansion, patios, and gardens, are used for classes and
activities or simply for study, conversation, and relaxation.

ACADEMIC BACKGROUND

Most teachers hold bachelor's degrees in Hispanic language and literature and are certified to teach Spanish as a Second Language. Two of the
teachers also hold master's degrees in applied linguistics.

CREDIT

Four-week sessions at Intstituto Cultural de Oaxaca have been accepted
for credit at colleges and universities in the U.S., including University of
Rochester, University of Wisconsin, Bard College, Cabrillo College, Mendocino College, and City College of San Francisco. Verify the requirements
for credit from your home institution prior to attending. The institute
will provide course descriptions, contact hours, and grading procedures,
as well as evaluations and transcripts to document student progress.

U.S. university credit is available from University of Southern Mississippi or National Registration Center for Study Abroad (NRCSA). Community college credit may be arranged through Seattle Central Community
College. *See "Getting College Credit," page 8.*

COSTS

Nonrefundable registration fee: $50

The tuition includes seven hours of instruction daily

Group classes:

One week	Two weeks	Three weeks	Four weeks
$115	$220	$325	$420

Private classes: $12/hour

Materials and books: $15 for each level of classes

LODGING

HOME STAY

Private room with breakfast: $15/day

Private room with three meals: $21/day

PROGRAMS AND SCHEDULES

INTENSIVE SPANISH

The school year at Instituto Cultural is divided into monthly sessions. Students may begin classes on any Monday; however, the school recommends beginning classes on the first day of a session. Two five-week sessions with emphasis on Oaxacan culture are offered in the spring and summer; there's also a special two-week Christmas session.

Monday – Friday schedule:

9 a.m. to noon: Intensive grammar instruction

Noon to 1 p.m.: Conversation

Afternoons: Two-hour cultural workshops (*talleres*)

One-hour language exchange (*intercambio*)

Cultural workshops include Oaxacan cooking, backstrap-loom weaving, conversation, Mexican History, Mexican music, salsa dancing, and ceramics. In the summer, two additional workshops are offered: History of Education in Mexico (especially for teachers) and Mexican cinema.

INTENSIVE SPANISH

Instituto Cultural Oaxaca offers many levels of intensive Spanish-language classes, ranging from the absolute beginning level to advanced classes. Students are placed according to their performance on a written and oral exam.

In the beginning levels, students concentrate on mastering vocabulary, simple sentence structure, and phonetics for use in everyday situations. In the intermediate levels, they learn more complex vocabulary, sentence structure, and application of grammatical rules to their reading, writing, and speaking. In the advanced classes, there's special emphasis on perfecting each student's oral and written comprehension through discussion of topics such as current events, politics, or short stories.

SPANISH FOR MEDICAL PROFESSIONALS

This program includes three to four hours of intensive one-on-one daily instruction in medical terminology and language skills necessary for interactions with patients. Group programs include visits to hospitals and medical clinics in the city of Oaxaca and neighboring towns.

SPANISH FOR BUSINESS PROFESSIONALS

This program includes three to four hours of intensive one-on-one daily instruction focusing on Spanish-language skills relevant to the student's occupation.

SPECIAL PROGRAM FOR ADVANCED PLACEMENT SPANISH LITERATURE TEACHERS

This is a group program (minimum five students) for teachers who are preparing to take the A.P. Spanish Literature exam. The objective is to present a clear and thorough understanding of the authors, and their works, covered in the exam.

PRIVATE CLASSES

Private classes may be arranged on request, except during January or in the summer months, which are the school's busiest seasons.

SPECIAL PROGRAMS

The Instituto Cultural Oaxaca will custom-design programs for universities, medical, academic, and business professionals.

METHODS

Instructors incorporate a wide variety of teaching techniques, using films, audio-visual aids, role-playing, music, and games. Students are encouraged to apply their language skills in conversational sessions, language exchanges with local residents, and cultural workshops.

TEXTBOOKS

Instituto Cultural Oaxaca publishes its own textbooks, written and edited by their teachers.

EXTRAS

CULTURAL PROGRAM. Weekly lectures, concerts, fiestas, and films are included. Lectures on history, art, archeology, and anthropology are given in Spanish.

WORKSHOPS. Instituto Cultural offers a variety of workshops to introduce students to the rich culture of Oaxaca. Taught by local artisans, musicians, and dancers, these workshops include regional dance, pottery, and weaving.

KITCHEN. There's a kitchen where cooking classes are held, and where coffee and cookies are provided in the morning.

LANGUAGE EXCHANGE. Students are given the opportunity to meet with local university students and professionals daily for an hour of conversation in Spanish and English.

EXCURSIONS. Optional weekend tours to pre-Hispanic sites and artisan villages near Oaxaca are offered at an extra cost of $14–$16. Destinations include the archeological sites of Monte Albán and Mitla and the villages of Tule, San Bártolo Coyotepec (black pottery), and Teotitlán del Valle (weaving).

WHAT DISTINGUISHES THIS SCHOOL?

WIDE VARIETY OF CLASSES. This school offers a wider variety of classes than other schools in the Oaxaca area. There are seven levels and twelve sublevels in the Intensive Spanish-language program to ensure that each student enters at the proper level. There are also many choices for advanced students, including literature and history classes.

ATMOSPHERE. Instituto Cultural de Oaxaca is located in a very impressive facility, a 19th-century estate with several buildings and patios surrounded by lawns and gardens.

CONNECTION WITH LOCAL ARTISANS. Cultural workshops or *talleres* are integrated into the daily schedule and serve to introduce students to the arts and crafts of Oaxaca, Mexico's center of *artesanía*. Especially interesting is the backstrap-loom-weaving workshop, which features one-on-one instruction with a local artisan.

INSTITUTO DE COMUNICACIÓN Y CULTURA

AT A GLANCE

Location: ✮✮✮✮
Facilities: ✮✮✮½
Programs: ✮✮✮✮
Overall Rating: ✮✮✮✮
Cost: $150/week (three hours/day) to $200/week (four hours/day)
Maximum number of students per class: five
Street Address:
    Macedonio Alcalá 307
    Oaxaca, Oaxaca, México 68000

Tel/Fax: 52 951-516-3443
Email: info@iccoax.com
Website: www.iccoax.com
Director: Yolanda García Caballero

Instituto de Comunicación y Cultura (ICC) is tucked behind a restored 16th-century building on a walking street in the historic center of Oaxaca. To get to the school, you walk through a beautiful old courtyard with a large fountain as its centerpiece. An elegant restaurant popular with local business people occupies this courtyard. Beyond the restaurant and through a passageway is Instituto de Comunicación y Cultura, occupying two buildings that open onto a patio and garden.

ACADEMIC BACKGROUND

Director Yolanda García Caballero holds a bachelor's degree in business as well as a certificate in teaching Spanish as a Second Language. She lived in the U.S. for several years, and founded the Instituto de Comunicación y Cultura upon her return to Oaxaca in 1986. She is also the founder and publisher of Oaxaca's English-language newspaper the *Oaxaca Times.* All teachers hold bachelor's degrees, and three also hold master's degrees in Spanish language and pedagogy.

CREDIT

Instituto de Comunicación y Cultura does not grant credit directly, but the following U.S. universities have offered credit programs at ICC: Clemson University, Howard University, and the University of New Mexico. Community college credit may be arranged through Seattle Central Community College. *See "Getting College Credit," page 8.*

COSTS

GROUP CLASSES

Regular class (fifteen hours/week): $150

Intensive class (twenty hours/week): $ 200

PRIVATE LESSONS

Regular Class (ten hours/week): $170

Intensive Class (fifteen hours/week): $260

Super-intensive Class (twenty hours/week): $340

Children's Program (ages six to fourteen)

Including housing with a local family and all meals: $250/week

Without housing assistance and without meals: $160/week

Special Program: $450/week

Five hours/week of Spanish-language study with cultural work-shops, field trips, housing, and all meals.

OPTIONAL WORKSHOPS

Writing workshop: $11/hour

Indigenous weaving: $10/hour plus $6 for the loom

Mexican and Oaxacan cooking: $50 including three hours of class, materials, and lunch

Tropical dance: $6/hour

LODGING

HOME STAY

Private room, including two meals a day: $15–$20/day

OTHER OPTIONS

As a free service, ICC makes arrangements for other types of student housing. Rooms in local hotels cost $20–$120/night for a private room with bath.

There are several youth hostels in Oaxaca that charge $3–$8 for a shared room with shared bath.

Furnished apartments with utilities cost from $300–$500/month.

Houses can be rented for $500–$800/month, including utilities.

PROGRAMS AND SCHEDULES

Regular classes meet from 9 a.m. to noon. Alternate schedules are noon to 3 p.m. and 4 p.m. to 7 p.m.

INTENSIVE SPANISH

BEGINNING SPANISH LANGUAGE I AND II. This is an introduction to the spoken language, with emphasis on oral comprehension. Whenever possible, the learning process is related to everyday life in Oaxaca.

INTERMEDIATE SPANISH I AND II. In these courses, students practice more complex structures, with special emphasis on reading comprehension as well as speaking and writing.

INTERMEDIATE SPANISH III. Students practice everyday conversation, with compound grammatical structures and special emphasis on written expression.

INTENSIVE ADVANCED SPANISH IV. This course provides advanced practice of the most complex structures in the Spanish language, incorporating everyday situations and literature.

INTENSIVE ADVANCED SPANISH V. This course is designed to improve and develop listening and speaking skills to the level of a native speaker.

WRITING WORKSHOP. Appropriate for intermediate and advanced students, this seminar is dedicated solely to written Spanish, including sentence structure, spelling, punctuation, and numbers.

ADVANCED GRAMMATICAL PROBLEMS. Designed for advanced students and Spanish teachers, this course is an in-depth study of special difficulties in the Spanish language.

PHONETICS. Presenting the theoretical basis of Spanish phonemes, this course is designed to correct the problems of native language interference.

TRANSLATION SPANISH-ENGLISH. This course emphasizes Spanish syntax and contrasts it with English. Exercises are based on translations of business and scientific documents.

READING COMPREHENSION. Designed for intermediate and advanced students, this course utilizes multiple reading strategies to improve reading comprehension.

MEXICAN 19TH CENTURY LITERATURE AND 20TH CENTURY LITERATURE. Focusing on excerpts from the works of Mexican writers, this course includes directed reading, study, and discussion.

CONTEMPORARY INDIGENOUS GROUPS OF MEXICO. This is a formal analysis of the Mexican ethnic groups and the problems they confront in modern Mexico.

SPECIAL PROGRAM

This program provides five hours of intensive Spanish instruction daily. From 9 a.m. to noon, Grammar in Action is presented; from 4:30 to 6:30 p.m., students attend conversational classes relating to their professions. All educational materials, two field trips, and optional workshops are included in the tuition.

BUSINESS SPANISH

Designed to provide the fluency in Spanish needed to conduct professional tasks, this course includes business vocabulary, telephone skills, the language of meetings and discussions, negotiations, presentations, and business-communication skills.

MEDICAL SPANISH

Focusing on how to communicate with Spanish-speaking patients, this course teaches the technical Spanish vocabulary of medicine in a realistic context.

SPANISH PROGRAM FOR CHILDREN

This program is appropriate for children age six and up. It includes three hours of Spanish daily using the Total Physical Response method as well as all class materials and optional afternoon workshops. The school recommends at least four children per class.

The course is divided into two ninety-minute sessions. The first session is dedicated to Spanish conversation, grammar in action, Spanish games and songs, and Mexican history. During the second session, the children visit museums, markets, libraries, or Oaxacan artisans. In the afternoons, they may participate in a weaving or dance workshop. On Fridays and Saturdays, the children visit a market, an archeological site, or the house of the famous painter Rodolfo Morales in the village of Ocotlán.

CHILD-CARE: Host families may be able to take care for children for very reasonable prices. In addition, for children under six, there are several daycare centers near the institute.

METHODS

The techniques at the Instituto Cultural Oaxaca emphasize the communicative approach to language teaching, but grammar and phonology are also an integral part of the courses. While learning basic communicative functions, students are encouraged to express their own ideas and feelings.

Children's classes are taught using the Total Physical Response method (TPR), which pairs an action with each word or phrase the children learn.

EXTRAS

INTERNET ACCESS. Students of the ICC have free Internet access to send and receive email.

AIRPORT TRANSFERS. The school provides transportation to and from the Oaxaca Airport free of charge.

Workshops. In addition to the regular courses, several workshops are offered at extra cost, including a writing workshop, traditional indigenous weaving (in Spanish), Mexican and Oaxacan cooking, and a tropical dance workshop.

Field trips. On Fridays and Saturdays, the school sponsors field trips to craft villages and archeological sites in the valley of Oaxaca. Adult students pay $15 for these trips, but they are included in the cost of the children's program.

What Distinguishes This School?

Number and variety of classes offered. For a small school, ICC offers a large variety of college-level classes that will appeal to university students. In addition to the standard intensive Spanish courses, there is a writing workshop, and courses in phonetics, reading comprehension, grammatical problems, translation, literature, and indigenous culture.

Children's program. ICC may be the only school in Oaxaca that offers a comprehensive children's program.

Solexico Oaxaca

At a Glance

Location: ★★★★
Facilities: ★★★★½
Programs: ★★★★½
Overall Rating ★★★★½
Cost: $93/week (three hrs./day) to $154/week (five hrs./day)
Maximum number of students per class: five
Street Address
    Abasolo 217 Edificio Canseco Landero
    Entre Juarez y Reforma
    Oaxaca 68000, Oaxaca, México

Tel: 52 951-501-1364
Fax: 52 951-516-5680
Email: oaxaca@solexico.com or liz@solexico.com
Website: www.solexico.com
Director: Oscar Barrera Flores
Foreign Promotions Coordinator: Elizabeth Petter

U pon entering a quiet courtyard, the noise of the street is forgotten. You are in the shady patio of a beautifully restored colonial home in the historic center of Oaxaca. This central patio, the focal point of Solexico, offers a snack bar and a few umbrella tables where students congregate between classes. Around the patio are Solexico's light and airy classrooms decorated with local handicrafts.

ACADEMIC BACKGROUND

Director Oscar Barrera Flores has a master's degree in academic administration. Most of the instructors hold master's degrees in linguistics or foreign-language teaching.

CREDIT

Community college credit may be arranged through Seattle Central Community College. *See "Getting College Credit," page 8.*

COSTS

Nonrefundable registration fee: $80

Regular Program (fifteen hours): $114/week

Regular Program (twenty-five hours): $167/week

Individual Program (twenty-five hours): $330/week

Executive Program: $438/week

Individual hour: $16

Materials: $17/book

DISCOUNTS

There are substantial discounts for students who enroll for eight weeks or more.

LODGING

HOME STAY

	Half board	*Breakfast only*
Private room (per day):	$21.00	$18.00
Shared room (per day):	$18.00	$15.00

OTHER OPTIONS

The school will also arrange for accommodations such as condominiums, houses, and hotel rooms. Prices are variable and usually do not include meals.

PROGRAMS AND SCHEDULES

Courses begin every Monday year-round. Group classes, fifty minutes long with breaks, are held from 9 a.m. to 2 p.m. Students in the Individual Program also meet with private tutors from 2:30 to 5:30 p.m. There are seven levels of language instruction, and students are given placement exams to determine their appropriate level.

REGULAR PROGRAM (FIVE HOURS / DAY)

These classes meet from 9 a.m. to 2 p.m. and include three hours of grammar instruction and two hours of conversation.

REGULAR PROGRAM (THREE HOURS / DAY)

Classes are held from 9 a.m. to noon and are composed of three hours of conversation and grammar.

INDIVIDUAL PROGRAM (FIVE HOURS / DAY)

This course includes two hours of group instruction in the morning and three hours of one-on-one instruction from 2:30 to 5:30 p.m.

EXECUTIVE PROGRAM (EIGHT HOURS / DAY)

Students in the executive program receive three hours of intensive, one-on-one instruction in addition to the five-hour group classes of the regular program. An executive lounge, executive assistant services, and a virtual office are also provided.

PRIVATE LESSONS

Private lessons are available in the afternoons for additional fees.

VOLUNTEER PROGRAMS

Students at Solexico Oaxaca may participate in selected volunteer activities, such as tutoring, organizing games, teaching arts and crafts, cooking, and even designing websites and leading tours. The following programs accept volunteers from Solexico:

PATRONATO PRO CASA. An orphanage for abandoned or mistreated boys between the ages of five and sixteen.

MILPAS DE OAXACA. A non-governmental agency that works with rural and indigenous youth to offer positive and educational activities.

CANICA (CENTRO DE APOYO AL NIÑO DE LA CALLE DE OAXACA). An organization that serves children who have been abandoned or taken from their families due to abuse.

PATRONATO ESTANCIA FRATERNIDAD. A shelter for the families of those who are ill and being treated in the General Hospital of Oaxaca.

MUNDO NUEVO. A nonprofit organization that promotes environmental conservation and finds ways to treat all types of pollution.

TIERRAVENTURA. A small ecological tour company providing trips throughout the state of Oaxaca, their goal is to show visitors the "real" Oaxaca, and to create sustainable tourism by helping local communities.

CASA HOGAR NUEVA VIDA. An orphanage for homeless children between the ages of one and eighteen.

If you're interested in applying to one of these volunteer programs, please email Solexico Oaxaca: oaxaca@solexico.com.

METHODS

Solexico uses a traditional grammatical approach to provide the structural basis of Spanish and the natural approach to conversation, with situations and excursions to apply the language.

TEXTBOOKS

Soléxico's books and materials were written by their academic director and have been updated and improved by the instructors.

EXTRAS

FREE INTERNET ACCESS. Each campus provides Internet-linked computers for student use.

PHONE & FAX. Students may receive telephone calls and faxes for free.

EXCURSIONS. The school offers day excursions to Monte Albán, Hierve el Agua (a waterfall and swimming area), "el Tule" tree, Mezcal distilleries, and local churches and convents.

Soléxico also offers two- and three-day excursions to the Pacific Coast beach areas of Puerto Escondido, Puerto Angel, and Huatulco. Other activities, such as trips to neighboring towns, visits to archeological zones, mountain-biking tours, rappelling, hiking, rock climbing, or paragliding are available at extra cost.

LIBRARY. The campus has a small library with books on history, art, and literature, as well as magazines and newspapers in Spanish.

LECTURES AND ACTIVITIES. During the conversation hours, lectures are given on Mexican history, Zapotecan culture, national holidays, and other cultural and historical topics of interest.

AFTERNOON WORKSHOPS. After-class activities include cooking, arts and crafts, salsa classes, singing Mexican songs, or attending a fiesta or picnic. Students at Soléxico meet once a week with the faculty and staff in a restaurant or café for a "Café Social," a time for informal conversation.

EXECUTIVE PROGRAM SERVICES. For students in the executive program, an executive lounge is provided to facilitate communication with their clients and home office.

SYLLABUS. A syllabus for each course is available by post or email from the main office in Playa del Carmen.

WHAT DISTINGUISHES THIS SCHOOL?

VOLUNTEER PROGRAMS. Soléxico Oaxaca offers students the opportunity to work with local residents and children through a variety of volunteer programs.

TWO CAMPUSES. Students may choose to study in a colonial city in the mountains at Soléxico Oaxaca or in the beach community of Playa del Carmen on the Caribbean Coast.

EXECUTIVE LOUNGE. Soléxico's executive lounge provides executive students with an area to read the newspaper, watch television, or simply relax. During school hours, a bilingual executive assistant will take and deliver phone messages, send faxes and emails, and type letters.

D.E.L.E. DIPLOMA. Soléxico offers preparation for the D.E.L.E. (the official diploma of Spanish as a Second Language).

COLLEGE PLACEMENT EXAMS. The school also offers preparation for college Spanish placement exams.

SAN MIGUEL DE ALLENDE

F ounded in 1542 by Fray Juan de San Miguel, a Franciscan monk, San Miguel de Allende retains its colonial atmosphere with cobblestone streets and beautiful Spanish-style mansions, many of which have been restored to their former splendor. Perhaps the most striking aspect of San Miguel is the Parroquía, the pink stone gothic church, with its lawn and topiaries, which dominates the tiny main plaza. Legend has it that the architect took his inspiration from picture postcards of the gothic cathedrals of Europe. The church appears to be somewhat out of proportion, probably because it was built by local Indians who had no idea what a gothic cathedral should look like.

In the early 1800s, the town of San Miguel added the phrase *de Allende* in honor of Ignacio Allende, a native son and a hero of Mexico's war of independence from Spain. Because of its role in the struggle for independence, the nearby state capital of Guanajuato and the area around it are called *La Cuna de la Independencia* (the Cradle of Independence).

Long known as an art center and a place where wealthy Americans own homes and galleries, this small city (population 80,000), still exudes considerable charm. The historic center is great for walking, with interesting sights around every corner, shady parks, fascinating shops, and numerous small cafés.

GETTING THERE

BY PLANE

FLYING INTO LEÓN / BAJÍO AIRPORT. The closest airport is León/Bajío near the city of León, which is about two hours by car or bus from San Miguel. If you arrive at the right time you can take the American Express bus that leaves the León/Bajío airport at noon, connecting with the flights from Houston and Dallas. The cost is $27/person. If you're unable to make a connection with a bus going directly to San Miguel, for about $25 you can get a taxi from the airport to the Guanajuato bus station, and then take one of the frequent buses from there to San Miguel. The bus fare is about $8.

FLYING INTO MEXICO CITY OR GUADALAJARA. Fares to one of these cities may be considerably lower than flying directly to León/Bajío Airport. San Miguel is more or less equidistant from Mexico City on the south and Guadalajara on the north.

BY BUS

FROM MEXICO CITY. There are a couple of ways to get to San Miguel from Mexico City by bus. Of the two options below, the first is the safest and fastest way. Option 2 costs less, but may take longer and is less secure because of the long taxi ride across Mexico City.

OPTION 1: The simplest route to San Miguel is the AeroPlus bus (tel. 52 555-786-9357) which leaves the Mexico City airport for Querétaro about every hour and costs $17. You'll find the AeroPlus buses just outside the doors in front of *Sala D* (National Gate D). To get to the bus-ticket counter, leave the international customs area and take the escalator to the second floor. Proceed directly through the food court into a windowed hallway and look for the AeroPlus ticket counter. After buying your ticket, make your way down the staircase to the right and look for the boarding area marked "Querétaro." The bus takes about three hours to get to Querétaro, where you can transfer to a bus headed for San Miguel.

When you arrive in Querétaro, you'll be in Terminal A. Go out the door, turn right, and walk to Terminal B. Buses for San Miguel leave from Terminal B every twenty minutes, alternating between two bus lines: Flecha Amarilla and Herradura de Plata. The trip takes a little over an hour and costs $4.

OPTION 2: If the AeroPlus bus isn't available, you can take a taxi from the Mexico City airport to the North Bus Station, (*Central de Autobuses del Norte*). *Always buy a ticket for an authorized taxi at the booth in the baggage area of the Mexico City airport. Under no circumstances should you hail a taxi on the street in Mexico City — unauthorized or pirate taxis have been involved in robberies and kidnappings.* Allow about twenty minutes by taxi from the airport to the *Central del Norte*, where you can take a bus directly to San Miguel for about $10. If there is a several-hour wait for the next bus to San Miguel, check the schedule for buses to Querétaro, where you can transfer to a bus going to San Miguel de Allende (see option 1).

FROM GUADALAJARA. Take a taxi from the airport to the main bus station (*Central de Autobuses*). Be sure to buy a ticket for an authorized taxi, and let the driver know that you're going to San Miguel de Allende so that you'll be dropped off at the right section of the enormous Guadalajara bus station. Buses that go directly to San Miguel de Allende charge about $15 for the five-and-a-half-hour trip. *"Directo"* service avoids stopping in the smaller towns along the way. San Miguel's bus station is the prettiest and cleanest I've seen in Mexico!

While there are only a few direct buses from Guadalajara to San Miguel each day, buses depart from Guadalajara every hour or two for Guanajuato, where you can transfer to a bus going to San Miguel de Allende. The trip takes four hours and the fares are between $11 and $15. In Guanajuato you can transfer to a bus to San Miguel. The trip from Guanajuato to San Miguel takes about ninety minutes and costs $4–$7. Some of the better and faster bus lines are Primera Plus/Flecha Amarilla, Futura/EstrellaBlanca/Turistar and ETN (Enlaces Terrestres Nacionales). Primera Plus/Flecha Amarilla allows you to see schedules and fares (*tarifas*) online at www.primeraplus.com.mx. Prices and comfort vary depending on which service you choose. ETN, Turistar, and Primera Plus are the most luxurious.

ACADEMIA HISPANO AMERICANA

AT A GLANCE

Location: ★★★★
Facilities: ★★★★★
Programs: ★★★★★
Overall Rating ★★★★½
Cost: $165/week (seven hours/day)
Maximum number of students per class: eight
Street address:
  Mesones 4
  37700 San Miguel de Allende
  Guanajuato, México

Tel: 52 415-152-0349 and 52 415-152-4349
Fax: 52 415-152-2333
Email: info@ahaspeakspanish.com
website: www.ahaspeakspanish.com
Director: Paulina Hawkins
Registrar: Carmen Araiza

From the street, the façade of Academia Hispano Americana is rather understated, consisting of a stone wall with heavy wooden doors. Once inside, however, you may feel that you have stepped back in time. The school occupies a charming, elegant 18th-century Mexican villa, and the modern classrooms open onto ancient patios and gardens. Luxuriant vines cover the old stone walls, and mature trees provide shade, adding to the peaceful atmosphere. Academia Hispano Americana was founded in 1959 and offers a wide variety of classes, including an intensive Spanish Program and an official Diploma in Spanish as a Second Language.

ACADEMIC BACKGROUND

Director Paulina Hawkins is originally from the U.S. but has lived in Mexico for many years. Most of the teachers hold academic degrees, and all have significant experience teaching Spanish as a Foreign Language. Because of their diverse professional backgrounds they can offer students a chance to learn specialized vocabulary in many fields such as banking, business, computer science, healthcare, and sports. Sergio Ortega has a master's degree in pedagogy and is a former elementary school teacher. Miguel Angel Muniz has a bachelor's degree in business administration and has taught Spanish for eight years. Domitila Arteaga is a certified nurse who has taught Spanish for fifteen years.

CREDIT

The regular program at Academia Hispano Americana is accredited by the Mexican Secretary of Education (SEP). The school issues its own transcripts. Twenty hours of instruction equal one unit of credit. The Ministry of Education of the state of Guanajuato accredits the Diploma in Spanish as a Second Language program. Although credit for courses taken at the Academia Hispano Americana has been transferred to many foreign colleges and universities, consult with your home institution to make sure you'll receive credit for your studies.

Community college credit may be arranged through Seattle Central Community College. *See "Getting College Credit," page 8.*

COSTS

Nonrefundable deposit: $50 (applied to tuition)

SPANISH IMMERSION CLASSES (THIRTY-FIVE HOURS / WEEK)

	Group Classes	Private Classes
Two Weeks:	$330:	$700
Three Weeks:	$430:	$1050
One Session (4 weeks):	$480	$1400
Two Sessions:	$860	$2800
Three Sessions:	$1190	$4200
Additional Sessions:	$330	$1400

One-on-one instruction: $14/hour

SPECIAL INTEREST CLASSES

one student: $14/hour	two students: $15/hour
three students: $16/hour	four students: $17/hour

Discounts continue at this rate, so a class with five students would cost $18, or $3.60/hour per student, and a class with six students would cost $19, or $3.17/hour per student.

Diploma in Spanish as a Second Language requires five four-week sessions.

TUITION

	Single Room	Double Room
First Session: $480	$644	$504
Second Session: $380	$644	$504
Third Session: $330	$644	$504
Fourth Session: $330	$644	$504
Fifth Session*: $610	$644	$504
Total Program: $2130	$3220	$2520

---

* Tuition for the diploma in Spanish includes an extra twenty hours of specialized vocabulary work.

LODGING

HOME STAY

Family placement fee: $20

Private room with three meals: $23/day

Shared room with three meals: $18/day

OTHER OPTIONS The school maintains lists of recommended hotels and bed & breakfast inns for students.

PROGRAMS AND SCHEDULES

Classes meet from 8:30 a.m. to 6:25 p.m. Monday through Thursday, and 8:30 a.m. to 12:30 p.m. on Fridays. Friday afternoons are reserved for special-interest courses and activities.

INTENSIVE SPANISH COURSE

The focus of this course is communication in Spanish. Students develop the ability to speak and understand spoken as well as written Spanish. They also acquire cultural information about Mexico. The course is a combination of the following core courses and seminars:

Spanish Conversation

Pronunciation and Diction

Writing Workshop

Grammatical Problems

Additional classes

History of Mexico

Study of the Mexican Mind

Modern Mexican Indian Groups

Mexican Themes

Mexican Folklore

Folk Singing and Folk Dancing

Current Events in Spanish

Novohispanic Literature

Mexican 19th Century Literature and Modernism

Twentieth Century Mexican Literature

The Novel of the Mexican Revolution

ONE-ON-ONE SPANISH

This is offered for students who have an urgent need to learn to communicate in Spanish, need to learn it for a special purpose, or do not function well in group classes. The pace is adjusted to the student's ability to absorb the material. A maximum of five hours is recommended per day. One-on-one instruction is available from 8:30 to 9:30 a.m., from 12:30 to 2:30 p.m., and from 4 to 6 p.m.

SPECIAL INTEREST SPANISH

These are courses for students who need help in a specialized vocabulary or are interested in specific areas of Mexican life. Individual or small-group lessons are available in a wide variety of areas: business and marketing, bookkeeping, banking, computer science, nursing, education, guitar, folk singing, folk dancing, Mexican cooking, interior decorating, tai chi, karate, and gymnastics. Some of these classes include visits to places where specialized vocabulary is used: schools, hospitals or clinics, banks, etc.

DIPLOMA IN SPANISH AS A SECOND LANGUAGE

This diploma (or certificate) course requires 600 hours of classroom work and 100 hours of professional practice. It can be completed in twenty weeks or five four-week sessions. Students study Spanish using ¡Vamos a hablar español!, Levels I through V, and attend the core courses listed above in the Intensive Spanish program. In addition, they attend a sociology seminar and take courses in Mexican history and literature, current events in Spanish, folk singing and dancing, and specialized vocabulary. The 100 hours of professional practice may be completed during the fourth and fifth sessions or in a sixth four-week session.

METHODS

Academia Hispano Americana uses a communicative approach, with texts that are based on rational-functional categories of language. Students are encouraged to practice the language in pairs or groups, with the teacher initiating the activities, assisting, and assuming a counseling role.

TEXTBOOKS

Vamos a hablar español I through V, which contains five levels of study and was written by the faculty.

EXTRAS

SPECIAL HELP. The school offers extra assistance free of charge for students who need it. A teacher is available for consultation between 8 and 8:30 a.m. and 9 and 9:30 a.m. daily. During office hours, 8 a.m. to 7 p.m., the office staff will help with living situations, money matters, and other problems.

FIELD TRIPS. The school organizes one-day field trips to places of historical interest, such as the colonial cities of Querétaro and Guanajuato, the town of Dolores Hidalgo, and the Atotonilco pilgrimage shrine and hot springs.

BUS INFORMATION. The school handbook lists all bus lines that serve San Miguel de Allende and includes telephone numbers, schedules, advice, and information on fares. This information is sometimes difficult to obtain outside the bus terminal.

WHAT DISTINGUISHES THIS SCHOOL?

WELL ESTABLISHED. Academia Hispano Americana was founded in 1959 and has operated continuously ever since.

DIPLOMA IN SPANISH AS A SECOND LANGUAGE. Academia Hispano Americana is officially authorized by the Ministry of Education of the state of Guanajuato to offer this five-month diploma or certificate program. A person who holds a Diploma in Spanish as a Second Language is qualified to work in a position where fluency in Spanish is necessary, in fields such as international commerce, sales, banking, public relations, medicine, and diplomacy.

ABILITY TO GRANT CREDIT. One semester unit of credit is given for every twenty hours the student spends in class. Each four-week session is typically worth four credits. The school can provide a list of colleges and universities that have accepted its credits for transfer.

WIDE VARIETY OF SPECIAL-INTEREST COURSES. Because the teachers have academic degrees and professional experience in many of areas, the school is able to offer special-interest classes ranging from bookkeeping and banking to computer science and interior decorating.

HISTORIC CAMPUS. The campus of Academia Hispano Americana is located in an impressive colonial mansion that was built in the 1700s. The classrooms are modern and well equipped, and students congregate in a series of plant-filled patios between classes. The thick masonry walls are covered with climbing vines, and a few well-placed trees provide shade.

INSTITUTO ALLENDE

AT A GLANCE

Location: ✫✫✫✫
Facilities: ✫✫✫✫✫
Programs: ✫✫✫
Overall Rating ✫✫✫✫
Cost: $117.50/week (four hours/day)
Street address:
 Ancha de San Antonio #20
 San Miguel de Allende 37700
 Guanajuato, México

Tel: 52 415-152-0226
Fax: 52 415-152-4538
Email: iallende@instituto-allende.edu.mx
Website: www.instituto-allende.edu.mx
Director: Rodolfo Fernández Martínez Harris
Financial Aid Director: Marc P. Taylor

Founded in 1950, Instituto Allende is a well-known art school associated with the University of Guanajuato. The institute offers a wide variety of art classes, which can be combined with Spanish classes. The campus occupies the former summer palace of Manuel Tomás de la Canal, which was constructed in 1734. There are many patios, gardens, and fountains throughout the property. The park-like grounds afford grand views of the town of San Miguel de Allende and the spire of its gothic church.

CREDIT

Instituto Allende grants credit for its courses through University of Guanajuato. Many universities in the U.S. and Canada have accepted transfer credits from this Mexican university. Before signing up, check with your college or university to see whether they'll accept credits from the University of Guanajuato. One credit is awarded for every fifteen classroom hours. Eight credits may be earned in a four-week cycle of Intensive Spanish, and other courses have proportional values. The Instituto is on the quarter system; three quarter credits equal two semester credits.

Students at Instituto Allende may also earn university credit through University of Southern Mississippi. Community college credit may be arranged through Seattle Central Community College. *See "Getting College Credit," page 8.*

COSTS

INTENSIVE SPANISH (four hours/day): $470 for four weeks

Two-hour Semi-intensive Spanish: $250 for four weeks

Conversational Spanish (one hour daily): $125 for four weeks

Spanish Verb Conjugation (three hours/week): $12.50/week

Introduction to Mexican Literature: $290 for four weeks

TOTAL IMPACT SPANISH

Three hours/day:

One week	Two weeks	Three weeks	Four weeks
$180	$325	$455	$585

Four hours/day:

One week	Two weeks	Three weeks	Four weeks
$230	$415	$585	$760

Five hours/day:

One week	*Two weeks*	*Three weeks*	*Four weeks*
$280	$505	$720	$890

Six hours/day:

One week	*Two weeks*	*Three weeks*	*Four weeks*
$320	$585	$855	$1010

Students may take Total Impact Spanish for fewer than three hours per day at a tuition rate of $13/hour.

LODGING

HOME STAY

Instituto Allende will provide a list of families that take in guests. Students may make their own arrangements to stay with a family or request help from the institute. Family stays include three meals a day.

Private room: About $22/day/person

Double occupancy room: About $20/day/person

OTHER ACCOMMODATIONS

The Instituto maintains a list of places for rent, from a one-bedroom apartment on campus at $250/month to a two-bedroom home with views of the city at $850/month. The school also has art-studio space for rent.

PROGRAMS AND SCHEDULES

The standard program consists of twelve four-week sessions per year. Students may enter at four-week intervals. Total Impact Spanish follows a more flexible calendar, beginning every Monday. Class schedules are shown on the school's website: www.instituto-allende.edu.mx.

Instituto Allende offers four levels of language instruction:

Level A (no knowledge)

Level 1 (beginner)

Level 2 (intermediate)

Level 3 (advanced)

INTENSIVE SPANISH

Designed to develop skills in listening, speaking, writing, and thinking in Spanish, this course also covers popular speech such as slang, gestures, sayings, and everyday expressions. Each course lasts four weeks, and classes are held from 9 a.m. to 1 p.m. and 4 to 6 p.m. daily. Class size is limited to six students.

TWO-HOUR SEMI-INTENSIVE SPANISH

Students who have less time can study Spanish for just two hours daily. This course is often taken by students who are also enrolled in art courses. Each course lasts four weeks, and classes are held from 9 to 11 a.m. or 3 to 5 p.m. daily.

CONVERSATIONAL SPANISH

This fifty-minute class is held daily, Monday through Friday from 12:10 to 1 p.m. The class is limited to ten students and is open to all levels.

SPANISH VERB CONJUGATION

A one-hour class on verb conjugation is held Monday, Wednesday, and Friday, 11 a.m. to noon. It includes one tense each week, starting with the present, and continuing with the preterit (simple past), imperfect, future, and subjunctive.

INTRODUCTION TO MEXICAN LITERATURE

This course introduces Mexican literature through the works of one author. Students discuss what they have read, and learn to write essays in Spanish. The class meets Monday through Thursday, 4–6 p.m.

TOTAL IMPACT SPANISH

For those who want to learn Spanish as quickly as possible, the Institute offers one-on-one instruction from three to six hours a day. All levels, from beginning to advanced, are taught, with special consideration given to professional or business requirements.

METHODS

Instructors use a communicative approach, presenting the patterns and structure of Spanish through directed, planned conversation. The instituto is alert to the latest trends in language teaching and adopts new techniques from time to time.

EXTRAS

FREE WORKSHOPS. Students in the Intensive Spanish program can attend workshops in Pronunciation and Diction, Advanced Grammar, Written Spanish, Everyday Spanish, Idiomatic Expressions, Reading, Mexican Traditions, Round Table Discussions, and Creativity.

FIELD TRIPS. The institute provides one-day and overnight field trips at extra cost. These trips visit colonial cities, archeological zones, ancient shrines, and traditional villages. Some typical destinations are Guanajuato, Querétaro, Mexico City, the ruins of Teotihuacán, and Lake Pátzcuaro.

CAFÉ. In the main courtyard on campus, there is an outdoor café where students can get snacks, sandwiches, coffee, juices, and soft drinks.

WHAT DISTINGUISHES THIS SCHOOL?

ART AND SPANISH. Instituto Allende is an old, established art school that has also been offering Spanish courses for many years. Art students who wish to learn Spanish can have the best of both worlds here by taking a combination of art classes and Spanish instruction.

ASSOCIATION WITH THE UNIVERSITY OF GUANAJUATO. Instituto Allende functions as a branch campus of the University of Guanajuato. The university issues transcripts to students who complete the Intensive Spanish program, and its credits are widely accepted by U.S. colleges and universities.

BEAUTIFUL CAMPUS. The large campus is a former hacienda that has been incorporated into the town of San Miguel de Allende. It is slightly elevated, and the garden area offers views of the town and its famous church.

INSTITUTO HABLA HISPANA

AT A GLANCE

Location: ★★★½
Facilities: ★★★½
Programs: ★★★
Overall Rating: ★★★½
Cost: $100/week (five hours/day)
Maximum number of students per class: ten
Street address:
  Calzada de la Luz #25
  Apartado 689, CP 37700
  San Miguel de Allende, Guanajuato, México

Tel: 52 415-152-0713 • Fax: 52 415-152-1535
Email: info@mexicospanish.com
Website: www.mexicospanish.com
U.S. Address (for payments):
  Angelica Rodriguez, Director
  Habla Hispana Spanish School
  220 N Zapata Hwy #11A
  Laredo, TX 78043, U.S.A.

Director: Angélica Rodríguez
General Manager: Attilio Tonelli

A s you walk along the cobblestone streets of San Miguel de Allende, it's not always easy to imagine what's behind the doors in those ancient stone walls. One of those doors opens into Instituto Habla Hispana, a small school with four classrooms and a central patio and garden. It's within walking distance of the historic center of San Miguel de Allende. General manager Attilio Tonelli is originally from Italy. He is friendly and welcoming, but it is his Mexican wife, Angélica Rodríguez, who designed the language programs. This school emphasizes instruction and highlights its faculty's qualifications, which are featured on the website.

ACADEMIC BACKGROUND

Angélica Rodríguez, founder and director of the school, is a graduate in Spanish of the Instituto Tecnológico of San Luis Potosí. She has been teaching Spanish as a Second Language for fifteen years. The principal teachers at Instituto Habla Hispana all have college degrees and many years of teaching experience. Socorro Olalde Chavéz and Jorge Arteaga Soto are graduates in Spanish of the Superior School of Querétaro and have taught Spanish as Second Language for more than twenty-five years. Martha Rodríguez Barbosa is a graduate in communication of the Instituto Hispano Inglés in San Luis Potosí and has been teaching Spanish for more than twenty years.

CREDIT

The school does not issue credits that are transferable to the U.S.; however, they will provide documentation needed for academic purposes. Consult with your home university to ascertain whether they'll grant credit for courses at Instituto Habla Hispana.

Community college credit may be arranged through Seattle Central Community College. *See "Getting College Credit," page 8.*

COSTS

Nonrefundable deposit: 40% of tuition

STANDARD PROGRAM (thirty hours/week)

1 week	2 weeks	3 weeks	4 weeks	5 weeks	6 weeks
$100	$200	$290	$380	$480	$580

Private Lessons: $12/hour

Private lessons for two or more students with the same teacher: $8/hour per student.

Lodging

Home Stay (including three meals a day)
Shared room: $17/day
Private room: $20/day

Other options

Habla Hispana maintains a list of hotels in San Miguel de Allende with phone numbers and addresses. Room rates start at about $35/night.

The school will provide contacts for apartment and house rentals. Rents vary from around $500/month for a one-bedroom apartment, to $5000 or more per month for a luxurious colonial-style house.

Programs and Schedules

The academic calendar is divided into twelve four-week terms, but Instituto Habla Hispana will accept students anytime throughout the term if space is available.

Standard Program

This program includes twenty hours/week of intensive Spanish as well as ten hours/week of seminars, workshops, and guided walking tours of San Miguel. Intensive Spanish classes are held from 9 a.m. to 1 p.m.; seminars are held from 4 to 5:30 p.m.

There are three levels of classes:

Nivel Principiante (Beginner)
Nivel Intermedio (Intermediate)
Nivel Avanzado (Advanced)

Methods

Instituto Habla Hispana uses a communicative approach. Emphasis is on verbal interaction in the classroom, and class placement is based more on fluency than on academic knowledge.

Textbooks

Textbooks written by the teachers and published by the school are included in the tuition.

EXTRAS

MAIL. Students may receive and send mail at the school.

TELEPHONE AND FAX. Students receive incoming telephone calls and faxes at the school at no extra charge. Outgoing calls or faxes to the U.S. cost about $1.50/minute.

EMAIL ACCESS. The school provides free email access. The first outgoing email page is free; additional pages cost U.S. 50¢ each. In addition, there are several Internet cafés within a block or two of the school that charge about $1/hour.

MONEY EXCHANGES. Students can exchange foreign currency for pesos with no commission.

SECURITY BOX. The school provides students a security box for their valuables.

EXCURSIONS. Upon request for a minimum of six students, the Institute organizes one- or two-day tours that cost $40/person and up. Destinations include Guanajuato, Dolores Hidalgo, Pozos, and a visit to a ranch near San Miguel for horseback riding and a Mexican lunch.

ESCORTED TRANSPORTATION. Transportation is available from Mexico City or Leon/Bajío Airport to the student's accommodation in San Miguel.

From Mexico City Airport

Private car (up to three people): $180

Minivan (up to six people): $195

From Leon/Bajío Airport

Private car (up to three people): $75

See the "Getting There" section in the general information about San Miguel for some less expensive transportation options.

WHAT DISTINGUISHES THIS SCHOOL?

SMALL AND PERSONAL. Instituto Habla Hispana is smaller than the other Spanish-language schools in San Miguel de Allende. They specialize in personal attention and track their students very carefully. Student placement is re-evaluated weekly, and students may, if necessary, transfer to a level more appropriate to their skills.

Yucatan and the Caribbean Coast

Cancún

Before 1975, the peninsula of Cancún was a beautiful but primitive area frequented by local fishermen and a few adventurers who came to dive in its crystal-clear waters. In the late 1960s, the area was chosen by the Mexican government as the future site of a modern resort city. Those plans have succeeded spectacularly. Today Cancún is a tourist mecca and its *"Zona Hotelera"* (Hotel Zone) boasts dozens of high-rise hotels interspersed with shops, restaurants, bars, and discotheques. The influx of visitors has brought prosperity to what used to be one of the poorest areas in Mexico. It has also spread development up and down the formerly sleepy Caribbean coast.

Many first-time visitors don't realize that there are two Cancúns: the *Zona Hotelera* and *Ciudad Cancún* (Cancún City), where almost everyone who works in the hotel zone lives. Ciudad Cancún functions and looks like a normal Mexican town. It has its main plaza, its churches, a bus station, and even a market. Although there are many small hotels, shops, and restaurants in Ciudad Cancún, they serve locals and visitors alike, in contrast to the twenty-mile-long *Zona Hotelera,* which exists only for tourists.

Cancún is a good location from which to visit the Mexican Caribbean coast, the offshore islands, and nearby Mayan ruins. Spectacular snorkeling and diving are just a ferry ride away on the islands of Cozumel and Isla Mujeres. The ruins of Tulum, the only seaside Mayan city, and Cobá, a huge and largely unexcavated site, are only a bus ride away. You can also head for the interior. The ancient Mayan city of Chichén Itzá can be visited on a day trip, although I recommend you stay overnight and tour the site in the early morning before the tourist buses arrive.

Climate

Temperatures in Cancún vary from warm to hot all year round. The best time to come is November through February, when the high temperatures tend to be in the 70s and 80s. It's always humid, but during the summer it's also hot, with high temperatures in the 90s and lows in the high 70s. In summer there are usually thundershowers in the afternoons. Cancún is also subject to tropical storms and hurricanes, which tend to hit between July and October.

Getting There

Many airlines, including Mexicana, Aeromexico, Continental, American, Alaska, and U.S. Air, fly directly from U.S. cities to Cancún. The airport is ten miles south of town and has two terminals with shuttles between them. Upon arrival at the Cancún airport, you'll need to get transportation to Ciudad Cancún if you're staying with a family or in a small hotel or hostel. If you're staying in a condo or large hotel, you may need to go to the Hotel Zone or Zona Hotelera. Make sure to get specific directions from your school before leaving.

A private taxi from the airport to Ciudad Cancún or the Hotel Zone (*Zona Hotelera*) costs $35 – $40. Some van services are almost as expensive. If you're going to Ciudad Cancún, the best option is to take the nonstop ADO bus that drops you off at the bus station (*Central Camionera)* in the downtown area. The cost is only 15 pesos each way (about $1.50). These buses run from 5 a.m. to past midnight, and you can catch them outside Terminal 2. If you're going to the *Zona Hotelera*, there are inexpensive shuttle vans (*colectivos*) that also leave from the airport, stopping at hotels to let off passengers, then going back through Ciudad Cancún. You can buy a ticket for about $8 from the booth to the far right as you exit the airport terminal. Then you may have to wait in line until the shuttle is ready to leave. These shuttles run a very long route and are only practical if you're going to the Hotel Zone. Since Ciudad Cancún is the last stop on that route, it could take you two or three hours to get there! All of this information and more is available on the website of a travel agency called Do Cancún!: www.doCancún.com. To get the airport transportation details, click on "Travel Info" and "Transportation." This excellent website also has detailed information on activities, tours, shopping, and much more.

EL BOSQUE DEL CARIBE

AT A GLANCE

Location: ★★★½
Facilities: ★★★★
Programs: ★★★★
Overall Rating: ★★★★
Cost: $135/week (three hours/day) to $187/week (five hours/day)
Maximum number of students per class: six
Street Address:
   Avenida Nader 52 SM 3
   77500 Cancún, Quintana Roo, México

Tel: 52 999-884-1065
Fax: 52 999-892-7548
Email: info@cancun-language.com.mx
Website: www.cancun-language.com.mx
Director: Eduardo Sotelo Nava
Administrative Director: Natalie Steiger de Sotelo

Cancún isn't the best place to learn Spanish, because it attracts large numbers of English-speaking tourists. If you plan to be in the area, however, El Bosque del Caribe is a bona fide Spanish-language school in Ciudad Cancún, which is more of a traditional Mexican town than the nearby beach area. For students interested in scuba diving, El Bosque del Caribe is one of the few schools that offer PADI diving certification in combination with Spanish-language instruction. Located in a small compound just off one of the main avenues, the school is inviting, friendly, and informal, and students appear to enjoy themselves learning Spanish in a non-threatening atmosphere. Eduardo Sotelo Nava and his wife, Natalie, seem to operate the school as though the students were guests in their home.

ACADEMIC BACKGROUND

The director, Eduardo Sotelo Nava, was certified as a teacher of Spanish as a Second Language by Universidad Autónoma del Estado de Morelos in Morelia, Michoacán. He taught Spanish at Ideal Latinoamericana in Cuernavaca for three years, worked in Switzerland for five years, and has attended various seminars on second-language learning. Administrative Director Natalie Steiger de Sotelo holds a degree in publicity and economics from Switzerland. Both Eduardo and Natalie are multilingual. All of the principal instructors have bachelor's degrees or have been trained in teaching Spanish as a Second Language.

CREDIT

Community college credit may be arranged through Seattle Central Community College. *See "Getting College Credit," page 8.*

COSTS

Nonrefundable enrollment fee: $100

Intensive Course (twenty-five hours/week): $187/week

Mini Course (fifteen hours/week): $135/week

Private Lessons: $20/hour or $320 for twenty hours

Business program (thirty hours/week): $240/week

Combined study program–Cancún and Cuernavaca, family stay included

One week in Cuernavaca plus one week in Cancún: $820

One week in Cuernavaca plus two weeks in Cancún: $1150

NOTE: *The classes in Cuernavaca are held at Ideal Latinoamericana.*

DIVING PROGRAM WITH PADI CERTIFICATION

Including twenty-five-hour intensive Spanish course, one week: $587; two weeks: $724

Including fifteen-hour mini Spanish course, one week: $485; two weeks: $620

Spanish and Flamenco Dance Course (four hours/week):

   Including twenty-five-hour intensive Spanish course: $342/week

   Including fifteen-hour mini Spanish course: $290/week

NOTE: *The Flamenco classes begin on specific dates and are held with a minimum of five students per group. More details on the dance and diving packages can be found on the school's website: www.cancun-language.com.mx.*

LODGING

HOME STAY

Home-stay lodging includes room and three meals a day with a Mexican family.

   Private room: $180/week

   Shared room: $160/week

SCHOOL RESIDENCE (MEALS NOT INCLUDED)

Two on-campus apartments are available, each accommodating one or two students.

   Private room: $160/week

   Shared room: $140/week

Student House in Downtown Cancún (meals not included)

   Private room: $95/ week

   Shared room: $75/week

HOTEL ACCOMMODATIONS (RATES VARY BY SEASON)

Downtown Cancún from $49/night

On the beach from $70/night

PROGRAMS AND SCHEDULES

Classes start every Monday and meet from 8 a.m. to 1 p.m. The first part is devoted mostly to grammar, followed by conversation and vocabulary building through dialog, discussions of culture and customs, games, songs, videos, and other exercises. Students are placed into one of seven levels of instruction according to their ability to speak Spanish.

BEGINNERS 1 (APPROX. FOUR WEEKS)

Covers the basic tenses of Spanish verbs, grammar, and basic vocabulary required for "Survival Spanish."

BEGINNERS 2 (APPROX. FOUR WEEKS)

Students learn more vocabulary and additional verb tenses in order to take part in simple conversations.

INTERMEDIATE 1 (FOUR TO FIVE WEEKS)

This course provides more practice with verb tenses and pronouns so that students can use the different grammatical structures in conversations on general topics, express their opinions, and read simple texts.

INTERMEDIATE 2 (APPROX. FOUR WEEKS)

Conversational skills are emphasized while reviewing the subjunctive mode, the direct, indirect and reflexive pronouns. Students will be able to take part in conversations and express opinions on non-specialized themes.

ADVANCED 1 (APPROX. FOUR WEEKS)

Students develop their conversation and composition skills so they can defend their ideas with valid arguments and a wide vocabulary.

ADVANCED 2 (APPROX. SIX WEEKS)

This is a continuation of Advanced 1 with further development of conversation, composition and editing techniques, as well as analysis of vocabulary.

SUPERIOR (NO LIMITS)

This class focuses on reading and discussion, analysis and expansion of vocabulary, advanced grammar, and translation. The objective is to be able to communicate in Spanish at the highest level.

For a more detailed description of what's covered in each level, see the school's website: www.cancun-language.com.mx

METHODS

Bosque del Caribe's teaching method is based on the seven-level ACTFL model (American Association of Teachers of Foreign Language). Classes include lectures and interactive exercises with grammar, oral, and written activities presented by two different teachers each day.

TEXTBOOKS

The textbooks used are *Dos Mundos* and *Pido la Palabra.* El Bosque del Caribe publishes its own beginning-to-advanced workbooks.

EXTRAS

AIRPORT PICKUP INCLUDED. The school will pick up students at the Cancún airport.

TEXTBOOKS INCLUDED. The cost of the workbooks is included in the tuition. There's no extra charge for the use of the textbooks.

FREE MIDMORNING SNACK. Every day at midmorning break, students congregate for a snack served in the patio area.

WHAT DISTINGUISHES THIS SCHOOL?

COMBINED STUDY IN CANCÚN AND CUERNAVACA. This program allows students to experience two very different parts of Mexico: a resort area on the Caribbean coast and a cosmopolitan city with a colonial heritage.

DIVE CERTIFICATION. Students may combine diving instruction with Spanish instruction and receive PADI certification.

FLAMENCO DANCE PACKAGE. This may be the only school in Mexico that offers a combination of Spanish-language instruction and Flamenco dance classes.

SEVEN-LEVEL ACTFL MODEL. The school has adopted the seven levels of language instruction developed by the American Association of Teachers of Foreign Language.

The Cancún Spanish Language Institute (CSLI)

At a Glance

Location: ★★★
Facilities: ★★★
Programs: ★★★½
Overall Rating ★★★
Cost: $150/week (three hours/day)
Maximum number of students per class: eight
Street Address:
   57 Avenida Bonampak, SM 2-A
   Cancún, Quintana Roo 77500, México

Tel: U.S. Office: 309-412-4332
Fax: None
Email: info@studyspanish-mexico.com
Website: www.studyspanish-mexico.com
Director: Francisco Romero
U.S. Contact: Lynda Wilson
Email: csli@studyspanish-mexico.com
U.S. Tel: 763-566-6840

L ocated in a multistory office building on one of Cancún's main avenues, the Cancún Spanish Language Institute is between downtown Cancún and the *Zona Hotelera*. Ciudad Cancún is within walking distance; the beach areas and the *Zona Hotelera* are accessible by bus. Despite its businesslike no-frills atmosphere, CSLI offers a variety of Spanish-language and related courses for college credit as well as PADI Scuba Diving certification. The co-owners are Francisco Romero, the onsite director and principal teacher, and Lynda Wilson, who is responsible for enrollment and marketing.

ACADEMIC BACKGROUND

Francisco Romero holds a master's degree in marketing from the Instituto Technológico de Estudios Superiores de Monterrey (ITESM). While at ITESM, he tutored non-native speakers in Spanish. He also studied and tutored in Spanish at McMaster University in Hamilton, Ontario, Canada. Before starting the Cancún Spanish Language Institute, he tutored foreign employees of Cancún businesses. Lynda Wilson has an MBA in marketing from the University of Minnesota. She was director of admissions and coordinator of student services for the Humphrey Institute of Public Affairs at the University of Minnesota for fifteen years.

CREDIT

Community college credit may be arranged through Seattle Central Community College. *See "Getting College Credit," page 8.*

COSTS

One-time nonrefundable registration fee: $50

Group Classes: $150/week

Private Tutoring: $15–$20/hour

Shared Tutoring: $12 per additional person/hour

Medical Spanish: $15–$20/hour

Airline Spanish: $15–$20/hour

Spanish and Scuba with PADI Certification: $662 for one week

Hourly rates for private tutoring, medical Spanish, and airline Spanish vary from $15/hour for ten or more hours per week, to $20/hour for fewer than ten hours/week.

Textbook (optional): $15

The use of a textbook is free, but you may also purchase a book to take home with you.

Discounts: If you enroll for more than four weeks, there's a discount of $20/week. The school also offers group discounts of up to $20/week per student, and waives the registration fee for members of a group.

LODGING

The school requires a $100 deposit to reserve student housing.

HOME STAY

Private or shared room, from $185/week (includes two meals a day). Home-stay cost varies with the location of the home, the number of daily meals, and whether the room has amenities such as air conditioning or a private bath.

OTHER OPTIONS

The school can reserve housing in the hotel zone, in downtown Cancún, or in the smaller towns of Punta Sam or Puerto Juárez. For details on rooms and rates, see the CSLI website: www.studyspanish-mexico.com.

CLASSES AND SCHEDULES

New classes start every Monday, year-round. Students may choose a morning or late-afternoon schedule. Morning classes meet 9 a.m. to noon; afternoon classes 4 to 7 p.m.

INTENSIVE SPANISH

BEGINNER 1. Intended for students who have little or no knowledge of the language, this course should give you enough Spanish for "survival" situations for travelers.

BEGINNER 2. This course is for students who can communicate using simple basic structures and a limited vocabulary. Upon completing Beginner 2, you should be able to take part in a variety of simple conversations using basic structures and vocabulary.

INTERMEDIATE 1. This course is intended for those who have completed the beginning courses or already have a good grasp of Spanish grammar and verbs in the present, imperative, and past tenses.

INTERMEDIATE 2. In this course, students review grammar and learn to use the subjunctive tenses. After completing Intermediate 2, you should have a wide vocabulary and good overall comprehension of the Spanish language.

High Intermediate, Advanced, and Superior (individual tutoring only). In these advanced courses, students learn synonyms of words and phrases, colloquial Spanish, and advanced Spanish grammar. You'll learn to speak the language in a more sophisticated manner and be capable of writing a letter or document with few spelling or grammatical errors. These classes are arranged on request.

Tutoring and Customized Groups

Students at all levels may also opt for individual tutoring in addition to or instead of group classes. The schedule is flexible and the program is tailored to your specific needs.

Spanish for Healthcare Professionals

Private tutoring sessions for healthcare professionals are held three to five times per week on a flexible schedule. In addition, healthcare students attend the regular group classes in general Spanish. The curriculum does not cover highly specialized medical terminology, but it provides the basic vocabulary needed to communicate with patients.

Spanish and Scuba

Cancún Spanish Language Institute offers PADI certification training with Scuba Cancún. Scuba classes meet each morning for six hours over five days, and the students take group Spanish classes in the late afternoon. Free transportation is provided from each student's lodging to the dive center. Students who are already certified divers can put together an a la carte program of dive excursions and Spanish classes with a private tutor on a flexible schedule.

Methods

CSLI teaches all language skills (reading, listening, speaking, and writing), with an emphasis on practical language for use in conversation. The curriculum has been developed following the Standards for Foreign Language Learning developed by the American Council on the Teaching of Foreign Languages (ACTFL).

TEXTBOOKS

Español Para Extranjeros, books 1, 2, and 3, by Ana María Maqueo, Universidad Nacional Autónoma de México (UNAM). These books are written entirely in Spanish.

EXTRAS

FREE REVIEW SESSIONS. An hour of conversation and review is available from noon to 1 p.m. or 7 to 8 p.m. at no extra cost.

ONLINE REGISTRATION. Students can resister online and pay by credit card.

EXCURSIONS. The school will arrange optional excursions for a minimum of six students; however, most students make their own arrangements for tours, and there's a link to a local tour agency on the CSLI website. Tours can be booked online; prices range from $30 to $110/person.

WHAT DISTINGUISHES THIS SCHOOL?

DIVING INSTRUCTION. The Cancún Spanish Language Institute is one of only a handful of schools that offer diving instruction and PADI certifications in addition to their Spanish-language courses.

U.S. CONTACT. Lynda Wilson is responsible for enrollment at CSLI and splits her time between Cancún and Minneapolis. Lynda can be contacted by phone or email and answers inquiries promptly in fluent English.

PLAYA DEL CARMEN

The small beach community of Playa del Carmen was previously just the departure point for ferries to the island of Cozumel. "Playa" as it is known locally, has now become a destination in its own right, although it's much more low-key than Cancún, its neighbor up the coast. The town has an old-fashioned beach-resort atmosphere, enhanced by the tropical climate, amazingly white beaches, and water in every imaginable shade of turquoise. So far, development has been limited to one or two large hotels on the outskirts. Many of the buildings in town are rustic Mexican or Mayan style, built of stucco or rough-hewn wood, with thatched roofs, and surrounded by lots of tropical foliage. Along the main street, a mix of locals and tourists stroll, shop, or stop for a drink or a meal in the many small cafés.

Playa del Carmen is a good location from which to visit the Caribbean Coast, the offshore islands, and nearby Mayan ruins. There's great snorkeling and diving along the Palancar reef just offshore. Cozumel Island is just a ferry ride away, and the ferry dock is right in town. By bus, you can visit the ruins of Tulum, the only seaside Mayan city, and Cobá, a huge and largely unexcavated site.

CLIMATE

The climate in Playa del Carmen is very similar to that of Cancún. Temperatures vary from warm to hot all year round. The best time to come is November through February, when the high temperatures tend to be in the 70s and 80s and there's often a strong sea breeze. Colder storms called nortes (northers) sometimes occur in winter. During the summer it's hot and humid, with high temperatures in the 90s and lows in the high 70s. In summer there are usually thundershowers in the afternoons, and there's always the possibility of tropical storms and hurricanes from July to October.

GETTING THERE

Many airlines, including Mexicana, Aeromexico, Continental, American, Alaska, and U.S. Air, fly directly from U.S. cities to Cancún. The airport is ten miles south of Cancún, in the same direction as Playa del Carmen, but traveling the additional thirty-five miles can be expensive. A private taxi from the airport to Playa costs about $60. There are other options, however. The least expensive is to take the Riviera bus. Tickets are 65 pesos (about $6.50) each way. The bus leaves from outside the main arrival hall at the Cancún airport. Just before you exit the terminal, there's a Riviera counter where you can buy a ticket. In Playa del Carmen the bus arrives at the main bus terminal on 5th Avenue and Juarez. Van transportation from the airport to Playa del Carmen costs about $25/person, with a minimum of two passengers. A van can be reserved online at www. docancun.com (click on Travel Info and Airport Transfers). If you'd prefer to take a taxi, go to any of the kiosks located around the terminal and buy a ticket. Then look for the authorized white, yellow, and black airport taxis. The fares are union controlled, so you won't be able to bargain for a lower price, but you can share a taxi with up to three other people, bringing the $60 fare down to about $15 each.

El Estudiante

At a Glance

Location: ★★★½
Facilities: ★★★½
Programs: ★★★
Overall Rating ★★★½
Cost: $369/week (five hours/day) including family stay
Maximum number of students per class: three
Street Address:
El Estudiante
Avenida 5 entre calles 14 y 16
Playa del Carmen, Quintana Roo, México

Tel/Fax: 52 984-873-0050
Email: info@playaspanishschool.com
Website: www.playaspanishschool.com
Director: Dieter Richter

El Estudiante is located right off the main street of Playa del Carmen, just a block from the Caribbean. The walls of the patio entryway are built in the style of the Mayan ruins, complete with polychrome painting and hieroglyphs. A small café serves *licuados* (smoothies), snacks, and sandwiches in the tree-shaded patio. There's also an Internet café where students can pick up their email or surf the Web. Classes are held upstairs on a large terrace under a palm-thatched *palapa* roof. This small school is very open and informal—no stuffy classrooms here!

ACADEMIC BACKGROUND

Director Dieter Richter holds a degree in architecture, has taught German to foreigners in Germany, and is certified to teach Spanish as a Second Language. Dieter has also worked on several Mayan archeological sites. Anabella Rodriguez, the head teacher, has a degree in communications from the University of Guatemala. Not all teachers have bachelor's degrees, but most have university studies in English and Spanish. The school has its own in-house training program that all teachers complete before beginning to teach Spanish.

CREDIT

Universidad de Chetumal, in the state capital, offers Mexican university credit for courses taken at El Estudiante. Community college credit may be arranged through Seattle Central Community College. *See "Getting College Credit," page 8.*

COSTS (LODGING INCLUDED)

STANDARD SPANISH COURSE

Fees include lodging with breakfast and twenty hours of instruction per week.

	Home Stay double	Home Stay single	Apartment double
One week:	$509	$555	$510
Two weeks:	$792	$885	$795
Three weeks:	$1056	$1195	$1060
Additional week:	$303	$348	$305

Prices are quoted in Euros on the school's website. The dollar prices above were calculated in February 2005 at $1.32/Euro.

Four-, eight-, and twelve-week programs are also offered at substantial discounts (see the school's website: www.playaspanishschool.com.

STANDARD PLUS 1 COURSE
Twenty-five hours/week, two weeks: $924

Tuition includes twenty hours of group lessons and five hours of private lessons weekly and home-stay accommodations with breakfast.

INTENSIVE COURSE
Thirty hours/week, two weeks: $1016

Tuition includes thirty hours of group lessons weekly and home-stay accommodations with breakfast.

INDIVIDUAL LESSONS
Twenty hours/week, two weeks: $1056

Tuition includes twenty hours of one-on-one instruction weekly and home-stay accommodations with breakfast.

NOTE: *These prices are shown for comparison only. Prices vary by type of accommodation. A more complete price list is shown on the school's website.*

Discounts are available for students of California community colleges and universities. For more information, contact the school at info@playaspanishschool.com.

LODGING

HOME STAY

Family accommodations in a double room with breakfast are included in the tuition. Single rooms are available for an extra $40/week.

OTHER OPTIONS

Single or double rooms are available in furnished apartments with access to a pool. Students living in apartments share a bathroom and a kitchen.

PROGRAMS AND SCHEDULES

Classes meet in morning and afternoon sessions from 9 a.m. to 1 p.m. and from 1:30 to 3:30 p.m. daily, Monday through Friday.

STANDARD COURSE, STANDARD PLUS 1 COURSE, AND INTENSIVE COURSE

In these courses, the daily schedule comprises a combination of grammar, reading, conversation, literature, and history classes. Conversation classes often feature excursions, thus using the community as a learning laboratory.

PRIVATE COURSE

This course features one-on-one instruction and can be tailored to the individual's needs.

METHODS

El Estudiante uses the communicative method, focusing on using the language in conversation.

TEXTBOOKS

The school publishes its own textbooks and manuals, which include both grammar and reading selections.

EXTRAS

FREE INTERNET ACCESS. El Estudiante's students have free Internet access at the Internet café in the same building as the school.

CAFÉ. At the entrance to the school, there's a small outdoor café that serves Mexican cuisine, healthy snacks, juices, and smoothies.

EXCURSIONS AND TOURS. El Estudiante offers day trips to the ruins of Cobá and the Punta Laguna Monkey Reserve. The excursions also include a visit to a Mayan family. The school sponsors a weekend tour to visit a recently discovered Mayan site, kayak in two lagoons, and swim in a *cenote,* a natural limestone pool.

WHAT DISTINGUISHES THIS SCHOOL?

OPEN, INFORMAL ATMOSPHERE. Classes are held in the open air, taking advantage of the tropical climate. The café is set in the garden area, encouraging students to relax and enjoy a drink or snack before or after classes.

MAYAN-LANGUAGE CLASSES. For archaeologists, ethnologists, and other interested people, El Estudiante offers classes in Maya taught by Mayan teachers.

Playalingua del Caribe
Centro Internacional De Lenguas

At a Glance

Location: ★★★★
Facilities: ★★★★
Programs: ★★★½
Overall Rating: ★★★★
Cost: $185/week (four hours/day)
Maximum number of students per class: six
Street Address:
    Calle 20, entre 5a y 10a Avenida
    77710 Playa del Carmen, Quintana Roo, México

Tel: 52 984-873-3876
Fax: 52 984-873-3877
Email: mail@playalingua.com
Website: www.playalingua.com
General Manager: Renzo Nani
Academic Director: Anne Calderón

Playalingua's inviting campus consists of two large Mayan-style buildings that surround a garden, pool, and patio area. One building houses seven air-conditioned classrooms, a library, an exhibition room, and administrative offices. The other contains lodging and a cafeteria. The friendliness of the faculty and staff contribute to the relaxed atmosphere. The school is in a residential area of Playa del Carmen, within walking distance of the beach.

ACADEMIC BACKGROUND

Academic Director Anne Calderon is originally from France but has lived in Mexico for twenty-five years. She has a bachelor's degree in applied languages and graduated from the School of Interpreters and Translators of Paris. She also completed a 200-hour course on the methodology of foreign-language teaching in Mexico City, and in-house training from a language school in Cancún. All teachers have previous experience and training in teaching Spanish as a Second Language, and most have bachelor's degrees in language or literature. For example, teachers Yereni Texon and Janet Quiroz have degrees in foreign languages, specializing in teaching Spanish to foreigners, and Fernando Romero has a degree in Spanish literature.

CREDIT

Community college credit may be arranged through Seattle Central Community College. *See "Getting College Credit," page 8.*

COSTS

Nonrefundable enrollment fee: $85

Intensive Spanish, four hours daily: $185/week

Intensive Spanish, two hours daily: $95/week

Private classes: $22/hour

Materials: $22

Excursions: $30–$50

Transfer to/from Cancún airport: $40

DISCOUNTS: Students who enroll for more than four weeks of Intensive Spanish receive the discounted rate of $170/week. Groups of ten students or more receive a 20 percent discount on tuition.

LODGING

HOME STAY

Including two meals a day, $150/week

OTHER OPTIONS

Lodging in on-campus rooms at the school, Mexican breakfast included.

Shared double room: $145/week
($135/week for more than four weeks)

Single room with balcony: $165/week
($155/week for more than four weeks)

Private room with private bath: $245/week
($225/week for more than four weeks

The school can provide information on hotels or studio apartments, which cost from $50 to $120/day. Hotels charge 20 to 50 percent more in the winter.

PROGRAMS AND SCHEDULES

INTENSIVE PROGRAM

Classes meet from 8:30 a.m. to 12:30, Monday through Friday. Seven levels of instruction are offered:

B-101 AND B 102 - BEGINNER SPANISH. At the end of the beginner level, students will be to speak in simple sentences and handle everyday situations such as shopping, asking for information in travel agencies, ordering in a restaurant, or renting a hotel room.

I-201 AND I-202 INTERMEDIATE SPANISH. After completing the intermediate level, students will be able to use all simple verb tenses and be able to converse on general topics. They will be able to talk about past events, express future plans and wishes, and give orders and advice.

A-301, A-302 AND A-303 ADVANCED SPANISH. Advanced students will be able to speak in an organized way about a great number of topics, both concrete and abstract, without making mistakes that could hinder communication with native speakers.

O-501 TO O-510 OPTIONAL COURSES. Conversation, history, and Mayan culture courses, such as ceramic painting, stone and woodcarving, Mexican cooking, and salsa dancing are offered for additional fees during late afternoon.

DIVE PROGRAM

Many levels of PADI certification are offered, from beginning to open-water diver and master diver. If you're a beginner, you can become a PADI certified diver in only four days. Courses include pool and classroom training, ocean and cenote or cave dives, theoretical support, and all necessary equipment. See the school's website for a complete description of this program. Diving classes are held in the mornings, and students take Spanish classes from 5 to 7 p.m.

METHODS

The teachers at Playalingua use their own method, which they developed and have worked with for four years. They are constantly making small changes and adding more support materials to improve instruction.

TEXTBOOKS

Pido la Palabra, Levels 1 to 5, published by La Universidad Autónoma de Méxixo

Lotería, Levels 1 to 5, published in Mexico by Trillas

Una vez más, a review of Spanish grammar

EXTRAS

LIBRARY. The school library contains Spanish-language reference books, as well as books on Mexican history, Mayan traditions, and many other aspects of Mexican culture. There's also a selection of novels in different languages.

TAPES. Audio and videotapes are available for student use.

CAFETERIA. The on-campus cafeteria is convenient for breakfast. It's also the place where students congregate for coffee breaks, Mexican cooking classes, and occasional dinners organized by the school.

INTERNET ACCESS. Playalingua has an Internet café with eight new computers for student use at a very low fee. In addition to surfing the Internet, students can burn CDs and print without leaving the school. The Internet café is open seven days a week.

SWIMMING POOL AND HAMMOCKS. Students can cool off in the pool and relax in a hammock right on campus.

EXHIBITION ROOM OF MAYAN ART. Art and handicrafts are exhibited for sale on campus.

EXCURSIONS. There are weekend excursions to water parks and archeological sites, as well as a two-day trip to Mérida, the capital of Yucatán. The school also offers information and tips on travel to Chiapas and Guatemala.

WHAT DISTINGUISHES THIS SCHOOL?

DIVE PROGRAM. Spanish instruction can be combined with diving instruction.

LODGING ON CAMPUS. The school is part boarding house, with twenty rooms, a studio, and apartments on campus to accommodate up to thirty students.

INTERNATIONAL SCHOOL. Playalingua is owned and operated by Europeans and accepts students from many different countries. English translations are less likely to be used in the classes because not all students are from English-speaking countries.

BEAUTIFUL CAMPUS. With its gardens and pool, Playalingua is a very inviting place to study.

FRIENDLY ATMOSPHERE. The friendly, helpful staff make students feel at home. Playalingua has many return students, and many others have studied there on the recommendation of former students.

Soléxico Playa del Carmen

At a Glance

Location: ★★★★
Facilities: ★★★★½
Programs: ★★★★½
Overall Rating: ★★★★½
Cost: $149/week (three hours/day) to $209/week (five hours/day)
Maximum number of students per class: five
Street Address:
 Avenida 35 s/n, entre 6 y 6 bis
 Playa del Carmen
 77710 Quintana Roo, México

Tel: 52 984-873-0755 • Fax: 52 984-873-0754
Email: info@solexico.com
juan@solexico.com
gerardo@solexico.com
Website: www.solexico.com
Director: Gerardo Diego
Marketing and Operations Director: Juan Carlos Delgado

Soléxico Playa del Carmen is just six blocks from the white sand beaches of the Caribbean. The school is designed in the open Caribbean style; palm-thatched Mayan-style pavilions set in a tropical garden serve as outdoor classrooms. A small snack bar occupies the center of the expansive lawn and garden area. This is a two-campus school, enabling students to combine courses here with courses at Soléxico's campus in the city of Oaxaca.

ACADEMIC BACKGROUND

Director Gerardo Diego holds a bachelor's degree in advertising and marketing from the University of Texas in Austin. After receiving his degree, he worked at an advertising agency, where he became head of the Hispanic department. Juan Carlos Delgado, the Marketing and Operations Director, has a marketing degree from Universidad Iberoamericana in Mexico City. He has worked for several different international companies. Most of the instructors at Soléxico have bachelor's degrees in language or literature.

CREDIT

Community college credit may be arranged through Seattle Central Community College. *See "Getting College Credit," page 8.*

COSTS

Nonrefundable registration fee: $80

Regular Program (fifteen hours/week): $149/week

Regular Program (twenty-five hours/week): $209/week

Individual Program: $398/week

Executive Program: $527/week

Scuba Diving Package 1: $670/week

Scuba Diving Package 2: $620/week

NOTE: *Tuition decreases slightly for multiple weeks. For a complete up-to-date fee schedule, see the school's website: www.solexico.com.*

Individual tutoring: $21/hour

Materials: $17 (each book)

Lodging

Home Stay

	Half board	Breakfast only
Private room (per day):	$25	$22
Shared room (per day):	$21	$19

Other options

The Solexico Residence. The residence has ten double rooms, all with air conditioning, cable TV and private bathroom. There's also a cafeteria where breakfast is served every day, and a Jacuzzi and grill.

Single room: $34/night

Double room: $27/night

Hotels and apartments. The school will also arrange for other accommodations such as condominiums, houses, and hotel rooms. Prices are variable and usually don't include meals.

Programs and Schedules

Courses begin each Monday year-round. Group classes, fifty minutes long with breaks, are held from 9 a.m. to 2 p.m. Students in the Individual Program also meet with private tutors from 2:30 to 5:30 p.m. There are seven levels of language instruction. Students are given placement exams to determine their appropriate level.

Regular Program (five hours / day)

These classes meet from 9 a.m. to 2 p.m. and include three hours of grammar and two hours of conversation.

Regular Program (three hours / day)

Classes are held from 9 a.m. to noon and are composed of three hours of conversation and grammar.

Individual Program (five hours / day)

This program includes two hours of group instruction in the morning and three hours of one-on-one instruction in the afternoon.

EXECUTIVE PROGRAM (EIGHT HOURS / DAY)

Students in the executive program receive three hours of intensive, one-on-one instruction in addition to the five-hour group classes of the regular program. An executive lounge, executive assistant services, and a virtual office are also provided.

PRIVATE LESSONS

For additional fees, private lessons are available in the afternoons.

SCUBA DIVING PROGRAM

The barrier reef in the Mexican Caribbean is one of the best places in the world to dive and snorkel. To take advantage of this aspect of its location, Solexico offers two combination Spanish and scuba diving packages.

SCUBA DIVING PACKAGE 1. This includes one week of private Spanish lessons, the registration fee, all materials, airport transfers, and the PADI Open Water Diver Certification.

SCUBA DIVING PACKAGE 2 (ONLY FOR CERTIFIED DIVERS). This includes one week of private Spanish lessons, the registration fee, all materials, transfers from and to Cancún International Airport, and a total of eight dives.

METHODS

Solexico uses a traditional grammatical approach to provide the structural basis of the language. They also use the natural approach to conversation, with situations and excursions to apply the language.

TEXTBOOKS

Soléxico's books and materials were written by their academic director and have been updated and improved by the instructors.

EXTRAS

FREE INTERNET ACCESS. The school provides Web-linked computers for student use.

PHONE AND FAX. Students may receive telephone calls and faxes free of charge.

LIBRARY. The school library is stocked with books on grammar, Mayan culture, religion, and travel in Mexico, as well as magazines and other Spanish-language publications.

CAFETERIA. There is an outdoor cafeteria area where students can purchase coffee, sandwiches, snacks, soft drinks, and juices.

VOLLEYBALL COURT. Solexico's expansive grounds also provide space for a volleyball court.

AFTERNOON WORKSHOPS. After-class activities include cooking, arts and crafts, salsa classes, singing Mexican songs, or attending a fiesta. Students at Soléxico meet once a week with the faculty and staff in a restaurant or café for a "Café Social," a time for informal conversation.

EXECUTIVE PROGRAM SERVICES. For students in the Executive Program, an executive lounge is provided to facilitate communication with their clients and home offices.

SYLLABUS. A syllabus for each course is available from the school and can be sent via post or email.

DIVING COURSES. Arrangements can be made for those who'd like to learn to dive. All levels of PADI certification are available.

OTHER ACTIVITIES. Solexico Playa del Carmen offers horseback riding, skydiving, wind surfing, yoga, and beach volleyball.

EXCURSIONS. The school organizes excursions to a number of places of interest in Quintana Roo and Yucatan: the Tulum ruins and Xel-ha lagoon, Sian-ka´an biosphere reserve, Cancún, Xcaret theme park, Cobá ruins and Cenote, Chichen Itzá ruins, Valladolid and Cenote Ikkil, and the colonial city of Mérida. These tours cost from $35 for day trips, to $100 for overnights.

WHAT DISTINGUISHES THIS SCHOOL?

DIVING INSTRUCTION. Solexico Playa del Carmen is one of only a handful of schools that offer diving instruction and PADI certifications in addition to their Spanish-language courses.

TWO CAMPUSES. Students may choose to study in a colonial city in the mountains at Solexico Oaxaca or in the beach community of Playa del Carmen on the Caribbean Coast.

EXECUTIVE LOUNGE. Soléxico's executive lounge provides executive students with an area to read the newspaper, watch TV, or simply relax. During school hours, a bilingual executive assistant will take and deliver phone messages, send faxes and emails, and type letters.

D.E.L.E. DIPLOMA. Soléxico offers preparation for the D.E.L.E. (the official diploma of Spanish as a Second Language).

COLLEGE PLACEMENT EXAMS. The school also offers preparation for college Spanish placement exams.

MÉRIDA

Mérida, the capital of the state of Yucatán, is an old, Spanish colonial city with a tropical flavor. Flowering vines and bougainvillea flourish in small parks and even on some of the old buildings near the main square (*Plaza Mayor*), where locals gather to stroll, shop, or listen to concerts. Overlooking the *Plaza Mayor* is the oldest cathedral in the Americas, which, in the early 16th century, was built of stones from a ruined Mayan city. Compared with some of the more ornate churches in the highlands, this one is rather plain looking, both inside and out, but it is beloved by the people of Mérida. Several other historic buildings surround the main square. *El Palacio del Obispo* (The Bishop's Palace), is now a contemporary art museum. *El Palacio de Montejo*, home of the Montejo family, original conquerors of the Yucatán, is embellished with strange images of conquistadors standing on the heads of Indians. The *Palacio de Gobierno* (Government Palace), its interior courtyard decorated with vivid murals depicting scenes from the history of Yucatan, also houses the state government offices and a small tourist information center.

About eight blocks from the Plaza Mayor is the Paseo de Montejo, a broad avenue bordered by huge mansions in the European style, built by wealthy owners of henequen plantations in the 18th and 19th centuries. Most of these mansions are no longer occupied by the original families, but they stand as a stately tribute to another era. Today, Paseo de Montejo is a fashionable district, and the avenue is lined with upscale shops, hotels, restaurants, and offices. One of the largest mansions, the Palacio Cantón, houses the *Museo Regional de Antropología*, which is worth a visit, as it contains artifacts from Yucatán's many Mayan archeological sites. One of the benefits of studying Spanish in Mérida is that it's close to major Mayan sites such as Chichén Itzá, Uxmal, and Dzibilchaltún, all of which can be visited on day trips. Of course, Mérida is not on the beach, but the beach town of Progreso is about an hour away by bus. Or, if you're off for the weekend, the Caribbean Coast is only four hours away.

Mérida has a regular system for its street layout and numbering. Streets running north-south have been given even numbers; those running east-west have odd numbers. Addresses are often given by *colonia;* for example, *Colonia México, Calle 66 entre* (between) *57 y 59.* The system is easy to use, except for the fact that in some cases there are two streets with the same number that do not connect and are in different *colonias*.

CLIMATE

From November to February the weather is warm but comfortable and sometimes breezy. In other months, it's just plain hot and humid, especially during the summer. Rain can occur any time of year, but is more frequent during the rainy season (July to October), when there are often afternoon tropical showers.

GETTING THERE

BY PLANE

Aeromexico and Aviacsa airlines have nonstop flights to Mérida from Miami. The fare is about $450. Aeromexico, Aviacsa, and Continental offer nonstop service to and from Houston for $350. Airfares from the West Coast of the U.S. are about $500. From the East Coast, the fares are $600 or more. Flights departing from other some U.S. cities may stop in Mexico City or Cancún.

Mérida's airport is about eight miles from the city center, on its southwestern outskirts, near the entrance to Highway 180. Taxi tickets to town cost about $11 and are sold outside the airport doors, under the covered walkway.

Flying into Cancún. Many airlines, including Mexicana, Aeromexico, Continental, American, and U.S. Air, fly directly from U.S. cities to Cancún. Flying to Cancún and taking the bus may be considerably less expensive than flying directly to Mérida.

If you fly into the Cancún airport, you must get to the *Central Camionera* (Central Bus Station) in Ciudad Cancún in order to catch a bus to Mérida. A private taxi from the airport to Ciudad Cancún costs $35–$40. Some van services are almost as expensive. The best option is to take the nonstop ADO bus that drops you off right at the *Central Camionera* at the intersection of Tulum and Uxmal avenues. The cost is only 15 pesos each way (about $1.50), and the trip takes fifteen minutes. The ADO buses run from 5 a.m. to past midnight. You can catch one outside Terminal 2, at the opposite end of the airport terminal from where international arrivals exit customs. Public shuttle vans (*colectivos*) also run from the airport into Cancún for about $8/person. These, however, take two to three hours, as they head first to the Hotel Zone, dropping off passengers along the way, and then returning to the airport through Ciudad Cancún.

By bus

ADO-GL and UNO buses leave Cancún's bus terminal for Mérida at regular intervals during the day. Some buses arrive in Mérida at the CAME bus terminal on Calle 70, between 69 and 71 in downtown Mérida. Others go to the Fiesta Americana Hotel just off the Paseo de Montejo. You can make a reservation or check departure times and prices at either of ADO's websites: www.adogl.com.mx or www.uno.com.mx. The fare for the ADO-GL bus from Cancún to Mérida is about $20. The UNO bus fare is about $30. The trip usually takes about four hours on either bus line.

By ferry

Through the 2003 winter season, a car ferry, the Yucatán Express, made weekly trips between Tampa, Florida, and the port of Progreso, near Mérida. This service was discontinued in 2003, but the company may reinstate it for the period November through April in 2005–06. This ferry offers some of the amenities of a cruise ship, with entertainment and lots of food. You can book passage one way or round-trip, with or without your car. "Passage Only" fares start at $120 round-trip. If you take your car, it will cost an additional $300. To determine the current status of this service, contact the Yucatán Express at 866-670-3939 in the U.S., or check their website: www.yucatanexpress.com.

BENJAMIN FRANKLIN INSTITUTE

AT A GLANCE

Location: ★★★★
Facilities: ★★★½
Programs: ★★★
Overall Rating ★★★½
Cost: $150/week (three hours/day)
Maximum number of students/class: four
Street Address:
    Calle 57 No. 474-A
    Merida, Yucatán, México
Tel: 52 999-928-0097 and 52 999-928-6005
Fax: 52 999-928-0097
Email: franklin@finred.com.mx
Website: www.benjaminfranklin.com.mx
Director: Guillermo Vales Duarte

The Benjamin Franklin Institute was founded in 1959 and dedicated to promoting U.S.-Mexican cultural relations. The institute is a binational center of the U.S. State Department (U.S.I.S.) and maintains a library of books and State Department publications that is updated frequently. Posters for many U.S. universities line the hallways, reflecting the fact that the Instituto Benjamin Franklin serves as an advising center for Mexican students who plan to study at foreign institutions. Classes are held in a picturesque old mansion, with balconies around a central patio, located in the downtown area near the *Plaza Mayor*. Although the institute's main program during the school year seems to be teaching English to local Mexican students, they also offer Spanish classes for university groups and individuals from the U.S., Canada, and Europe.

CREDIT

Academic credit can be granted through the Universidad de Yucatán. Check with your home university to determine the transferability of these credits. Community college credit may be arranged through Seattle Central Community College. *See "Getting College Credit," page 8.*

COSTS

Nonrefundable deposit (applicable toward course fees): $25

Intensive Spanish program

Spanish grammar and conversation: $15/hour

Four-week course: $600

Discounts: Special group rates are available.

TEFL Program (Teaching English as a Foreign Language)

Thirty hours of instruction and TEFL certification test: $70

LODGING

HOME STAY

Private room, meals included $15/day

OTHER OPTIONS

The school can also recommend inexpensive hotels, apartments, and boarding houses.

PROGRAMS AND SCHEDULES

Courses start every Monday year-round. Regular classes are held from 9:30 a.m. to 3:30 p.m. The school can also adapt a course to a student's personal schedule.

INTENSIVE SPANISH

Students take placement exams upon arrival to determine their appropriate level.

All Intensive Spanish courses feature grammar and conversation classes as well as guided tours to places of historic and cultural interest in the city. The conversation classes are designed jointly by the teacher and students.

SPECIAL CLASSES

Mexican history: Pre-Hispanic to present (several different classes)

Mexican culture emphasizing the Maya

Mexican literature

The socioeconomic situation of Mexico

METHODS

In addition to traditional classroom instruction, teachers use audio and video instructional aids. Excursions within the city, and interaction with Mexican students, are integral parts of the instructional program.

TEXTBOOKS

In its grammar classes, The Ben Franklin Institute uses two textbooks: *¡Díme!* and *Dos Mundos,* both published in the U.S. No textbooks are used in the conversation classes, but students are given handouts on various topics and current issues.

EXTRAS

INTERNET ACCESS is available at a nearby campus of the Universidad de Yucatán.

TOURS. Guided tours to places of historic and cultural interest in the city of Mérida are included in the Spanish program.

LIBRARY. The school maintains a rather large library of books in Spanish and English as well as U.S. State Department publications.

CERTIFICATE OF COMPLETION. Students receive a certificate showing that they have satisfactorily completed their Spanish-language study program.

WHAT DISTINGUISHES THIS SCHOOL?

ASSOCIATION WITH THE U.S. DEPARTMENT OF STATE (U.S.I.S.). This principally benefits Mexican students who are learning English; however, it's a credit to the institute to have been chosen as a binational center.

TEFL CLASSES AND TEST. Students can take a thirty-hour class in Teaching English as a Foreign Language for much less than this type of instruction would cost in the U.S. They can also take the TEFL certification test at Instituto Benjamin Franklin.

COLLEGE BOARD. Instituto Benjamin Franklin is authorized to administer the College Board test.

Centro de Idiomas del Sureste (CIS)

At a Glance

Location: ★★★½
Facilities: ★★★
Programs: ★★★★
Overall Rating: ★★★½
Cost: $185/week (three hours/day)
Maximum number of students per class: five
Street Addresses (three centers):
    CIS-PONIENTE
    Calle 11 No. 203-C entre 26
    Col. García Ginerés 97070
    Mérida, Yucatán, México

Tel: 52 999-920-2810
    CIS-NORTE
    Calle 14 No. 106 entre 25
    Col. México 97128
    Mérida, Yucatán, México

Tel: 52 999-926-9494
  CIS-52
  Calle 52 No. 455 entre 49 y 51
  Centro 97000
  Mérida, Yucatán, México
Tel: 52 999-923-0954
For all centers:
Fax: 52 999-926-9020
Email cis@sureste.com
Website: www.cisyucatan.com.mx
General Director: Chloe Conaway de Pacheco
Academic Coordinator: Regina Bendetz de Patrón

Centro de Idiomas del Sureste was founded in 1974 and occupies three buildings in different parts of Mérida. This school's principal occupation seems to be teaching English to local Mexicans, but it also has a small but active Spanish-language department. Spanish classes are usually held at CIS Poniente (West). The building is a plain-looking converted suburban house divided into several classrooms. There are outdoor patio areas where students gather between classes. Students who sign up for study-abroad programs in Mérida through Amerispan and NRC-SA are sent to CIS.

CREDIT

CIS is accredited through the Yucatán Department of Education, and students are issued an official transcript upon concluding their courses. U.S. university credit is available from the University of Southern Mississippi or the National Registration Center for Study Abroad (NRCSA). Community college credit may be arranged through Seattle Central Community College. *See "Getting College Credit," page 8.*

COSTS

Intensive Spanish Program (includes three hours of class daily in a small group format)
  Two weeks: $370
  Four weeks: $580
  Ten weeks: $1400

Additional weeks are charged at the rate of $135/week

An extra two hours of study daily may be added to any option above at a cost of $100/week.

Private tutoring: $15/hour

LODGING

HOME STAY

CIS encourages its students to stay with a local family (meals included).

Room with shared bath, no air conditioning: $135/week

Private room with bath and air conditioning: $180/week (single)

Private room with bath and air conditioning: $160/week (double)

PROGRAMS AND SCHEDULES

Courses start every Monday year-round, except the last two weeks of December.

INTENSIVE SPANISH PROGRAM

Group classes in grammar and conversation meet three hours per day, five days a week.

SUPER-INTENSIVE SPANISH PROGRAM: FIVE HOURS / DAY

For students who want maximum exposure to the language, CIS also offers an optional two-hour per day extra study package. The additional study may focus specifically on medical, legal, or business vocabulary, or on any other aspect of language learning requested by the student.

SPECIAL PROGRAMS

Cultural enrichment programs are available for Spanish teachers and other advanced learners in the summer and at other scheduled times. CIS will also design special-interest programs for groups in a variety of fields.

METHODS

CIS uses the "total immersion" method, in which the home stay is closely supervised by the school, so that academic input is reinforced by practical usage. Verbal skills are emphasized at all levels.

TEXTBOOKS

CIS uses both *Pido la Palabra* and *Schaum's Grammar Series*.

EXTRAS

CULTURAL ACTIVITIES. Two cultural activities are offered each week, such as a tour of Mérida or a visit to the ruins of Dzibilchaltún; these are included in the tuition.

WHAT DISTINGUISHES THIS SCHOOL?

ESTABLISHED PROGRAM. El Centro de Idiomas del Sureste offers the advantages of thirty years' experience in the teaching of foreign languages, as well as careful individual attention to the learning needs of its students.

ACADEMIC CREDIT. This is the only school in Mérida that has been approved for U.S. university credit by both the University of Southern Mississippi and the National Registration Center for Study Abroad (NRCSA).

Institute of Modern Spanish

At a Glance

Location: ✦✦✦✦
Facilities: ✦✦✦✦
Programs: ✦✦✦✦
Overall Rating: ✦✦✦✦
Cost: $190/week (four hours/day) to $312/week (six hours/day)
Maximum number of students per class: five
U.S. Mailing Address:
  413 Interamerica Blvd. WH1, PMB, MX 018-108
  Laredo, TX 78045

Fax: 775-213-0406
Tel: (toll-free) 877-463-7432 (877-4MERIDA)
Street Address:
  Calle 27 #493 entre 56A y 58
  Colonia Itzimna
  Mérida, Yucatán, México

Tel: 52 999-927-9975 or 52 999-926-4695

Email: 4merida@modernspanish.com or 2learn@modernspan-
ish.com
Website: www.modernspanish.com
Director: Janese Ott Cerón

The Institute of Modern Spanish is a small school located near the elegant Paseo Montejo in Mérida. The school is modern and comfortable, with air-conditioned classrooms, as well as an outdoor lounge and
a common area. Director Janese Ott Cerón is an American who is mar-
ried to a Mexican and makes her home in Mérida.

ACADEMIC BACKGROUND

Janese Ott Cerón has a bachelor's degree in Spanish from Truman State
University and a master's in applied linguistics and teaching English as
a Second Language from Iowa State University. All teachers hold bachelor's degrees and have experience teaching Spanish as a Second Language.
Teachers also receive training in specific classroom techniques during instructional workshops at the school.

CREDIT

Simpson College in Indianola, Iowa, offers a credit program every spring
for their students only. Other students have been able to receive credit
from their home universities for their studies at the Institute of Modern
Spanish. Check with your home university to determine whether they
grant credit for courses at this school. Community college credit may be
arranged through Seattle Central Community College. *See "Getting College Credit," page 8.*

COSTS

GROUP INSTRUCTION, HOME STAY INCLUDED

Twenty hours of instruction: $323/week

Twenty-five hours of instruction: $361/week

NOTE: There is a recommended minimum of two weeks of study; however, private instruction, semi-intensive (six hours daily), and intensive
programs (eight hours daily) may be taken for one week.

GROUP INSTRUCTION (CLASSES ONLY)

Twenty hours/week: $190/week

Twenty-five hours/week: $240/week

Thirty hours/week: $312/week

INTENSIVE INSTRUCTION (FORTY HOURS / WEEK, CLASSES ONLY)

Weeks 1 and 2: $394/week

Weeks 3 and 4: $384/week

Weeks 5 and 6: $369/week

Intensive instruction is a combination of group and private classes.

LODGING

HOME STAY WITH THREE MEALS INCLUDED

Shared room: $140/week

Private room: $175/week

Private room and private bathroom: $210/week

A home stay may also be included in tuition for a slight reduction in fees (see above).

OTHER OPTIONS

Student housing in dormitories with a shared kitchen is available. The charge is $22/night, no meals included.

The school can recommend and reserve hotel accommodations for those who would prefer not to stay with a family or in a dormitory.

DISCOUNTS

Tuition is discounted for study programs of eight weeks or more.

There is a 10 percent discount for ESL, Spanish, or bilingual teachers (a letter from your employer is required).

There is a 10 percent discount for retired persons (age 58 and over).

Two or more students who arrive and depart on the same dates and stay with the same host family receive a 10 percent discount.

PROGRAMS AND SCHEDULES

Individual placement tests may be taken before arrival online or via mail or fax. Classes meet from 8 a.m. to 2 p.m. An eight-hour-per-day program is available that also includes a two-hour afternoon or evening session.

Students typically spend two or three hours daily in beginning, elementary, intermediate, or advanced Spanish-language classes, along with two hours of Spanish Conversation or special-interest classes.

SPANISH-LANGUAGE CLASSES

BEGINNING SPANISH (SPANISH 100, FORTY TO FIFTY HOURS)

This course provides the basics of survival Spanish. Students are introduced to the structure and usage of the language, including forming simple sentences.

ELEMENTARY SPANISH I & II
(SPANISH 150 AND 151, FORTY TO FIFTY HOURS EACH)

These courses present Spanish in the context of Mexican culture. Instruction is in Spanish with selected readings from authentic texts to illustrate grammar and syntax. Both speaking and writing are emphasized.

INTERMEDIATE SPANISH I & II
(SPANISH 250 AND 251, FORTY TO FIFTY HOURS EACH)

These courses provide further practice in speaking, listening, reading, and writing skills in Spanish, focusing on fluency and cultural understanding.

ADVANCED SPANISH I & II
(SPANISH 350 AND 351, FORTY TO FIFTY HOURS EACH)

Advanced students work toward full fluency in speaking and writing in both informal and formal contexts. Advanced listening and reading practice is provided.

SPANISH CONVERSATION
(SPANISH 105, 120, 220 AND 320, FORTY TO FIFTY HOURS)

Students participate in conversation and role-playing at a level appropriate for their language knowledge.

SPECIALIZED CLASSES

Spanish for Teachers
Spanish for Business
Local Political/Socioeconomic Development
Mayan Culture

History of Yucatán

Spanish American Literature

METHODS

IMS uses a method based on the concept of language learning called Integrated Spanish Language Learning. Their programs integrate Spanish-language classes with a family stay, and replace memorization of grammar rules with a total cultural experience, focusing on practical and culturally applicable language.

TEXTBOOKS

Grammar classes use *Schaum's Outline of Spanish Grammar, Spanish Two Years,* and *Advanced Spanish in Review.* The staff is working to combine all the materials they use for conversational Spanish in order to publish their own textbook.

EXTRAS

FREE CITY TOUR. All packages (classes with home stay) include a Panoramic City Tour.

EXCURSIONS. Excursions are available to the Mayan ruins of Chichén Itzá, Uxmal, and Dzibilchaltún.

WHAT DISTINGUISHES THIS SCHOOL?

LOCATION. The Institute of Modern Spanish is located in a middle-class suburban neighborhood in Mérida. Host families live within walking distance. Living and studying in such an area allows students to experience the day-to-day life of the average Mexican.

THE DIRECTOR. Janese Ott Cerón has a BA in Spanish and a TESL certification as well as a master's in applied linguistics. She is well qualified to teach, and is very enthusiastic about the school, which she founded while in graduate school.

COURSE NUMBERING SYSTEM. The school has adopted a numbering system similar to the system used in many U.S. colleges and universities, making it easier to distinguish equivalent classes for academic credit transfer.

EMPHASIS ON HOST FAMILIES. The director is personally acquainted with all the families, who are chosen for their proximity to the school and their warm and caring attention to students.

Instituto de Lengua y Cultura de Yucatán

At a Glance

Location: ✯✯✯
Facilities: ✯✯½
Programs: ✯✯✯½
Overall Rating: ✯✯✯½
Cost: $175/week (four hours/day) to $195/week (five hours/day)
Maximum number of students per class: six
Street Address:
   Calle 13 #448 entre 34 y 36
   Fracc. Montejo
   Mérida, Yucatán, México

U.S. Address (for registration):
   413 Interamerica Blvd.
   WH1 PMB MX-018-155
   Laredo Texas, 78045

Tel. 52 999-927-0993
Tel: 52 999-948-1908
Fax: 52 999-927-0993
Email: inf@ilcymex.com
ilcymex2000@yahoo.com
Website: www.ilcymex.com
Director: Cecy Novelo
International Director: Jessica Kuiper

Instituto de Lengua y Cultura de Yucatán is a very small school located in an older suburban house near the Paseo de Montejo. Although the exterior is rather plain, the interior is nicely decorated in Mexican style. The school has a homey atmosphere, with the former living room and patio serving as common areas.

ACADEMIC BACKGROUND

Director Cecy Novelo has a background in psychology and pedagogy. She has twelve years' experience teaching Spanish and has taught for the University of Ohio study-abroad program since 1993. International Director Jessica Kuiper graduated from Davenport University with a bachelor's degree in international business. She decided to make Mérida her home after studying at Instituto de Lengua y Cultura de Yucatán.

CREDIT

Community college credit may be arranged through Seattle Central Community College. *See "Getting College Credit," page 8.* The medical program is approved for CME (Continuing Medical Education) credit through the state of California.

COSTS

Nonrefundable registration deposit $100 ($200 for CME course); the deposit is applied toward total tuition and/or accommodations.

GROUP INSTRUCTION (CLASSES ONLY)

Twenty hours/week: $175/week
Twenty-five hours/week: $195/week

GROUP INSTRUCTION (INCLUDING SHARED FAMILY HOUSING)

	20 hrs./week	25 hrs./week
One Week:	$310	$345
Two Weeks:	$620	$695
Three Weeks:	$930	$1,035
Four Weeks:	$1,190	$1,325

ONE-ON-ONE PROGRAM (CLASSES ONLY)

	20 hours/week	25 hours/week
One Week:	$295	$370
Two Weeks:	$590	$745
Three Weeks:	$830	$1,045
Four Weeks:	$1,115	$1,390

Additional weeks are prorated.

INTENSIVE PROGRAM (EIGHT HOURS / DAY, CLASSES ONLY)

One Week: $390
Two Weeks: $748
Three Weeks: $1,074
Four Weeks: $1,369

MEDICAL SPANISH PROGRAM
(GROUP INSTRUCTION, INCLUDING SHARED FAMILY HOUSING)

Twenty to twenty-five hours of instruction: $450/week

MEDICAL SPANISH PROGRAM (GROUP INSTRUCTION ONLY)

Twenty hours/week: $300
Twenty-five hours/week: $380
Optional five-hour CME course: $80/week
Private room upgrade: $40/week

Lodging

Home Stay (including three meals a day)

A home stay may be included in a group program for a discounted package rate (see above).

Shared Room: $150/week

Single Room: $180/week

Programs and Schedules

A new session begins every Monday for all levels of Spanish. Classes are held from 9 a.m. to 1 p.m. or from 3 to 7 p.m., Monday through Friday.

Standard Program

Four fifty-minute sessions daily are devoted to Spanish grammar and conversation.

There are four instructional levels: Beginning, Elementary, Intermediate, and Advanced.

Special Classes

Mayan, Yucatecan, and Mexican History

Yucatecan and Mexican Traditions

Mexican Economy and Latin American Literature

Business Spanish

Medical Spanish

Legal Spanish

Spanish for the Diplomatic Professions

Medical Spanish

Maricopa Integrated Health System, Clínica Adelante, Inc., and Instituto de Lengua y Cultura de Yucatán have joined to offer up to twenty-five hours of Continuing Medical Education or CME credit to healthcare professionals who complete this program. The courses are intended to help medical personnel understand and communicate more effectively with their Hispanic patients. There are four levels of instruction in the program: Basic Medical Spanish I and II; and Intermediate/Advanced Medical Spanish I and II.

METHODS

Teachers use current foreign-language teaching methods as well as real-life experiences to reinforce classroom learning.

TEXTBOOKS

Since learning is primarily based on real experience with the language, textbooks aren't used in the classes, but the teachers do provide relevant handouts.

EXTRAS

SEASONAL PACKAGE PROGRAMS. Special package programs that include tuition, housing and excursions are offered throughout the year. For up-to-date information on these packages, see the school's website: www. ilcymex.com.

EXCURSIONS. The institute offers tours, arranged by a local travel agent, to Mayan sites and other attractions.

WHAT DISTINGUISHES THIS SCHOOL?

MEDICAL PROGRAM FOR CME CREDIT. This is the only Spanish-language school in Mérida where medical professionals can earn CME credit.

THE INTERNATIONAL DIRECTOR IS A FORMER STUDENT. Jessica Kuiper is a former student of ILCY. In 1999, she spent a semester abroad at ILCY and received a certificate for 450 hours of Spanish as a Second Language. Jessica is from the U.S., and answers all inquiries from English speakers.

The Spring Bell School

At a Glance

Location: ★★★½
Facilities: ★★★★
Programs: ★★★
Overall Rating: ★★★½
Cost: $225/week (four hours/day)
Maximum number of students per class: five
Street Address:
    Calle 56 entre 25 y 29 #330
    Colonia Itzimá
    Merida, Yucatán, México

Tel/Fax: 52 999-948-0015
Email: ed_albor@hotmail.com
Website: www.geocities.com/ed_albor/springbell.html
Director: Eduardo Albor

This relatively small school shares a large, modern facility in a residential area of Mérida with the University of Mérida Journalism Department and functions as the university's Spanish department for foreign students. The area is nicely landscaped and classrooms are spacious, light, and airy. There's a small outdoor café in front of the building where students congregate during breaks. Spring Bell Spanish school prides itself on giving individual attention to each student. The director is personally involved in making sure the students are picked up at the airport, oriented to the city, and placed with compatible families.

ACADEMIC BACKGROUND

Director Eduardo Albor has a master's degree in business and marketing, three years of university study in psychology, and an English certificate from the University of Michigan. Each faculty member has at least a bachelor's degree. Instructors Edgardo Medina and Fausto González are attorneys who previously taught at the University of Yucatán. Gabriela Cardozo and Pauline Ruiz have degrees in communication and are high school teachers. Juan Carlos Jordan is a medical doctor who knows English, French, and German in addition to his native Spanish. He teaches Spanish and also trains other teachers at Spring Bell School.

CREDIT

Students can receive up to five units of Mexican university credit through the University of Mérida at no extra cost. Check with the counseling department of your home university to see if these credits will be accepted for transfer. Community college credit may be arranged through Seattle Central Community College. *See "Getting College Credit," page 8.*

COSTS

TWO-WEEK YUCATECA PROGRAM

This program includes twenty hours of instruction per week, home-stay accommodations, and field trips to the ancient Mayan cities of Chichén Itzá and Dzibilchaltún. The cost varies with the number of students in the group.

One: $950 per person   Two: $900 per person

Three: $850 per person   Four: $825 per person

Five: $800 per person

FOUR-WEEK YUCATECA PROGRAM

This program includes twenty hours of instruction per week, home-stay accommodations, and field trips to Chichén Itzá, Dzibilchaltún, Chelem Beach, and a weekend trip to the famous Caribbean resort city of Cancún.

One: $1550 per person

Two: $1500 per person

Three: $1450 per person

Four: $1400 per person

Extra week of instruction (twenty hours): $250 (class only)

TWO-WEEK SIMPLY SPANISH PROGRAM

This program includes four hours of daily classroom instruction (Monday through Friday) but does not include field trips.

One: $450 per person

Two: $450 per person

Three: $425 per person

Four: $400 per person

FOUR-WEEK SIMPLY SPANISH PROGRAM

One: $800 per person

Two: $800 per person

Three: $750 per person

Four: $725 per person

Extra week of instruction (twenty hours): $250 (class only)

LODGING

HOME STAY (PAID TO THE SCHOOL)

Full room and board with a Mexican host family $130/week.

OTHER OPTIONS

The school can make arrangements for an apartment or hotel for students who prefer not to stay with a family.

PROGRAMS AND SCHEDULES

This school operates all day, Monday through Friday. Morning classes are held from 8 a.m. to noon or 9 a.m. to 1 p.m. Afternoon and evening classes are held from 3 to 7 p.m. or 4 to 8 p.m.

Three levels of Spanish-language instruction are offered:

Spanish 301, Beginning level

Spanish 302, Intermediate level

Spanish 303, Advanced level.

Students who complete four weeks of instruction (eighty hours) can earn five Mexican university credits.

SPECIAL COURSES (TWO WEEKS AND THREE CREDITS EACH)

Spanish 310 – Mexican History and Culture

Spanish 320 – Mexican Economy

METHODS

Spring Bell School uses the Integrated Learning method, focusing on immersion into the Spanish-speaking Mexican culture. Memorization of textbook grammar and language rules is avoided in favor of a conversational approach.

TEXTBOOKS

Español para extranjeros Levels 1, 2, and 3, by María Maqueo, is used in all classes, supplemented by magazines, newspapers, and other relevant books.

EXTRAS

FREE INTERNET ACCESS. Students have Internet access through the University of Mérida.

FREE AIRPORT PICKUP SERVICE. The school will pick you up at the airport and deliver you to your host family.

LIBRARY. Students have access to the library at the University of Mérida.

WHAT DISTINGUISHES THIS SCHOOL?

PERSONAL ATTENTION. Director Ed Albor is enthusiastic about his school and anxious for students to enjoy their stay in Mérida. He personally makes sure they are picked up at the airport upon arrival, and communicates frequently with students and their host families.

MEXICAN UNIVERSITY CREDIT. Because of Spring Bell School's connection with University of Mérida, students may earn Mexican university credit for their studies at no extra cost.

Cypress House

Order Form

SPANISH — LIVE IT AND LEARN IT!
BY MARTHA RACINE TAYLOR

✍ No. of books ordered @ $18.95 each	Subtotal ☞	
○ *Please put me on your book catalog mailing list.*	7.75% sales tax (CA residents only) ☞	
Shipping & handling: $3.00 USPS or $6.00 UPS or priority mail, plus $1.00 for each additional book.	Shipping & handling ☞	
Name	**Total** ☞	

Address	Ship to
City State Zip	Address
○ Check enclosed *Charge to:* ○ VISA ○ MasterCard ○ Discover ○ AmEx	City State Zip
Card Number	Expiration Date
Authorized Cardholder Signature	Daytime Phone Number (required)

Send your order to:

CYPRESS HOUSE

155 Cypress Street • Fort Bragg, CA 95437

or call 1-800-773-7782

You can also fax your credit card order to 707-964-7531

or visit our website at www.cypresshouse.com